Asia's New Geopolitics:
Military Power and Regional Order

Desmond Ball

Lucie Béraud-Sudreau

Tim Huxley

C. Raja Mohan

Brendan Taylor

'A sober assessment of how a number of factors, new and old, impact the state of geopolitics in the region. The in-depth and timely analysis of COVID-19, the lack of regional architecture, shifting balances of power and the intensification of rivalries and military build-ups – especially China's – serves as a warning of the potentially troubled future for this dynamic and strategically critical region.'

– Oriana Skylar Mastro, Stanford University and the American Enterprise Institute

Asia's New Geopolitics:
Military Power and Regional Order

Desmond Ball

Lucie Béraud-Sudreau

Tim Huxley

C. Raja Mohan

Brendan Taylor

IISS The International Institute for Strategic Studies

The International Institute for Strategic Studies

Arundel House | 6 Temple Place | London | WC2R 2PG | UK

First published September 2021 by **Routledge**
4 Park Square, Milton Park, Abingdon, Oxon, OX14 4RN

for **The International Institute for Strategic Studies**
Arundel House, 6 Temple Place, London, WC2R 2PG, UK
www.iiss.org

Simultaneously published in the USA and Canada by **Routledge**
52 Vanderbilt Avenue, New York, NY 10017

Routledge is an imprint of Taylor & Francis, an Informa Business

© 2021 The International Institute for Strategic Studies

The International Institute for Strategic Studies is an independent centre for research, information and debate on the problems of conflict, however caused, that have, or potentially have, an important military content. The Council and Staff of the Institute are international and its membership is drawn from almost 100 countries. The Institute is independent and it alone decides what activities to conduct. It owes no allegiance to any government, any group of governments or any political or other organisation. The IISS stresses rigorous research with a forward-looking policy orientation and places particular emphasis on bringing new perspectives to the strategic debate.

The Institute's publications are designed to meet the needs of a wider audience than its own membership and are available on subscription, by mail order and in good bookshops. Further details at www.iiss.org.

British Library Cataloguing in Publication Data
A catalogue record for this book is available from the British Library

Library of Congress Cataloging in Publication Data

ADELPHI series
ISSN 1944-5571

ADELPHI 478–480
ISBN 978-1-032-18736-5

Contents

Professor Desmond Ball was Special Professor in the Strategic and Defence Studies Centre, Australian National University, having been head of the centre from 1984 to 1991. He was the author of more than 40 books or monographs on technical intelligence subjects, nuclear strategy, Australian defence and security in the Asia-Pacific region. Professor Ball served on the Council of the IISS from 1994 until 2000 and was Co-chair of the Steering Committee of the Council for Security Cooperation in the Asia Pacific from 2000 until 2002. He was appointed Officer of the Order of Australia (AO) in 2014 prior to his passing in October 2016.

Dr Lucie Béraud-Sudreau is Director of the Arms and Military Expenditure Programme at the Stockholm International Peace Research Institute (SIPRI). Her research interests focus on European and Asian arms trade, military spending and the arms industry. She was previously a Research Fellow for Defence Economics and Procurements at the IISS and an analyst at the French Ministry of Armed Forces.

Dr Tim Huxley was Executive Director of IISS–Asia until April 2021, where he played a leading role in organising the annual IISS Shangri-La Dialogue and the IISS Fullerton Forum, leading IISS research on the Asia-Pacific and editing the annual *IISS Asia-Pacific Regional Security Assessment*. Dr Huxley has worked for many years in the overlap between strategic studies and Asian area studies. His research and writing focus particularly on Southeast Asian states' security and defence policies, and the security roles of the major powers in the Asia-Pacific region. He was awarded an OBE for services to security in Asia in the UK's 2021 New Year Honours.

Professor C. Raja Mohan is Director of the Institute of South Asian Studies, National University of Singapore, and is one of India's leading foreign-policy commentators. He was previously Professor of South Asian Studies at Jawaharlal Nehru University, New Delhi, and at the S. Rajaratnam School of International Studies, Nanyang Technological University, Singapore. Professor Mohan has also been associated with a number of think tanks in New Delhi and was the founding Director of Carnegie India. He writes a regular column for the *Indian Express* and was previously the Strategic Affairs Editor for the *Hindu* newspaper.

Professor Brendan Taylor is Professor of Strategic Studies at the Strategic and Defence Studies Centre, Australian National University, having been head of the centre from 2011–16. He is a specialist on great-power strategic relations in the Asia-Pacific, East Asian 'flashpoints' and Asian security architecture. He is the author or editor of 12 books, including *The Four Flashpoints: How Asia Goes to War* (Black Inc., 2018) and *Dangerous Decade: Taiwan's Security and Crisis Management* (IISS, 2019).

ACKNOWLEDGEMENTS

This *Adelphi* book was initially conceived as part of a project funded by the MacArthur Foundation by Adam Ward, former Director of Studies at the IISS. The authors express their gratitude to Adam for his role in the project.

Immense thanks are also due to the editor of the *Adelphi* series, Benjamin Rhode, for his forbearance and support while we were completing the book, and to Jeffrey Mazo for his extremely thoughtful edit of the manuscript.

Bradley Wood from the Australian National University provided valuable research assistance.

A major factor that complicated completion was the October 2016 passing of one of the original co-authors, Desmond Ball, after a courageous and lengthy battle with cancer. It was one of Des's dying wishes to see this book published. We are thus particularly grateful to Des's family – Annabel, Katie, Matthew and James – for giving us their permission to publish his essential contributions posthumously. We hope that we have done justice in our own contributions to Des's impeccably high scholarly standards. His life and work remain an inspiration and this book is dedicated to his memory.

Lucie Béraud-Sudreau, Tim Huxley, C. Raja Mohan and Brendan Taylor
Stockholm, Singapore and Canberra, March 2021

GLOSSARY

A2/AD	anti-access/area denial
ADIZ	Air Defence Identification Zone
ADMM	ASEAN Defence Ministers' Meeting
ADMM+	ASEAN Defence Ministers' Meeting-Plus
AFP	Armed Forces of the Philippines
APC	armoured personnel carrier
ARF	ASEAN Regional Forum
ASEAN	Association of Southeast Asian Nations
BRI	Belt and Road Initiative
C4ISR	command, control, communications, computers, intelligence, surveillance and reconnaissance
CCG	China Coast Guard
CCP	Chinese Communist Party
CDG	Cyber Defense Group
CICA	Conference on Interaction and Confidence-Building Measures in Asia
DMZ	Demilitarized Zone
DPP	Democratic Progressive Party
EAS	East Asia Summit
EEZ	exclusive economic zone
ELINT	electronic intelligence
FOIP	Free and Open Indo-Pacific
FPDA	Five Power Defence Arrangements
HADR	humanitarian assistance and disaster relief
IAF	Indian Air Force
ICBM	intercontinental ballistic missile
IFV	infantry fighting vehicle
INCSEA	Incidents at Sea Agreement
INF	Intermediate-Range Nuclear Forces

IRBM	intermediate-range ballistic missile
JASDF	Japan Air Self-Defense Force
JGSDF	Japan Ground Self-Defense Force
JMSDF	Japan Maritime Self-Defense Force
JSDF	Japan Self-Defense Forces
KMT	Kuomintang
LACM	land-attack cruise missile
LoC	Line of Control
MAF	Malaysian Armed Forces
MoU	Memorandum of Understanding
MRBM	medium-range ballistic missile
NLL	Northern Limit Line
PCA	Permanent Court of Arbitration
PLA	People's Liberation Army
PLAAF	People's Liberation Army Air Force
PLAN	People's Liberation Army Navy
PLASSF	People's Liberation Army Strategic Support Force
Quad	Quadrilateral Security Dialogue
SAF	Singapore Armed Forces
SAM	surface-to-air missile
SCO	Shanghai Cooperation Organisation
SEATO	Southeast Asian Treaty Organization
SLBM	submarine-launched ballistic missile
SRBM	short-range ballistic missile
SSBN	nuclear-powered ballistic-missile submarine
TCOG	Trilateral Coordination and Oversight Group
THAAD	Terminal High Altitude Area Defense
TNI	Tentara Nasional Indonesia

UAV   uninhabited aerial vehicle

UN   United Nations

UNSC   United Nations Security Council

VFA   Visiting Forces Agreement

VPA   Vietnam People's Army

WHA   World Health Assembly

WMD   weapons of mass destruction

CHAPTER ONE

A region in flux

Geopolitics can be conceived of as an exercise in the peaceful use of military power;[1] it is the stuff of the 'grand chessboard', of tectonic power shifts, the art of the long view.[2] The long-standing perceived importance of military power in the international order, and hence of geopolitics, went into eclipse with the passing of the superpower stalemate at the end of the Cold War. In Asia, most observers were optimistic that the region's burgeoning economic interdependence and its nascent multilateral institutions would together create a new era of peace and prosperity.[3] Yet Asia's institutions are increasingly conspicuous by their absence, and initially promising mechanisms for avoiding and managing crises have also unravelled as simmering tensions have flared across the region. Three visions for the future of the region – a US-led 'Free and Open Indo-Pacific' (FOIP), a Chinese-centred order, and an Association of Southeast Asian Nations (ASEAN)-inspired 'Indo-Pacific Outlook' – are now vying to replace the post-Second World War US-led Asian order.

In this *Adelphi* book we examine the growing geopolitical rivalries, defence-procurement trends and developing military capabilities in Asia in the context of the present ill-equipped regional security architecture and a fraying international order. Looking at Northeast, Southeast and South Asia in turn, we consider whether and how the collective effects of the ways regional states are employing military power to defend and advance their long-standing territorial claims will allow one of the three competing visions to triumph, or whether the struggle between these competing frameworks will continue for decades.

The evolving Asian order

Even as the COVID-19 pandemic brought many parts of the globe almost to a standstill during 2020, Asia's geopolitical rivalries intensified. Chinese naval vessels and military aircraft entered the waters and skies around Taiwan with unprecedented frequency. The deadliest clashes in decades erupted along the disputed Sino-Indian border. North Korea's nuclear and missile development continued apace, challenging the extended-deterrence guarantees long given by America to its Asian allies. As China and the US edged towards partial 'decoupling', there was even talk in policymaking and analytical circles of a 'new Cold War', underscored by an expansion in military exercises and naval stand-offs in the increasingly contested waters of the South China Sea and the Indian Ocean.

A decade ago, hopes were high that Asia's burgeoning security architecture would reduce the risk of such flare-ups and serve to manage major crises when they occurred. The expansion of the annual East Asia Summit (EAS) from its original 16 Asian states to include the US and Russia in 2011 and the establishment the previous year of the ASEAN Defence Ministers' Meeting-Plus (ADMM+), comprising the same countries, were cited as evidence that an optimal regional cooperative footprint had been found.[4] But this was overly optimistic. In June 2020, for example, Pyongyang announced that it was severing all communication lines with South Korea – which it described as an 'enemy' – before blowing up a liaison office that the two countries had agreed to establish during an April 2018 inter-Korean summit.[5] And the deadly China–India border clash in June 2020 occurred despite an agreement on a new military hotline between the two countries at an informal summit in April 2018, in the city of Wuhan, between Indian Prime Minister Narendra Modi and his Chinese counterpart Xi Jinping.[6]

As hopes for an effective Asian security architecture crumble, the post-1945 rules, norms and institutions that helped maintain peace and stability in the region (and indeed globally) are also atrophying. Some observers have even suggested that the so-called 'rules-based international order' has already ended.[7] Concern that the unravelling of the old order may foreshadow a much darker strategic future in Asia is apparent in regional governments' statements on security and defence. Vietnam's 2019 defence white paper, for example, argued that territorial disputes in the region are 'likely to become more complex, potentially leading to conflicts, threatening regional stability, peace, and prosperity, and triggering a regional arms race'.[8] Japan's 2020 defence white paper noted that 'uncertainty over the existing order is increasing' due to an accelerating and intensifying 'inter-state competition across the political, economic and military realms, in which states seek to shape global and regional order to their advantage as well as to increase their influence'.[9] Australia's July 2020 'Defence Strategic Update' warned that 'major power competition, coercion and military modernisation are increasing the potential for and consequences of miscalculation. While still unlikely, the prospect of high-intensity military conflict in the Indo-Pacific is less remote … including high-intensity military conflict between the United States and China.'[10] Three broad strategic trends underlie these concerns: declining US willingness to underwrite Asia's security order, rising US–China tensions and weakening Asian multilateralism.

US engagement

The willingness and ability of Washington to continue under-writing the rules and principles which have traditionally defined the limits of permissible action in the Asia-Pacific, coupled with the balance of military power needed to enforce them,[11] are increasingly in doubt. Allan Gyngell, a former head of Australia's Office of National Assessments, noted with regard to the COVID-19 pandemic that 'it is hard to think of a global crisis over the past fifty years to which Washington has offered the international community so little response'.[12] No international order lasts indefinitely, and it is likely, particularly given the re-emergence of power centres in China, India and possibly Indonesia, that Asia's US-led order would eventually succumb. There is, however, a strong case that the 'America First' posture during the presidency of Donald Trump has hastened the incumbent order's decline.

Trump's disdain for alliance relationships undermined one of the central pillars of that order. He made his intentions clear on the campaign trail in March 2016, when he signalled a desire to withdraw American forces from Japan and South Korea and to support the development of nuclear weapons by those two treaty allies.[13] Following his historic June 2018 summit with North Korean leader Kim Jong-un in Singapore, Trump again expressed his wish to bring US troops home from the Korean Peninsula.[14] He subsequently accused Japan and South Korea – regarded traditionally as the cornerstones of America's Asian alliance network – of taking 'tremendous advantage' of the US, and he demanded they quadruple the financial contribution they each make towards the costs of the US military presence.[15]

The incoming administration of President Joe Biden pledged to renew and strengthen America's commitment to its Asian allies, even though the administration of Barack Obama, in which Biden served as vice president, had also called on US allies to increase their defence contributions, albeit less crudely and confrontationally than Trump.[16] And Trump's emphasis on allied burden-sharing was part of a much deeper pattern. Half a century earlier, then-president Richard Nixon's July 1969 announcement at a press conference in Guam that America's Asian partners must assume greater responsibility for their own defence sent a shockwave through the alliance system, especially against the backdrop of US failure to make headway against communist forces in Vietnam.[17] Upon entering office in January 1977, Jimmy Carter tried to make good on a campaign promise to remove US ground forces from South Korea, only to be stymied by bureaucratic and congressional opposition.[18] Questions regarding the future of the US-led order re-emerged in the wake of the Cold War, precipitating reductions in American forces in the region that were eventually halted as a result of the 1995 US 'Security Strategy for the East Asia-Pacific Region', which required that the US maintain a minimum forward presence in Asia of approximately 100,000 military personnel.[19]

US–China tensions

Nixon was able to consolidate the US position in Asia through a historic normalisation of diplomatic relations with China, a bold geopolitical play that shifted the Cold War balance of power back in America's favour.[20] The bargain he struck with Beijing, however, has to a significant degree unravelled, and with it the engagement strategy that successive US administrations had hoped would tame if not transform China.[21] During the Obama era, for example, Sino-US tensions intensified over Beijing's increasingly repressive internal policies; allegations of Chinese intellectual-property theft, cyber espionage and political-influence operations; and the militarisation of the

South China Sea.[22] Attitudes towards China had hardened across the US political spectrum and also, significantly, in the traditionally pro-Beijing business community. The Trump administration identified long-term strategic competition with China as America's most important international challenge, and responding to that challenge as the country's top foreign-policy priority.[23] Many prominent US strategic commentators suggested that a new Sino-American cold war was already under way.[24]

The global pandemic that began in early 2020 accelerated this deterioration in US–China relations. Neither country initially responded well to the COVID-19 outbreak. In China, local officials in Wuhan and elsewhere in Hubei province (where the virus first appeared), and perhaps also in the higher echelons of the Chinese Communist Party (CCP), almost certainly failed to disclose information about the spread of the virus.[25] On the US side, Trump was slow to react, claiming initially that the risk to the American people and economy was limited. Beijing responded by zeroing in on Trump's failures, aiming to deflect domestic criticism and to repair the significant damage done to China's international image. Chinese medical personnel and supplies were also sent to places hit hard by the pandemic – including some in Asia, such as the Philippines.[26] Trump in turn responded with an anti-Chinese narrative, insisting that COVID-19 should be referred to as the 'Chinese' or 'China' virus – a characterisation supported by more than half the American public.[27] He clearly had an eye on the November 2020 presidential election; during the campaign, Biden charged that Trump's lacklustre COVID-19 response stemmed from the fact that he had been too conciliatory towards China and too accepting of Beijing's COVID-19 assurances. China subsequently emerged as a major campaign issue, further straining Sino-American ties.[28]

These strains were evident in the absence of US–China cooperation during the pandemic, in sharp contrast to the experience of past crises, such as the 2008–09 global financial crisis when cooperation was so close that it prompted calls for the establishment of a US–China 'Group of Two' or G2.[29] During the pandemic, however, calls in the US for the 'decoupling' of the countries' economies, already under way to some degree, have become more raucous.[30] A complete decoupling of the two economies remains unlikely given their high degree of interdependence, particularly in the financial sphere,[31] but the COVID-19 crisis has also highlighted American dependence on Chinese supply chains, and continued economic disengagement seems inevitable as this vulnerability is addressed.

Asian multilateralism

Asia's multilateral groupings in general have struggled to respond to any of Asia's major crises over the course of the past three decades: the North Korean nuclear crises of 1993–94, 2010 and 2017; the 1995–96 Taiwan Strait crisis; or the 1997–98 Asian financial crisis, to name but a few. In the aftermath of the financial crisis, for example, the frequency of multilateral gatherings in the region decreased sharply, as many member states could not afford to attend.[32] And while multilateral institutions often display an institutional 'stickiness' that allows them to survive well beyond their use-by date, the very *raison d'être* of some long-standing regional groupings is already being challenged. The pandemic's damaging economic effects will further weaken these bodies.

Multilateral forums should, in theory, serve as venues for mediating and dampening geopolitical rivalries. In practice, however, such gatherings sometimes also become arenas where those rivalries are played out. For example, while the annual IISS Shangri-La Dialogue in Singapore has provided an important platform for Asian security dialogue, including through the opportunities it provides for private bilateral meetings, it has often also seen Sino-American and Sino-Japanese tensions come to the fore.[33]

At the global level, the May 2020 gathering of the World Health Assembly (WHA) was a tense affair, as the European Union and Australia advanced a co-sponsored resolution – which China initially resisted, but ultimately supported – calling for an 'independent' review of the handling of the pandemic. A simultaneous Taiwanese bid to secure WHA observer status languished at Beijing's insistence, an exclusion the United States' then-secretary of state Mike Pompeo described as 'spiteful'.[34] Xi also used this gathering to burnish his country's leadership credentials, pledging US$2 billion in international assistance in response to the pandemic over the next two years at the same time that the Trump administration froze US funding for the World Health Organization.[35]

The return of geopolitics

The continuation of these broad strategic trends is neither inevitable nor irreversible. The pandemic's scale and severity, and equally serious global challenges such as climate change and strategic arms control, could yet convince Beijing and Washington of the need to cooperate, potentially through new or reimagined multilateral forums.[36] There are historical precedents: for example, in the aftermath of the October 1962 Cuban Missile Crisis, Moscow and Washington saw the need for more robust crisis-management mechanisms, and established a hotline connecting the Kremlin to the Pentagon.[37]

Some have argued that the severe economic downturn prompted by the pandemic could also undermine the will and capacity of governments to use military means to attain national goals.[38] This may be overly optimistic. In reality, different political systems and leaders are unlikely to react uniformly to the financial strictures imposed by the pandemic. Indeed, authoritarian countries, notably China, are less likely to feel constrained by domestic political considerations in deciding military budgets and capability-development efforts.

In the post-COVID-19 world, the salience of military power will almost certainly increase. Historically, the importance of military power has largely been taken as a given. The nature and scope of international order has been shaped primarily by what the major powers were willing and able to fight over. As Michael Howard observed in 1964:

> The power which states exercise in international affairs is compounded of many attributes, economic, diplomatic, cultural and ideological as well as military. But military power, the capacity to use violence for the protection, enforcement or extension of authority, remains an instrument with which no state has yet found it possible to completely dispense. Indeed, it is not easy to see how international relations could be conducted, and international order maintained, if it were totally absent. The capacity of states to defend themselves, and their evident willingness to do so, provides the basic framework within which the business of international negotiation is carried on.[39]

Two classic examples of this nexus between military power and international order are the nineteenth-century Concert of Europe and the twentieth-century Cold War. The collective willingness of the European great powers to use force to prevent any one of them from achieving hegemony largely preserved order for almost a century after 1815.[40] Similarly, the willingness and ability of the US and the Soviet Union to defend their respective spheres of influence, including through nuclear deterrence, defined the bipolar order of the Cold War.[41]

In 1990, US president George H.W. Bush famously proclaimed the birth of a 'New World Order' in which the rule of law would supplant the 'rule of the jungle'.[42] Political scientist Francis Fukuyama went further, proclaiming that the 'end of history' had arrived because closed, authoritarian societies lacked the requisite creativity to compete economically or militarily and would thus need to embrace liberal capitalism if they were to survive and thrive.[43] Edward Luttwak argued that states (and blocs of states) would increasingly seek to advance and defend their interests through economic rather than military means, in a world where traditional geopolitics had been supplanted by 'geo-economics'.[44]

Some analysts questioned the validity of applying such ideas to Asia, arguing instead that the region was emerging as a likely 'cockpit of great power conflict'.[45] But most post-Cold War Asia watchers foresaw a new era of peace and prosperity.[46] Even the region's geopolitics, to the extent they remained relevant, were seen as pointing towards peace.[47] Developments over the past decade in Asia and beyond, however, have undermined this optimism. It has become increasingly clear that what US commentator Charles Krauthammer termed the 'unipolar moment' – a period during which US military superiority was so overwhelming that no potential adversary could seriously contemplate a challenge[48] – is fading. The military instruments of statecraft, diminished during the brief post-Cold War peace and prematurely consigned to the annals of history, are making a comeback. Russia's invasion of Georgia in 2008 provided an early indication that history might not have ended after all, while its annexation of Crimea in 2014 led commentators to pronounce that geopolitics had returned.[49] In Asia, China's assertive territorial moves in the East and South China seas reinforced this message.

Over the last 30 years, academics, journalists and busi-nesses interested in Asia's evolving international relations have focused much attention on geo-economics and the evolution of regional institutions. The economic instruments of statecraft are becoming increasingly important as geopolitical rivalry returns, and the strategic significance of China's Belt and Road Initiative (BRI) and other geo-economic developments are justifiably seizing the interest of the relevant expert and government communities. There has been, however, a parallel tendency to underestimate the importance of the role played by military power in the region's evolving dynamics. This could be dangerous if states also underestimate how quickly military confrontation can escalate.[50] Understanding the stra-tegic postures of competing Asian powers more fully should help to address these risks.

The analysis of the peaceful use of military power is equally important. States more often employ military power in this way – coercing an opponent through the *threat* of harm or destruc-tion, without actually taking offensive action – to advance their objectives. As the term implies, this 'peaceful' use of military power can even be used in efforts to avoid major conflict, either through supporting diplomatic processes or as a last resort if diplomacy fails. And yet, precisely because the peaceful use of military power is often subtle and poorly defined, it is difficult to analyse. Robert J. Art has compared the war-waging use of military power to a powerful flood and the peaceful use to a gravitational field that exerts its effects imperceptibly.[51]

Strategic interregnum

Even if armed conflict can be avoided (which cannot be taken as given),[52] Asia may not settle on a new strategic order anytime soon. Of the three alternative models currently vying to replace the current order – a revived US-led vision for a

FOIP; a China-centred model based around Beijing's BRI; and an Indonesian-inspired approach emphasising leadership through the ten-member ASEAN[53] – none appears to be a clear favourite. This suggests the possibility of a protracted, potentially decades-long strategic interregnum.

A 'Free and Open Indo-Pacific'

The FOIP vision marks an attempt to expand and adapt the established but weakening US-led order to contemporary circumstances. The first hint of this approach came early in the Obama presidency, with leading figures such as secretary of state Hillary Clinton using the term 'Indo-Pacific' when articulating the administration's 'rebalance' to the Asia-Pacific.[54] Wanting to disassociate his presidency from Obama's, Trump subsequently rebranded the rebalance, most notably in his November 2017 address to the Asia-Pacific Economic Cooperation summit in Danang, Vietnam, where he outlined his administration's FOIP vision.[55] Several major policy documents (including the Department of Defense's June 2019 'Indo-Pacific Strategy Report' and the Department of State's 'A Free and Open Indo-Pacific: Advancing a Shared Vision' in November 2019) subsequently highlighted the FOIP's four underpinning principles: respect for sovereignty and independence; peaceful resolution of disputes; free, fair and reciprocal trade, based upon open and transparent investment and connectivity; and adherence to international rules and norms, including freedom of navigation and overflight.[56] Most observers have suggested that any changes by the Biden administration to Trump's Indo-Pacific strategy will be more stylistic than substantive. In a series of telephone conversations with regional leaders in November 2020, for example, Biden reverted to Obama's favoured formulation of a 'secure and prosperous' Indo-Pacific.[57]

Other governments have also adopted the 'Indo-Pacific' terminology and vision. Australia and Japan even preceded America down this path. The Australian government was the first to refer formally to the region as the 'Indo-Pacific' in its 2013 Defence White Paper, and some officials in Canberra reportedly used the term as early as 2005.[58] Abe Shinzo advanced such ideas during his tenure as Japan's longest-serving prime minister, for example his 2012 proposal for a 'democratic security diamond' to guard the maritime commons from the Indian Ocean to the Western Pacific. Tokyo formalised its own FOIP strategy in 2016.[59] India, too, has been a supporter: in a keynote address to the June 2018 IISS Shangri-La Dialogue in Singapore, for example, Prime Minister Modi spoke of Washington's and New Delhi's 'shared vision of an open, stable, secure and prosperous Indo-Pacific Region'.[60] When ministerial-level officials from Australia, India, Japan and the US met on the sidelines of the United Nations General Assembly in September 2019 in the Quadrilateral Security Dialogue (or Quad), one Australian newspaper described it as a 'significant victory' for an 'alliance of democracies promoting a "free and open Indo-Pacific"'.[61] Likewise, a March 2021 'virtual summit' of the four countries' leaders was heralded by some commentators as the Quad's coming of age.[62] The Quad was originally launched in 2007, but Australia withdrew in 2008 and the dialogue was only revived in 2017.

A Chinese sphere of influence

Unsurprisingly, Beijing has been dismissive of the FOIP, believing it to be both ineffective and aimed at 'containing' or, at the very least, 'constraining' Chinese power and ambition. In 2018, Chinese Foreign Minister Wang Yi described the FOIP as a 'headline grabbing' idea that 'like the sea foam in the Pacific or Indian Ocean … may get some attention, but

soon will dissipate'.[63] Chinese academic Feng Zhang has attributed Beijing's 'nonchalant' response to FOIP to four factors: a
realisation that it over reacted to the Obama administration's
Asian 'pivot' or rebalancing strategy; confidence in its growing
'strategic leverage' to meet the FOIP; its superior resources,
relative to the Quad members, for funding regional economic
initiatives; and a belief that sufficient 'strategic space' exists
to advance its aims given America's inability to implement its
preferred vision in this highly variegated region where non-
aligned preferences remain powerful.[64]

Beijing is advancing an alternative, China-centred model for
Asian order, the contours of which have become increasingly
clear following Xi's rise to power in late 2012, when he became
chairman of the Central Military Commission and secretary of
the CCP (and then president in March 2013). His approach has
been more strident than that of any of his recent predecessors,
drawing comparisons with communist China's founding leader
Mao Zedong. Xi has made clear that his overriding goal is to
make China wealthy and powerful again. A stronger China,
he maintains, will never again be subjected to the ignominy
suffered during the so-called 'century of humiliation' (1839–
1949), when the once-powerful Middle Kingdom was carved
up by foreign powers. Preserving and strengthening CCP rule
is Beijing's fundamental, and non-negotiable, objective. With
each passing year, Xi has thus looked to consolidate his domestic position. In March 2018, for example, China's National
People's Congress voted to remove limits on the presidential
term of office, effectively allowing Xi to serve as China's 'leader
for life' should he choose.[65]

The centrepiece of Xi's vision for Asian order is the ambitious BRI, a massive infrastructure-development programme
covering transport, energy and communications. One element
(the 'belt') of this two-pronged programme binds China's

poorest western provinces to Europe through Central Asia. The other connects its southernmost coastal provinces to Southeast Asia, South Asia and Oceania through a 'Maritime Silk Road of the twenty-first century' running through the South China Sea, the Indian Ocean and down to the South Pacific.[66] The BRI is said to have been inspired by the 'Silk Road' network of trade routes established during the Han Dynasty (202 BCE–220 CE), which bound the ancient world together in commerce. Underwriting the BRI is a set of new Chinese-led financial institutions, such as the Asian Infrastructure Investment Bank and the 'Silk Road Fund'.[67]

There is debate over whether the BRI is motivated primarily by a desire for Chinese dominance over Asia or by domestic determinants. Economist Peter Cai, for example, argues that while geopolitical considerations are undoubtedly part of Xi's calculus, Beijing's overriding objective is to correct worsening economic disparities across the country by stimulating growth in China's poorest regions. He also contends that the BRI is an attempt by Beijing to remedy China's deepening problems of excess capacity (for example in steelmaking) by dumping surplus goods and even migrating entire factories elsewhere in Asia. In so doing, Beijing also intends to export Chinese technological and manufacturing standards, making these the norm across the region.[68] Other commentators contend that what Beijing is portraying as a purely economic initiative is deeply geopolitical. For example, Nadège Rolland argues that, through the BRI, Xi is aiming to use China's burgeoning economic weight to dominate the entire Eurasian continent without having to wage war or indeed provoking any kind of countervailing response from elsewhere in the region. The BRI would hedge against possible disruptions to maritime supply routes, and deeper strategic space would help counter efforts to contain the country's rise.[69]

China's formal rejection of alliances is reflected in its largely non-aligned international posture. Beijing has instead initiated a series of multilateral mechanisms, such as the Shanghai Cooperation Organisation (SCO) – comprising China, India, Kazakhstan, Kyrgyzstan, Pakistan, Russia, Tajikistan and Uzbekistan – and the 27-member Conference on Interaction and Confidence-Building Measures in Asia (CICA). For example, in a January 2017 white paper, 'China's Policies on Asia-Pacific Security Cooperation', Beijing gave pride of place to ASEAN-led mechanisms that exclude the US, such as the ASEAN Plus One (ASEAN with China) and ASEAN Plus Three (with China, Japan and South Korea) processes.[70] Some contend that Xi now aims to use the BRI incrementally to knit together this seemingly disparate collection of groupings in support of a Chinese-led order.[71] This may have been behind his call at the 2014 gathering of the CICA for a new 'Asia for Asians' security architecture.

Many commentators are thus convinced that Xi's ultimate objective is to establish a traditional sphere of influence in Asia, within which China can act to rewrite international rules and norms in line with its growing economic and strategic weight. According to this view, Beijing will seek to reclaim territories lost during the century of humiliation – most importantly Taiwan – by coercion and even the use of military force. International boundaries could even be redrawn under a Chinese-led order, as is arguably already occurring in the South China Sea.[72]

Yet there is significant uncertainty over the geographic limits of Xi's vision, and particularly whether his aspirations extend beyond Asia. Some commentators contend that they do, and that establishing regional dominance in Asia is merely a stepping stone to realising larger global aspirations.[73] They point to Xi's address to the January 2017 World Economic Forum in Davos, where he portrayed Beijing as the new champion of free trade and globalisation, as well as his October 2017 report to China's National Party Congress, in which he articulated his vision for transforming China into a 'global power'.[74]

ASEAN's Indo-Pacific outlook

Most Southeast Asian countries would rather not choose between the US-led and Chinese-centred visions for regional order, in part because they fear their sub-region would be marginalised should either prevail. They also regard deepening Sino-American rivalry, as reflected in these competing visions, as undesirable. At worst, such rivalry risks embroiling them in a destabilising military conflict that would severely undermine their hard-won economic success. Short of such a calamity, Southeast Asian nations are concerned at the prospect of having to side definitively with either China or the US, rather than continuing to enjoy the benefits of interacting with each. As Singapore Prime Minister Lee Hsien Loong wrote in mid-2020, 'Southeast Asian countries, including Singapore, are especially concerned, as they live at the intersection of the interests of various major powers and must avoid being caught in the middle or forced into invidious choices'.[75]

ASEAN has been relatively slow to join the contest to define Asia's new security order, largely because of its consensus-style approach, which requires unanimity before decisions are taken. In June 2019, however, ASEAN announced its own 'Outlook on the Indo-Pacific' at the organisation's 34th annual summit in Bangkok. As its title suggests, the ASEAN Outlook shares some similarities with Indo-Pacific visions advanced by other countries. Like India, for instance, the Outlook emphasises 'inclusivity'. But it also reflects important differences. The ASEAN Outlook, for example, treats the Asia-Pacific and the Indian Ocean as distinct (albeit interconnected) territorial spaces. It emphasises cooperation over competition. Most importantly, the Outlook envisages a central role for ASEAN and ASEAN-led mechanisms, such as the annual ASEAN Regional Forum (ARF), the EAS and the ADMM+.

As with the vision for a US-led order, the ASEAN Outlook revives an existing approach and adapts it to the present. Following the end of the Cold War, Southeast Asian policy elites sought to extend the ASEAN model – which was established in 1967 with a focus on open trade and cultural cooperation – into the security sphere and onto an under-institutionalised region. Their pioneering efforts, which included establishing the ARF in 1993–94, were greeted with initial US and Chinese suspicion. Washington worried that these fledgling arrangements could, over time, supplant its network of Asian alliances, while Beijing feared they could become venues where regional countries would join forces against China. The failure of the region to marshal an indigenous response to the 1997–98 Asian financial crisis, however, gave further impetus to the idea of building an East Asian Community, leading to the establishment of the EAS in 2005.

Jakarta was the primary driver behind the 2019 ASEAN Outlook. As early as 2013, Indonesian foreign minister Marty Natalegawa had proposed an 'Indo-Pacific Treaty of Friendship and Cooperation', building upon ASEAN's 'Treaty of Amity and Cooperation' that all of ASEAN's dialogue partners – including Australia, China, India and the US – had already signed. Soon after he took office in 2014, President Joko Widodo (popularly known as 'Jokowi') outlined the need for Indonesia to expand its strategic outlook to become a 'Global Maritime Fulcrum' bridging the Indian and Pacific oceans. The campaign that culminated in the ASEAN Outlook, however, got under way between 2017 and 2018, when the Indonesian foreign ministry produced a draft document entitled 'Indonesia's Perspective for an ASEAN Outlook on the Indo-Pacific: Towards a Peaceful, Prosperous and Inclusive Region'. A March 2019 'high level dialogue on Indo-Pacific cooperation' in Jakarta involved representatives from all 18 EAS member countries. ASEAN leaders endorsed the document in Bangkok three months later. The final document closely resembled the Indonesian draft.[76]

The visions for US-led and Chinese-centred Asian order both, to be sure, claim to afford ASEAN pride of place. In its November 2019 report on implementing the Indo-Pacific vision, for example, the US State Department claimed that 'ASEAN sits at the geographical center of the Indo-Pacific and is central to our vision'.[77] Most ASEAN countries, however, take such pronouncements with a pinch of salt. They have noticed the patchy attendance of senior US figures at ASEAN-centred multilateral gatherings. Trump, for example, missed the ASEAN summit, Southeast Asia's most important annual meeting, in 2018 and 2019, and departed early from the 2017 summit.[78] His predecessor Obama was absent from the 2013 summit,[79] while Condoleezza Rice twice missed the ARF during her four years as secretary of state during the George W. Bush administration.[80] As Singaporean analyst William Choong has put it, 'extra-ASEAN regional powers such as India, Japan and the United States have expressed support for ASEAN central-ity. In practice, major powers would only profess ASEAN centrality … when it suits their interests.'[81]

A region of sub-regions

Constructing and maintaining order over a region as vast and diverse as Asia is challenging. This was true even under the decades-long US-led security order, characterised as one of 'partial' or 'incomplete hegemony'.[82] Asia's scale and complexity have led security analysts to conceive of the region as comprising three largely separate sub-regions: Northeast Asia, Southeast Asia and South Asia. Barry Buzan and Ole Wæver have described these as three distinct 'security complexes', a concept they defined as meaning 'a group of states or other entities [possessing] a degree of security interdependence sufficient both to establish them as a linked set and to differentiate them from surrounding security regions'.[83] The Northeast Asian security complex emerged during the late nineteenth and early twentieth centuries, as a rising Japan incorporated Korea and Taiwan into its empire and engaged (partly through conflict) with a quasi-independent China. The Southeast Asian and South Asian regional security complexes, by contrast, were products of the decolonisation that followed the Second World War.[84]

Asia's diversity and, hence, its analytical division into three sub-regions is also partly a product of geography. The Himalayas, for example, serve as a formidable geographical barrier to interaction between South Asia and the rest of the region.[85] But this division also reflects the economic and military weakness of Asian countries in the aftermath of the Second World War, which further limited opportunity for interaction and security interdependencies beyond their most immediate neighbours. Rapid economic growth in many Asian countries from the 1960s onwards, and the military modernisation it facilitated, significantly lowered these barriers. China's growing economic and military weight, for example, enhanced its capacity to project power into Southeast and South Asia. Buzan and Wæver propose that this eventually led to a merging of the Northeast and Southeast Asian security complexes, while also giving rise to a new China-centred Asian 'supercomplex' wherein inter-regional connections between East and South Asia were strong and sustained, but not sufficiently so to override sub-regional security dynamics.[86]

While none of the visions for US-led, Chinese-led or ASEAN-centred order has materialised, a strong case could be made that Asia's strategic trajectory is heading inexorably towards greater integration.[87] Yet the sub-regional approach remains highly relevant and useful as a prism through which to view Asia's contemporary and emerging security challenges. A more integrated Asia would not remove the need to understand the various and often quite disparate sub-regional security dynamics within that larger complex. This was certainly one of the key lessons Asian security analysts learned in the aftermath of the Cold War. History did not end in Northeast Asia, for example, where deep-seated animosities and nationalisms (between, for example, Japan and the two Koreas, and between China and Taiwan) that had been suppressed below the over-arching superpower contest rapidly resurfaced. Southeast Asia, by contrast, gradually left behind (or at least glossed over) the divisions and conflicts that had characterised its recent past, prompting speculation about its transformation into a 'security community' where inter-state conflict would be virtually unthinkable.[88] Despite an undeniable subsequent rise in security connections and interaction between Asia's sub-regions, such variations persist. For example, notwithstanding the weakening of Asian multilateralism, a phenomenon that the COVID-19 crisis has highlighted and possibly exacerbated, such institutions remain far more prevalent in Southeast Asia than in either Northeast or South Asia.

Degrees of political integration across Asia and its sub-regions have, moreover, ebbed and flowed for centuries. Major crises have often promoted disintegration. In the decades before the Second World War, for example, Imperial Japan's bid for regional dominance had the makings of an East Asian security complex, as Tokyo acquired colonies in Korea and Taiwan, territory in China, control of almost all Southeast Asia, and a foothold in the South China Sea.[89] Yet the defeat in 1945 of Tokyo's ambitions for a 'Greater East Asia Co-Prosperity Sphere' led to the division of East Asia into two largely autonomous sub-regions. More recently, during the 1990s, some Southeast Asian governments hoped for greater Indian engagement as a counterweight to growing Chinese power and influence. India's inclusion in the ARF reflected such thinking. But the 1997–98 Asian financial crisis temporarily put those hopes on hold.[90] To the frustration of those who would like the Quadrilateral Security Dialogue to succeed, India has remained reserved about engaging more directly in Asian security beyond South Asia and the Indian Ocean. And, as a former permanent secretary of Singapore's foreign ministry, Bilahari Kausikan, has cautioned, even Southeast Asia's future coherence is by no means assured.[91]

The sub-regional approach is certainly not without its shortcomings. Just as a top-down analysis can overlook vital local security dynamics, a bottom-up approach risks missing the wood for the trees. To mitigate that possibility, it is essential to acknowledge and address the critical interconnections between Asia's sub-regions and to watch for indications of the trajectory of Asia's security order. In the final analysis, however, the prospect that no pan-regional vision for order will prevail in the foreseeable future makes the traditional sub-regional approach critical for analysing strategic postures in Asia.

CHAPTER TWO

Disputes and tensions in Northeast Asia

The increased prosperity of Northeast Asia over the last generation is striking; China and Japan now have the second- and third-largest national economies in the world. But Northeast Asia is also wracked with inter-state tensions and disputes, and the potential for escalation to large-scale conflict, with horrendous social and economic consequences, is palpable. China, Japan, North Korea, South Korea and Taiwan are all vigorously acquiring new and diverse weapons systems, including advanced conventional arms and long-range missiles. In some cases they have nuclear-weapons programmes, as well as some of the most modern C4ISR (command, control, communications, computers, intelligence, surveillance and reconnaissance) systems and advanced cyber-warfare programmes. As these states develop their military capabilities, there are signs that 'action–reaction' dynamics are at work, which could further heighten tensions and increase the risk of conflict.

Northeast Asia also suffers from a dearth of regional security structures to help mitigate inter-state tensions. There was speculation during the late 2000s that the Six-Party Talks – involving China, Japan, the two Koreas, Russia and the US

– could evolve into a more formal Northeast Asian 'Security and Peace Mechanism', but this ad hoc diplomatic effort to address the North Korean nuclear problem instead unravelled.[1] Smaller, 'minilateral' initiatives have been hostages to the region's deep-seated animosities. Trilateral cooperation between Japan, South Korea and the US, for example, which flourished during the late 1990s and early 2000s under the auspices of the Trilateral Coordination and Oversight Group (TCOG), has languished for much of the past decade, largely due to differences between Tokyo and Seoul rooted in their shared history. Cooperation between Beijing, Tokyo and Seoul has progressed at glacial pace for similar reasons. When the China–Japan–South Korea trilateral summit met in Chengdu, China to celebrate its 20th anniversary in December 2019, for example, it was the first meeting between the leaders of the three countries in 15 months.[2] A planned December 2020 summit was postponed due to disagreements between Seoul and Tokyo.[3]

Every major Northeast Asian power is engaged in more or less serious bilateral disputes with at least two of the others. South Korea has disputes with three, and China and Japan with each of the other four. Most of the disputes concern territory – competing sovereignty claims, contested legitimacy and disagreements about borders. Many are about maritime boundaries, especially claims to 200-nautical-mile exclusive economic zones (EEZs).[4] All these disputes are in key respects interconnected; measures taken by one party to enhance its position with another will tend to exacerbate tensions with a third party.

Many of these issues are unlikely to lead to conflict. Some, such as those between China and North Korea, are quiescent. Others could be addressed or even resolved through negotiation. In April 2013, for example, Tokyo and Taipei signed a fisheries agreement facilitating reciprocal fishing rights within a designated zone in the East China Sea, incorporating the disputed Senkaku/Diaoyu islands.[5] All the disputes nevertheless remain sources of tension, suspicion and (potentially) misunderstanding. And three of Asia's major potential flashpoints – Taiwan, the Korean Peninsula and the East China Sea – are in Northeast Asia.

The Taiwan flashpoint

Taiwan is arguably the most likely focus for future inter-state conflict in Northeast Asia: in March 2021, the commander of United States Indo-Pacific Command, Admiral Phil Davidson, told a US Senate committee that China might try to seize the island 'in the next six years'.[6] Between 2008 and 2016, when Taiwan was controlled by then-president Ma Ying-jeou and the Nationalist Party (Kuomintang, or KMT), economic relations between China and Taiwan prospered, cross-strait tourism burgeoned and the possibility was even floated of a peace treaty to formally end the civil war (1927–49) that effectively concluded with the communist victory on the mainland and the KMT's retreat to Taiwan. But warming relations with China encountered domestic opposition, giving rise to the 'Sunflower' protest movement which included occupation of Taiwan's parliament in March–April 2014 and directly inspired Hong Kong's street protests in 2019–20. Relations between Beijing and Taipei deteriorated markedly following the landslide electoral victory in January 2016 of Taiwan's first female president, Tsai Ing-wen, and her Democratic Progressive Party (DPP). Tsai convincingly won a second term in January 2020. The DPP maintains that Taiwan is already independent, as the 'Republic of China', and has rejected Beijing's demands that, as a precondition for resuming talks, Tsai accept the '1992 Consensus', which espouses that there is only 'One China' even if the two sides agree to disagree over its precise definition.[7]

Beijing's interpretation of the 1992 Consensus asserts that it has full sovereignty over the One China, and it maintains its policy of 'reunification', by force if necessary. China currently targets approximately 1,200 short-range ballistic missiles (SRBMs), 400 land-attack cruise missiles (LACMs) and an unknown number of medium-range ballistic missiles (MRBMs) at the island. The military balance inevitably and inexorably continues to move in the mainland's favour, denuding Taiwan's deterrent capabilities and increasing Beijing's options for employing force to obtain its objectives.[8]

Since the early 2000s, Beijing has been developing capabilities for delaying or deterring US assistance in the event of a conflict with Taiwan. This anti-access/area-denial (A2/AD) strategy includes capabilities for attacking key US warships and aircraft (especially US carrier battle groups) and for incapacitating American C4ISR systems. China's growing A2/AD capabilities comprise traditional weapons such as submarines and anti-ship missiles as well as information-warfare (IW) and cyber-warfare techniques and anti-satellite systems, for the purpose of 'information dominance'. These capabilities should not, however, be over estimated: US superiority in advanced technologies remains considerable. Its C4ISR capabilities are extraordinarily powerful, even when subject to 'asymmetric' attacks, and its ingenuity with respect to conceptual innovation is unparalleled.

There is nevertheless a considerable danger that miscalculation and misadventure, with consequential escalation, could arise from cross-strait provocations. The most troubling of these is the growing number of sorties by Chinese military aircraft into Taiwan's Air Defence Identification Zone (ADIZ).[9] These even routinely cross the median line of the Taiwan Strait, until 2020 the tacitly acknowledged boundary separating China and Taiwan, and stimulate Taiwanese air-defence systems. The

Map 2.1: **The Taiwan Strait**

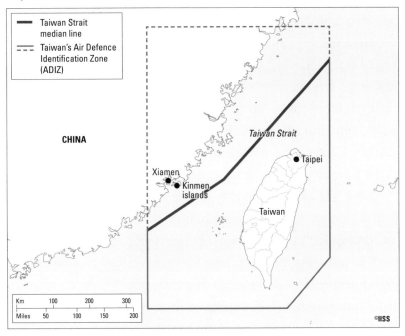

Chinese People's Liberation Army Air Force (PLAAF) began flying along the median line in 1996, with more than 400 sorties in 1998 and more than 1,200 in 1999. On a single day in late 2004, the Chinese flew more than 30 sorties that approached the median line.[10] Significantly, in November 2016 the PLAAF began flying strategic bombers around Taiwan, sometimes as solo flights, sometimes in conjunction with fighters, electronic-warfare aircraft and transport aircraft. April 2018 saw bomber flights around Taiwan conducted on three consecutive days for the first time. The following month, bombers arriving from different directions flew simultaneously around the island.[11]

Taiwan's defence ministry reports that the island's air force had to scramble aircraft 2,972 times during the first ten months of 2020 and conducted a total of 4,132 missions (including training and regular patrols), a 129% increase on the whole of 2019.[12] A similar trend was evident at sea, with Taiwanese ships undertaking 1,223 missions to intercept Chinese vessels between January and early November 2020 – an increase of 400 over the previous year.[13] Taiwan's foreign minister Joseph Wu said that, with Chinese air and naval drills around Taiwan reaching 'unprecedented' levels, the prospect of a military clash in the Taiwan Strait is rising precipitously.[14] In March 2020, coinciding with the PLA's first night-time exercise near Taiwan, China's maritime militia reportedly rammed a Taiwan Coast Guard vessel operating near the Kinmen Islands (occupied by Taiwan, but close to the Chinese mainland).[15] In October 2020, two Taiwanese fighter aircraft reportedly drove a Chinese fighter out of the island's ADIZ. This contrasts with past Taiwanese practice, where Chinese aircraft were typically monitored from a distance of approximately 30 kilometres so as to minimise the risk of collision, but is consistent with Tsai's March 2019 pledge to 'forcefully expel' Chinese transgressions of the median line.[16] In September 2020, China's foreign ministry confirmed Beijing's new position that 'there is no so-called median line of the strait'.[17]

The Korean Peninsula

The Demilitarized Zone (DMZ) which divides North and South Korea roughly along the 38th parallel is in reality one of the most heavily militarised areas on earth. More than one million troops, 20,000 armoured vehicles and artillery pieces, over a million landmines, and numerous fortified positions are squeezed into a small area on either side of the zone. The two Koreas are technically still at war; the Korean War (1950–53) ended with a ceasefire and a peace treaty has never been concluded.

More than 80 serious incidents have occurred on the border since the 1960s, most recently Pyongyang's June 2020 demolition of the Inter-Korean Liaison Office in Kaesong.[18] Many incidents had the potential to escalate into large-scale conflict.[19]

Map 2.2: **Korea**

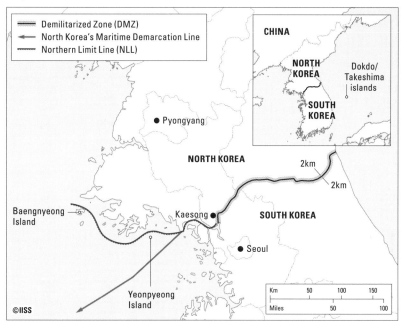

Most have occurred near either the DMZ or its seaward extensions. The two sides disagree on their maritime boundary in the Yellow Sea: South Korea recognises the Northern Limit Line (NLL) drawn unilaterally by the UN Command in August 1953, while North Korea has drawn a demarcation line roughly equidistant between the coasts of North and South, well to the south of the NLL.[20]

Tensions eased somewhat after a crisis in 1993–94 over Pyongyang's burgeoning nuclear-weapons programme, but spiked again dramatically in March 2010 with the sinking of a South Korean corvette, the *Cheonan*, near Baengnyeong Island in the Yellow Sea, killing 46 of the 104-man crew. An investigation concluded that the cause was a torpedo from a North Korean submarine, but Pyongyang denied any involvement. Later that year, two South Korean soldiers and two civilians were killed when North Korea fired approximately

200 artillery shells at Yeonpyeong Island, just south of the NLL. Pyongyang released a statement claiming that the island lies inside North Korea's 'territorial waters' and that 'a prompt powerful strike' had been necessary as 'a self-defensive measure' in response to 'extremely reckless military provocation' from the South.[21]

The year 2017 was especially tense on the peninsula. Following a North Korean intercontinental ballistic missile (ICBM) test in July 2017, Trump pledged to unleash 'fire and fury like the world has never seen' against Pyongyang if it continued to threaten the US.[22] Later reports suggested that the US and North Korea came closer to military conflict than many commentators had assumed. In an underreported response to the ICBM launch, for example, the US Army test-fired a tactical missile to signal to Pyongyang its ability to decapitate North Korea's leadership.[23] In December 2017 the US Air Force also reportedly performed a 'simulated air attack' on North Korea involving B-1 bombers and other aircraft crossing the NLL.[24]

Seoul diverged from this more assertive American approach, however, especially after Moon Jae-in, a progressive, was elected as president in May 2017. Moon warmly welcomed a North Korean delegation (which included Kim Jong-un's sister, Kim Yo-jong) to the February 2018 Winter Olympics in the South Korean city of Pyeongchang. This prompted a flurry of inter-Korean diplomacy, including three Kim–Moon summits. At the third summit, in Pyongyang in September 2018, several confidence-building measures were agreed, including the establishment of no-fly zones along the border, the cessation of military exercises close to the DMZ and the removal of several military guard posts in the area.[25] Moon also served as an inter-locutor between Kim and Trump, facilitating a summit between them in Singapore in June 2018. Trump and Kim met on two further occasions, in Hanoi in February 2019 and at the DMZ the following June. These encounters delivered little, however, beyond the vague four-point statement produced at their initial meeting in Singapore, and at working-level US–North Korea talks in Stockholm in October 2019, the North Koreans walked out after only eight hours.[26]

Kim and Chinese leader Xi Jinping did not meet at all in the first five years they were in power (in contrast, Kim's father Kim Jong-il visited China at least seven times during his ten-year rule).[27] Between March 2018 and 2020, however, they met five times, usually just before or just after other major summits, such as the first inter-Korean summit of April 2018 and Kim's Singapore and Hanoi summits with Trump. This emerging pattern led to depictions in the Chinese media of Xi as an elder statesman and mentor to Kim.[28] Kim also met Russian President Vladimir Putin near Vladivostok in April 2019.[29] As the previously hermit-like Kim found his feet on the global stage, his connections to Seoul seemed increasingly perfunctory. When Trump and Kim met at the DMZ in June 2019, for example, Moon was permitted only the briefest of interactions with his North Korean counterpart, even though he was technically the host. By August 2019, North Korea's state-run Korean Central News Agency was referring to Moon disparagingly, describing him as an 'impudent guy'.[30]

The stalling of US–North Korean diplomacy did not lead to a resuscitation of the inter-Korean process. Instead, North Korea withdrew from a number of the confidence-building measures agreed in Pyongyang in September 2018, with the underlying sources of the inter-Korean dispute still unresolved. The Kim Jong-un regime retreated from the diplomatic limelight and again became shrouded in secrecy. In April 2020 there were erroneous reports of Kim's death after the North Korean leader was not seen in public for several weeks.[31]

The East China Sea

Sporadic Chinese intrusions into Japan's EEZ increased rapidly after 1996, when Japan expanded its claims to include the disputed Senkaku/Diaoyu islands, Okinotorishima and other islands in the East China Sea, overlapping with existing Chinese claims. These intrusions increasingly involved warships, including submarines, as well as 'oceanographic research' and signals-intelligence ships.[32]

Much of the activity focused on the area around Okinotorishima, in the Philippine Sea midway between Taiwan and Guam. One report speculated that the PLA Navy (PLAN) was surveying the seabed to support future submarine operations as part of Beijing's A2/AD strategy to prevent the US Navy from coming to Taiwan's defence.[33] In November 2004, a Japan Maritime Self-Defense Force (JMSDF) patrol aircraft detected a Chinese *Han*-class nuclear attack submarine near the Sakishima islands and tracked it for three days, during which it sailed submerged between Ishigaki and Miyako islands, at the southern end of the Ryukyu island chain.[34] In September 2008, an unidentified (but almost certainly Chinese) submarine was detected south of the entrance to the Bungo Strait between Kyushu and Shikoku islands, some 60 km southwest of Shikoku's southernmost point, and 7 km inside Japan's territorial waters. The submarine, spotted with a 'periscope-like object' poking out of the water, was evidently on a reconnaissance mission.[35]

In September 2010, a Chinese fishing trawler, the *Minjinyu 5179*, deliberately rammed a Japan Coast Guard vessel near the Senkaku/Diaoyu islands. Departing from past practice, Tokyo arrested the vessel's captain and detained his 14-man crew. A statement from China's foreign ministry said Japan's actions were 'absurd' and 'violated international law and rudimentary common sense in international matters', and warned that 'if

Map 2.3: **East China Sea**

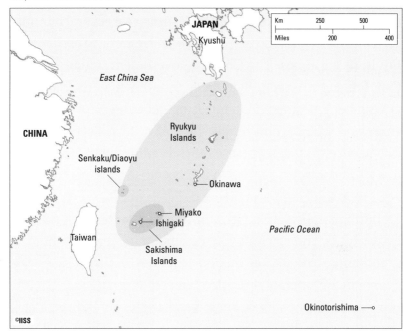

Japan continues in this reckless fashion, it will taste its own bitter fruit'.[36] Beijing cancelled bilateral exchanges, and Chinese travel companies began a boycott of Japan that continued even after the release of the crew, whose detention had lasted six days. The diplomatic crisis was resolved with the release of the Chinese captain, without charge, 11 days later.

Tensions flared over the Senkaku/Diaoyu islands in September 2012, after the Japanese government purchased some of the disputed features from their private owner, ostensibly to pre-empt the notoriously nationalistic mayor of Tokyo, Ishihara Shintaro, from using municipal funds to do the same. The purchase prompted the largest anti-Japanese demonstrations in China for almost a decade. In late 2012, a small Chinese maritime-surveillance aircraft penetrated Japanese airspace over the islands, the first such incident since 1958. Tensions reached a peak in January 2013 when, in two separate incidents, PLAN ships directed fire-control radar at a Japanese helicopter and a JMSDF destroyer for several minutes. This was the closest the two countries have come to exchanging fire in recent times. The Chinese government initially denied that fire-control radar had been used, while the Japanese government decided that releasing recordings of the radar emissions would compromise its ability to collect electronic intelligence (ELINT). Chinese officials admitted in March 2013 that a fire-control radar had in fact been used, but in a way that was 'accidental' and 'not planned'.[37]

Tensions subsided in November 2014 after the first meeting between Xi and Japan's then-prime minister Abe Shinzo, a 20-minute discussion on the sidelines of the Asia-Pacific Economic Cooperation leaders' meeting in Beijing. In the run-up to that encounter, Beijing and Tokyo announced a new 'four-point consensus' for improving China–Japan ties. The agreement included acknowledging that the two sides held differing 'positions' (or 'views', in the Japanese translation of the document) regarding the disputed islands, a promise that they would use 'dialogue and consultation' to prevent East China Sea issues from boiling over, and a pledge that they would 'gradually resume political, diplomatic and security dialogue through various multilateral and bilateral channels'.[38] In mid-2018, Beijing and Tokyo launched a new 'communication mechanism', which included a hotline connecting senior defence officials from the two sides and was designed to avoid accidental clashes between Chinese and Japanese military ships and aircraft.[39] In October 2019, the Chinese and Japanese militaries conducted joint military exercises for the first time in eight years.[40]

Chinese incursions into Japan's EEZ nevertheless continued to increase. In 2019, for example, more than 1,000 Chinese government vessels, including China Coast Guard (CCG) ships, entered the disputed waters. This was an 80% increase on the previous year and the highest frequency of incursions since at least 2012.[41] The CCG now maintains a near-permanent presence in the islands' 'contiguous zone', the area lying between 12 and 24 nautical miles offshore, between territorial waters and the inner edge of the EEZ (the UN Convention on the Law of the Sea permits freedom of navigation for all states in contiguous zones as well as EEZs). Between April 2019 and August 2020, Chinese vessels were present in the contiguous zone on 456 out of 519 days. During the previous 17-month period they entered the zone on only 227 out of 516 days.[42] When CCG vessels have actually entered the territorial waters within 12 nautical miles of the Senkaku/Diaoyu islands, they have loitered for increasingly long periods. On one occasion in July 2020, for example, they stayed for almost 40 hours, the longest such incursion on record.[43]

Meanwhile, Japan has also increasingly had to respond to Chinese aircraft approaching its ADIZ. From 1 April 2019 to 31 March 2020, Japan Air Self-Defense Force (JASDF) fighter jets were scrambled on 675 occasions in response to approaching Chinese drones, fighters, bombers and surveillance aircraft. This represented 71% of all JASDF scrambles during that period.[44]

Other disputes and tensions

Japan and Russia

The relationship between Tokyo and Moscow is also burdened by unresolved disputes and incessant tensions, most notably over competing claims to the southernmost Kuril Islands (which Japan calls the 'Northern Territories'), which the Soviet Union occupied in the aftermath of Japan's defeat in 1945. Tokyo's 'Basic Position' is that the islands are 'inherent territories of Japan that continue to be illegally occupied by Russia'.[45]

Map 2.4: **Kuril Islands**

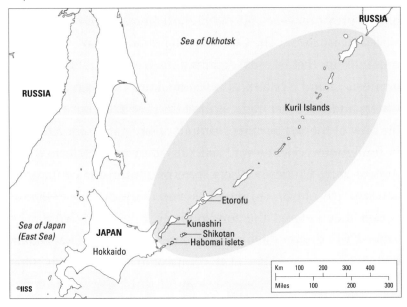

The dispute has prevented the two countries from signing a treaty formally ending the Second World War.

Tokyo's stance towards Moscow eased somewhat in 2013, reflecting Abe's view that closer cooperation could help to resolve the Kuril dispute. This rapprochement stalled briefly after Russia's March 2014 annexation of Crimea, but the sanctions Japan imposed as a result were no more than token, and by 2016 Russo-Japanese cooperation had resumed.[46] In September 2018, Putin unexpectedly proposed that Moscow and Tokyo sign a peace treaty 'without preconditions'.[47] Japan initially rejected this idea, arguing that the territorial disputes needed to be resolved before any treaty could be finalised. Two months later, Tokyo moderated this position, suggesting that treaty negotiations could be advanced based on a 1956 'joint declaration' between the two countries. But Moscow and Tokyo interpret that declaration differently: Moscow maintains that it is only required to return the Habomai islets and the island of

Shikotan (which together encompass only 7% of the disputed territory), while Tokyo holds that there must also be continued negotiations over the two larger islands of Kunashiri and Etorofu even after the Habomai islets and Shikotan have been returned.[48] The Japanese and Russian foreign ministers, Motegi Toshimitsu and Sergey Lavrov, recommended negotiations over the disputed territories in December 2019, agreeing to establish working-level talks on joint economic activity in the islands. But their meeting was overshadowed by Russia's seizure of five Japanese vessels fishing in the disputed waters.

Abe's successor as prime minister, Suga Yoshihide, who took office in September 2020, appears unlikely to display the same degree of personal commitment to addressing the territorial dispute, although during his first press conference he did express a desire to build a 'stable relationship' with Russia.[49] Putin cites Japan's alliance with the US as a stumbling block to peace. Moscow appears particularly concerned that the US intends to deploy intermediate-range missiles to Japan following the 2019 demise of the Intermediate-Range Nuclear Forces (INF) Treaty. Meanwhile, Russia has continued to visibly increase its military presence on and around the disputed islands. In 2016, for example, it deployed anti-ship missiles on Etorofu and Kunashiri. It has also conducted large-scale military exercises nearby, drawing protest from Tokyo. In March 2019, for example, 500 Russian troops participated in exercises on Etorofu and Kunashiri in which they practised how to prevent an enemy force from landing.[50] Japan's 2019 defence white paper referred to reports regarding the potential deployment of Russian fighter aircraft to Etorofu.[51]

During the Cold War, Japan was concerned with intrusions into its ADIZ by Soviet aircraft. In the 1980s the Soviet Union conducted more than 300 surveillance flights around Japanese airspace each year. This activity began to decrease in 1988 as the Soviet Union neared collapse, and such flights were relatively infrequent over the following decade. However, Russian flights close to Japanese airspace became more frequent again in the late 1990s.[52] During the year from 1 April 2019 to 31 March 2020, JASDF fighters intercepted Russian aircraft on 268 occasions, representing 28% of all JASDF scrambles during that period.[53]

Many of the Russian flights deliberately skirt the edge of Japanese airspace to test the strength and responsiveness of Japan's air defences. In February 2019, for example, JASDF fighters intercepted four Russian strategic bombers and four fighters flying in two separate formations over Japan's east and west coasts. Russia's defence ministry claimed that these were 'routine' flights which did not violate Japan's airspace.[54] On other occasions, however, Moscow's intentions have been less clear. In October 2020, for example, a Russian Mi-8 helicopter appears to have strayed accidentally into airspace off the northern Japanese island of Hokkaido, prompting Japan to scramble fighters in response. Tokyo subsequently complained to Moscow, which claimed that the helicopter did not belong to the Russian armed forces.[55]

Japan and North Korea
Japan officially portrays North Korea as the most immediate threat to its security, although there is substantial evidence that the government uses North Korean activities as a justification for a defence programme that it sees as necessary in response to the growing threat it perceives from China. While the main issues from Japan's point of view are North Korea's nuclear and missile programmes, North Korea's abduction of Japanese citizens during the Cold War also remains a source of grievance. During the 1970s and 1980s, North Korea abducted at least 17 (and perhaps as many as 70–80) Japanese citizens in

order to use them as 'cultural trainers' for North Korean spies. Pyongyang acknowledged the abductions in 2002, when Kim Jong-il met with his Japanese counterpart Koizumi Junichiro and five abductees were returned to Japan. Pyongyang declared that this resolved the matter, but Tokyo maintains that 'North Korea's assertions regarding the abductions issue have not provided any satisfactory account or convincing evidence, and therefore, the Government of Japan finds them unaccep-table'. Indeed, the Japanese government continues to place the highest priority on the abductions, insisting that 'without the resolution of this issue, there can be no normalization of relations between Japan and North Korea'.[56] When Trump met with family members of the abductees in May 2019, he noted that Abe had raised this issue in all of their meetings to date.[57]

Tokyo's deep concerns about North Korea's nuclear and missile programmes date to 1998, when Pyongyang launched a multi-stage *Taepodong*-1 ballistic missile whose path took it over Japan. The fear that the *Taepodong* could carry a nuclear warhead was raised after North Korea conducted its first nuclear test in October 2006. In March 2009, when North Korea was preparing to launch a *Taepodong*-2 missile, saying that it would carry a communications satellite, Japan's defence minister ordered the Japan Self-Defense Forces (JSDF) to shoot down any North Korean object that entered Japanese airspace. North Korea responded by threatening war against Japan in such an event.[58] In August and September 2017, Pyongyang test-fired *Hwasong*-12 intermediate-range ballis-tic missiles (IRBMs), which on both occasions flew over Hokkaido.[59] In December 2019, after formally announcing the end of its self-imposed moratorium on nuclear-weapon and long-range-missile testing, Pyongyang declared that Japan would again witness 'a real ballistic missile' flying over the country 'in the not distant future'.[60]

Japan and South Korea

Japan and South Korea have an outstanding dispute over ownership of the Dokdo (in Korean) or Takeshima (in Japanese) islands in the southern Sea of Japan (East Sea), about halfway between the two countries (see Map 2.2).[61] The islands were annexed by Japan in 1905, primarily because the Imperial Japanese Navy was interested in the possibility of building watchtowers and a telegraph station.[62] The main island is currently occupied by South Korea, which has built lodgings, lighthouses and a 'monitoring facility' there.[63]

Since 2018, relations between Japan and South Korea have deteriorated. In December 2018, for example, a South Korean destroyer locked its fire-control radar onto a Japanese P-1 maritime-patrol aircraft. Seoul and Tokyo disputed the details of this episode: South Korea claimed that the Japanese aircraft flew 'menacingly' close to its warship and demanded an apology; Tokyo denied the allegations, and both sides issued video, audio and photographic evidence purportedly supporting their respective claims. Despite working-level talks and a separate meeting between the foreign ministers of the two countries, there was no agreement on what had happened and several planned bilateral military activities were cancelled.[64] During a meeting on the sidelines of the June 2019 IISS Shangri-La Dialogue, Japan's then-defence minister Iwaya Takeshi asked his South Korean counterpart, Jeong Kyeong-doo, to prevent a recurrence of the episode and expressed Tokyo's keenness to conclude talks on this issue. Though again denying the Japanese allegations, the South Korean minister said Seoul would make 'active efforts to improve relations with Tokyo'.[65]

Yet tensions flared again in late July 2019, after two Russian surveillance aircraft flew twice through the airspace over Dokdo/Takeshima. South Korean fighters were scrambled in response, reportedly firing hundreds of warning shots.[66] Tokyo objected to the actions of both sides, formally lodging a protest with Seoul and stating that 'in light of Japan's stance regarding sovereignty over Takeshima, the South Korean military aircraft's having carried out warning shots is totally unacceptable and extremely regrettable'.[67]

Moon reached out to Suga as soon as the latter took office, and they conducted a 'telephone summit' in September 2020.[68] There have also been suggestions that the Biden administration will work actively to mend the rift between its two Northeast Asian allies, engendering a return to the trilateral cooperation which has periodically proven viable, most notably in the TCOG.[69] There is little evidence so far, however, that either Seoul or Tokyo is willing to de-emphasise the deep-seated historical animosities that divide them, which include not only their territorial dispute but also the issue of compensation for the victims of Japan's use of Korean forced labour, including prostitution, during the Second World War.

Japan and Taiwan

Japanese cooperation with Taiwan, previously discreet, has been more explicit since December 2020, when Japan's Deputy Defence Minister Nakayama Yasuhide surprised many commentators by calling upon the incoming Biden administration to 'be strong' in its support for Taipei and to regard the island's security as a 'red line'.[70] But Japan also has disputes with Taiwan, some arising from the sovereignty issue regarding the Senkaku/Diaoyu islands, where Taiwan's claim parallels China's, and some from zealous enforcement by the Japan Coast Guard of strict laws concerning foreign fishing in Japanese waters. In April 2016, for instance, the Japan Coast Guard detained the crew of a Taiwanese vessel that was fishing 150 nautical miles from Okinotorishima, around which Japan claims a 400,000 km² EEZ. The crew were released after paying a 'security deposit' of US$54,000, with assistance from the Taiwanese government.[71]

The Japan–Taiwan fisheries agreement of April 2013 was revised in 2015 to increase the time crews from both countries could spend in designated fishing zones around the Senkaku/ Diaoyu islands, and in 2018 to specify the methods they were permitted to use. Following the April 2016 incident, Tokyo and Taipei also agreed to convene an annual dialogue on cooperation in maritime affairs. This dialogue met for the fourth time in Taipei in December 2019, when discussions included maritime safety, scientific research, ocean environmental protection and fisheries cooperation. The 2017 iteration of the dialogue produced an agreement on search-and-rescue operations near Okinotorishima.[72]

A relatively small number of Taiwanese military aircraft fly close to Japan's ADIZ, occasionally causing the JASDF to respond. In October 2017, for example, Japanese fighters scrambled to identify an aircraft that was conducting a test flight from Taiwan.[73] However, Japan reported no such incidents involving Taiwanese aircraft in the two-year period between April 2018 and March 2020, perhaps reflecting closer cooperation between Tokyo and Taipei.[74]

China and North Korea

Although the 1,416 km China–North Korea border is currently quiescent, there are four areas of significant dispute. One concerns Mount Paektu, at the source of the Yalu and Tumen rivers. It is occupied by China, which regards it as recompense for supporting North Korea during the 1950–53 war. But the mountain carries considerable historic and symbolic significance for Pyongyang, which claims some 33 km² around the summit. North Korea asserts that it was the birthplace of Kim Jong-il (although Soviet records indicate he was born in Russia), and that Kim Il-sung, Kim Jong-il's father, used it as a base for fighting against the Japanese during their period of colonial rule (1910–45).[75] Kim Jong-un has visited this sacred mountain (on one occasion famously emulating his grandfather by riding a white horse) before making major policy pronouncements.[76] Another dispute involves dozens of islands in and some of the banks of the Yalu and Tumen rivers, where there is no agreed demarcation line. Pyongyang and Beijing each claim the island of Shindo in the Yalu estuary. Finally, the maritime boundary between North Korea and China has been unresolved since 1977, when Pyongyang unilaterally declared a 200-nautical-mile EEZ in the Yellow Sea, intruding into the Gulf of Beihai.[77]

These territorial disputes have not, however, caused major strains in the China–North Korea relationship. China is North Korea's leading supplier of food and fuel, while Pyongyang's primary focus continues to be regime survival. This has led it to de-emphasise disputes with China. Similarly, Beijing regards North Korea as an essential strategic buffer, particularly in the context of China's growing strategic competition with the US. The two countries cooperate across their disputed border, with joint infrastructure-development projects including a new Namyang–Tumen road bridge and an electricity-sharing scheme linked to the Sup'ung Dam on the Yalu River.[78] While North Korea was quick to close its border with China in January 2020 to prevent the transmission of COVID-19, and in late August ordered that violators be shot, there are no indications of any diminishing desire for continued cooperation from either Pyongyang or Beijing.[79]

China and South Korea

The relationship between China and South Korea has generally been harmonious since the two countries normalised their diplomatic relations in 1992. However, they too have several boundary disputes. China argues that its maritime boundary should be determined by a 'natural prolongation' approach, which extends its continental shelf about two-thirds of the way across the Yellow Sea and covers half of the maritime zone to which South Korea would be entitled if an 'equidistance line' was drawn between the two coasts, as has been Seoul's preferred approach since the 1960s.[80] They also dispute a submerged feature, known internationally as Socotra Rock (South Korea calls it Ieodo, China calls it Suyan), which sits in a busy waterway that is also thought to hold substantial gas and mineral resources.[81] It lies 149 and 247 km respectively from the nearest South Korean and Chinese islands. Its highest point is 4.6 metres below sea level at low tide, but South Korea has built a research station and a helipad on top.

This dispute has, on occasion, turned violent. A South Korean coastguard (KCG) official was killed in December 2011, while a crewmember on a Chinese fishing vessel died in October 2012 after being hit by a rubber bullet fired by the KCG.[82] In late 2013, after China established an East China Sea ADIZ that encompassed the rock, South Korea extended its ADIZ to it as well.[83] In February 2018, South Korea's air force scrambled more than ten aircraft after a Chinese fighter entered its ADIZ for more than four hours without prior notification.[84]

From defence modernisation to arms racing

Northeast Asia's geopolitical disputes and tensions and growing prosperity since the beginning of the century have together led to significantly greater defence spending. Aggregate Asian defence expenditure (including Northeast Asia, Southeast Asia, South Asia and Australasia) was an estimated US$457.6bn in 2020, approximately 25% of the global total. Northeast Asia accounts for about two-thirds of this, with China alone accounting for 42% in 2020.[85] Northeast Asia also accounts for a significant proportion of Asian defence procurement, including much of the more advanced new equipment purchased for national armed forces.

China is clearly the largest defence spender in Asia. How much Beijing actually spends on its armed forces is uncertain. China's official defence budget for 2020 was US$178bn, but this excludes several categories that other countries would typically include in their formal defence-budgeting processes, such as acquisitions of foreign weapons, and also certain personnel benefits and some of its research-and-development expenditure.[86] The IISS estimates that China's actual defence expenditure in 2020 was US$193bn, a 75% increase on 2010.[87] It is now the second-largest defence spender in the world, after the US. Japan, whose Ministry of Defense has secured funding increases for nine successive years, ranks eighth in the world, just behind France and Germany, with defence expenditure of US$49.7bn in 2020. South Korea ranks tenth with US$40.4bn.[88]

The sustained and rapid build-up of defence capabilities in Asia since 2000 can be characterised as the second phase of a region-wide enhancement that began in the late 1980s, but it differs in important ways from the first, which was truncated by the Asian financial crisis of 1997–98. Most importantly, there is substantial evidence of action–reaction dynamics that had not been operating in the earlier phase, indicating a complex emerging arms race in Northeast Asia, principally involving acquisitions of naval equipment.

The first phase saw Asian defence expenditure increase at an unprecedented rate, with the region's share of global military expenditure nearly doubling from 11% in the mid-1980s to 20% in 1995. Asia's share of global expenditure on arms transfers more than doubled, from 15% in the mid-1980s to 33% in 1993, reaching 41% in 1998.[89] The extraordinary rates of economic growth across most of the region provided the necessary resources. There was, however, little evidence of action–reaction dynamics. Asian military-procurement programmes during this period are best explained as driven by a desire for enhanced self-reliance in the context of a rapidly changing and increasingly uncertain regional security environment, and mostly involved modernisation, or the replacement of obsolescent equipment acquired in the 1960s and 1970s. This replacement process often involved substantial increases in qualitative capabilities, especially with respect to weapons, sensors and electronic-warfare systems.[90]

By around 2000, nearly all the countries which had been severely affected by the financial crisis had resumed increasing defence budgets. In Northeast Asia, South Korea, which was the hardest hit by the crisis, increased its defence spending by 6.2% in the 2000–01 fiscal year; by 2007 its annual real increase had grown to almost 9%.[91] China, of course, hardly faltered during the crisis; its defence budget increased by an average of 10% per year in the period 2000–16. This rate has since declined to 5–7% per year, reflecting slower Chinese economic growth.[92] Overall, Northeast Asian states have substantially improved their military capabilities over the last 20 years as a result of such budget increases. They have moved well beyond the levels of capability improvement considered adequate for defence modernisation in the 1990s.

There is, moreover, considerable evidence of action–reaction dynamics at work in these second-phase capability developments, which involve major procurement programmes in which indigenous defence industries play major roles. Important areas of capability improvement where action–reaction dynamics are evident include major naval capabilities; ballistic and cruise missiles, and missile-defence systems; and information-warfare and cyber-warfare capabilities.

The emerging naval arms race

Northeast Asian states are engaged in a serious strategic naval competition. They possess increasingly capable 'blue-water' navies, with modern surface combatants, aircraft carriers (sometimes euphemistically called 'amphibious transport ships' or 'helicopter destroyers') and submarines, as well as new land-based aircraft in both maritime-patrol and strike roles. They are conducting maritime surveillance and ELINT collection with increasing intensity and intrusiveness. They have acquired and deployed large numbers of long-range anti-ship missiles with over-the-horizon targeting capacity. Submarine- and ship-launched LACMs are also proliferating. Action–reaction dynamics are particularly evident with regard to modern surface combatants (destroyers and frigates); large 'amphibious transport ships', helicopter carriers and 'sea-control ships'; and submarines and anti-submarine-warfare capabilities.

With over 300 ships, China's PLAN has now overtaken the US Navy in terms of hull numbers to become the world's largest. The scale of China's naval shipbuilding has been particularly impressive: between 2014 and 2018 it launched more ships than the number of existing ships serving in any of the individual navies of Germany, India, Spain and the United Kingdom.[93] Approximately 70% of China's fleet can now be classified as 'modern' in terms of contemporary standards of ship production, compared to less than 50% in 2010.[94] The PLAN has 130 major surface combatants and 60 submarines (comprising four nuclear-powered ballistic-missile submarines (SSBNs), six nuclear-powered attack submarines (SSNs) and 50 diesel-powered attack submarines).[95] Over the last five years, its most significant new ships have included six Type-055 guided-missile cruisers, 23 Type-052D guided-missile destroyers and a Type-075 large amphibious assault ship.[96]

The Type-055 cruisers are likely to become the primary escort for China's aircraft carriers in blue-water operations. The US Defense Intelligence Agency describes them as 'one of the most advanced and powerful ships in the world, boasting a large array of advanced-capability weapons and sensors developed domestically'.[97] The Type-052D destroyers carry a variety of cruise missiles, surface-to-air missiles (SAMs) and anti-submarine weapons.[98] The Type-075 large amphibious assault ship can carry up to 30 helicopters in addition to landing craft and hundreds of troops, further enhancing China's power-projection capabilities. A second is under construction and others are reportedly planned.[99]

China also currently operates two aircraft carriers, with more in prospect. Its first carrier, the *Liaoning*, was purchased second-hand from Ukraine in 1998. It entered service in 2012 and has been used primarily in a training role. China's first indigenously built carrier, the *Shandong*, entered service in December 2019 and is a slightly larger version of the *Liaoning*. The *Liaoning* can carry 18–24 J-15 multi-role fighters and 17 helicopters; the *Shandong* can accommodate 32 J-15s and 12 helicopters.[100] These carriers are significantly smaller than their American counterparts, which can carry up to 100 aircraft, and the fact that neither is fitted with a catapult-launch system limits how quickly their fighters can be launched. China's third aircraft carrier has been under construction since 2018, while work on a fourth carrier is reportedly imminent. These vessels will almost certainly be larger than their predecessors and are expected to be fitted with electromagnetic catapult-launch systems.[101] China originally envisaged a six-strong carrier fleet, but cost and technical difficulties may lead to delays to the final two vessels.[102]

Similarly, despite cost and technical challenges, China has pressed ahead with an impressively paced submarine-construction programme. Based on its current production rate, the PLAN could have a fleet of 100 boats by 2035.[103] Perhaps most significantly, the US Department of Defense expects China to begin construction of the new Type-096 SSBN in the early 2020s.[104] This successor to the Type-094 SSBN will almost certainly be armed with JL-3 submarine-launched ballistic missiles (SLBMs) with an estimated range of 9,000 km, going a long way towards making China's nuclear second-strike capability credible. The JL-3 was tested several times in 2018–19.[105]

After the PLAN and the US Navy, the JMSDF is the third-most-powerful navy in the region; it may be the only one besides the US that could hold its own in a conflict with China. Its capability developments are undoubtedly intended to offset China's growing naval power. In December 2018, Tokyo confirmed long-standing speculation that its two largest warships – *Izumo*-class 'helicopter-carrying destroyers' – would be modified to allow them to carry the F-35B short-take-off and vertical-landing variant of the Joint Strike Fighter. This modification will essentially mean these vessels become light aircraft carriers. Tokyo refers to these vessels as 'multi-purpose destroyers', because of historical sensitivities stemming from Japan's aggressive use of aircraft carriers during the Second World War.[106] The *Izumo* class is significantly smaller than US or even Chinese carriers, and will be able to carry only around 20 F-35Bs. There is also speculation that Tokyo may convert the JMSDF's two older and smaller *Hyuga*-class through-deck 'helicopter destroyers' to operate F-35Bs, even though the number of aircraft each could carry would be even smaller.

Largely in response to developments in Chinese naval capability, Japan is also expanding its already formidable submarine fleet. The JMSDF presently operates 22 submarines, including 11 potent *Soryu*-class attack boats commissioned since 2009. Like China's newer *Yuan*-class submarines, the

Soryu uses an air-independent propulsion system which extends its range, and the latest two use lithium-ion batteries to extend it even further.[107] In October 2020, Japan launched the first of seven planned *Taigei*-class attack submarines, slightly larger and quieter than the *Soryu* class. When these enter service from 2022, they will allow the JMSDF to retire some of its older boats.[108]

Growing Chinese and Japanese submarine capabilities have in turn encouraged a significant enhancement of South Korea's submarine force. Speculation (sometimes overstated) regarding Pyongyang's apparent efforts to develop a 'new' type of conventionally powered ballistic-missile submarine with an associated SLBM capability, and to refurbish its existing fleet of some 70 conventional and coastal submarines, has further contributed to Seoul's anxiety over sea-based threats.[109] In the early 1990s South Korea only had four operational submarines; now it has 18. These include nine older boats and seven more modern ones, all based on German designs. Sea trials for the indigenously designed *Chang Bogo* III class, which is significantly larger and better-armed than its predecessors, commenced during 2019, and a second was launched in November 2020.[110] Nine such boats are expected to enter service by 2029.[111]

Taiwan is similarly trying to expand its submarine capabilities. It currently has two Second World War-era former US boats, the oldest operational submarines in the world. These can no longer fire torpedoes, although they can still lay mines. It also has two modified *Zwaardvis*-class boats it acquired from the Netherlands in the late 1980s.[112] Long-standing difficulties in obtaining replacements from abroad, largely due to Chinese pressure against external suppliers or their governments, led Taiwan to launch an ambitious 'Indigenous Defense Submarine' (IDS) programme in late 2016. It envisages introducing eight diesel-powered submarines into service within a decade. Construction of the first commenced in November 2020, with completion expected by 2024.[113] Taiwan's complete lack of submarine-building experience – and limited track record in producing naval vessels more generally – is a formidable obstacle for the programme, but it is drawing on external support and expertise. In March 2021, for example, Taiwan's defence minister Chiu Kuo-cheng confirmed that the Biden administration had approved the sale of three (unspecified) pieces of equipment considered key to the IDS programme.[114]

Nuclear weapons and missile developments

The proliferation of weapons of mass destruction (WMD) and long-range missile systems is proceeding rapidly and extensively in Northeast Asia. This is a much more complicated and potentially more volatile process than the bipolar superpower strategic nuclear arms race of the Cold War. There are several bilateral competitors, some of which are engaged in multiple rivalries. The expansion of the Chinese and North Korean nuclear arsenals, alongside uncertainties among US allies and partners over the reliability of US extended nuclear deterrence, could also influence Japan, South Korea and Taiwan to exercise their own nuclear options.[115] The dynamics, moreover, now involve not only relative nuclear capabilities but also interactions between nuclear postures and conventional capabilities.

China is the most important nuclear-weapons power in Asia, with an estimated stockpile of 350 warheads and an active development programme for both warheads and delivery systems. This makes China the third-largest nuclear power in the world. Although its nuclear force remains considerably smaller than both Russia's 4,310-warhead and America's 3,800-warhead stockpiles,[116] Beijing is highly likely to expand its nuclear-warhead inventory so as to maintain a credible second-strike capability, particularly as the US strengthens its missile defences.[117]

North Korea's nuclear programme has also accelerated since 2000, particularly under the leadership of Kim Jong-un. Pyongyang's first nuclear test was conducted under Kim Jong-il in October 2006. With a yield of less than one kilotonne, the test was regarded by most analysts as a 'fizzle'. A second test, in May 2009, yielded around two kilotonnes, which was still insufficient to demonstrate an operational nuclear-weapons capability.[118] The four tests conducted under Kim Jong-un, however, have generated progressively larger yields, with the latest, in September 2017, at an estimated 140–250 kilotonnes, which implies a thermonuclear or boosted-fission device.[119] How many operational nuclear weapons North Korea possesses is uncertain. According to one estimate, Pyongyang most probably has enough fissile material for 60 weapons, and has assembled 10–20 warheads, the majority of which have a likely yield of 10–20 kilotonnes.[120]

There is also considerable proliferation of ballistic-missile technology in Northeast Asia. China has produced a full suite of ICBMs, SLBMs, IRBMs, MRBMs and short-range tactical ballistic missiles. A new ICBM (the long-anticipated DF-41) and a new hypersonic boost-glide system (the DF-17) were introduced at a parade in 2019. The DF-41 is a solid-fuel, road-mobile missile capable of delivering multiple nuclear warheads to different targets. The DF-17, whose delivery system flies at more than five times the speed of sound, threatens to confound existing missile-defence systems. While Beijing maintains that the DF-17 will carry a conventional payload (it is report-edly in the process of replacing some of its older DF-11 and DF-15 SRBMs, some of which are targeted on Taiwan, with the DF-17),[121] there is speculation that it will ultimately be dual-capable, much like China's DF-26 IRBM.[122]

Like its nuclear-weapons programme, North Korea's missile programme has advanced significantly under Kim Jong-un. In July 2017, Pyongyang successfully tested an ICBM (the *Hwasong*-14) for the first time. In November 2017 it successfully tested the larger *Hwasong*-15, whose estimated range of 13,000 km could potentially reach anywhere in the continental United States. There are, however, doubts as to whether North Korea has developed the re-entry vehicle needed to deliver a nuclear warhead over such a distance.[123] In October 2020, North Korea paraded its newest ICBM, presumed to be the *Hwasong*-16. Although considerably larger than its predecessors and thus conceivably able to deliver a heavier payload, the size of the missile will constrain its mobility. It will almost certainly need to be fuelled at the launch pad, increasing its vulnerability to pre-launch attack. Several years of flight-testing will likely be required before the *Hwasong*-16 is fully operational.[124] North Korea also tested three new SRBMs in 2019. In March 2020 it conducted nine short-range missile tests – the most ever in a single month.[125] Pyongyang's new generation of SRBMs are solid-fuelled, making them quicker to launch and probably more accurate than their predecessors. At least some of them could be dual-capable.[126]

Other Northeast Asian states have begun to expand their indigenous missile capabilities in response to these Chinese and North Korean developments. After starting its own missile programme in the late 1960s, Taiwan focused on developing anti-ship cruise missiles and SRBMs, primarily because of US pressure to limit its weapons to 'defensive' systems. During the Tsai administration, however, Taiwan's interest in developing longer-range missiles able to strike Chinese military bases and critical infrastructure has grown. Its missile-development programme has proceeded quietly to avoid antagonising both Beijing and Washington, but at least two new medium-range cruise missiles are reportedly under development: the *Yun Feng* LACM with an estimated range of 1,000–2,000 km and a supersonic 2,000-km-range variant of the *Hsiung Feng*-II cruise missile.[127] Some reports also claim that Taiwan possesses a small number of indigenously developed ballistic missiles that could be used for deep strikes against the mainland.[128] Apart from these home-grown systems, in October 2020 the US approved the sale to Taiwan of 400 *Harpoon* anti-ship missiles and associated equipment, along with 135 extended-range Standoff Land Attack Missiles (SLAM-ERs), a *Harpoon* derivative compatible with Taiwan's F-16 aircraft.[129]

South Korea's system for responding to nuclear weapons and WMD is underpinned by three elements. The 'Strategic Strike' system (known as the 'Kill Chain' before it was rebranded in 2019) relies heavily upon *Hyunmoo*-II SRBMs and *Hyunmoo*-III and *Haeseong* cruise missiles[130] to pre-empt an impending North Korean nuclear attack. The second element, 'Overwhelming Response' (known as 'Korea Massive Punishment and Retaliation' until 2019), would be executed *after* a North Korean attack and would use missiles to eliminate the North's military and political leadership, with the aim of effecting regime change. The third leg is 'Korean Missile Defense', a multi-layered missile-defence network currently under development. It includes low-tier missile-defence capabilities (variants of the US *Patriot* system, which Seoul acquired second-hand from Germany in 2008) and the indigenously developed *Cheongung* medium-range surface-to-air-missile (M-SAM) system. There is also a sea-based component: South Korea's three *Sejong* KDX-3 guided-missile destroyers are fitted with *Aegis* combat systems and armed with SM-2 SAMs. In October 2019, a further three KDX-3 ships were ordered.[131]

In response to North Korea's burgeoning SLBM capabilities, Seoul is also acquiring, from Israel, additional *Green Pine* radars, which can detect and track targets out to a range of 800 km, to supplement two that became operational in 2012. Finally, South Korea continues to develop its indigenous long-range air-defence system (L-SAM), intended to intercept North Korean missiles in their terminal phase, and due to become operational in 2023–24.[132]

South Korea is adamant that it will not be part of any US-led missile-defence architecture, hence its focus on developing indigenous anti-missile systems. This reluctance was reinforced when China responded furiously to Seoul's 2016 decision to allow deployment of US Army Terminal High Altitude Area Defense (THAAD) missile-defence systems to counter the growing North Korean missile threat. Beijing charged that THAAD radars were capable of looking deep into Chinese territory, thereby undermining China's nuclear deterrent.[133]

Japan's missile defences, by contrast, are highly integrated and inter-operable with those of the US. Japanese missile-defence cooperation with the US began in the mid-1980s, when Tokyo agreed to jointly conduct research related to the Strategic Defense Initiative. Since the early 2000s, when Tokyo decided to acquire its own missile-defence capability (in large part due to the 1998 North Korean test that overflew Japan), there has been US–Japanese cooperation in the design, production and deployment phases. The two countries are currently working together, for example, to complete development of the advanced SM-3 Block IIA interceptor missile for use on *Aegis*-equipped destroyers. The missile completed its first successful intercept test in 2017.[134] The US Navy and the JMSDF have also been conducting joint missile-defence exercises for the past decade. The JASDF joined these exercises in 2018, and the Japan Ground Self-Defense Force (JGSDF) in 2019.[135]

Like South Korea's, Japan's missile-defence network is multi-layered. Lower-tier missile defence is provided by some 120 *Patriots* deployed throughout the country. Since 2006 the US has deployed *Patriot* Advanced Capability-3 units on Okinawa. To provide upper-tier missile defence, Tokyo had planned to acquire two *Aegis Ashore* units, which provide similar capabilities to ship-based *Aegis* systems. It retreated from this commitment in June 2020, ostensibly over concerns that the system's boosters could land on populated areas but more likely due to a combination of cost, technical difficulties and implementation delays.[136] Tokyo will instead rely on *Aegis*-equipped destroyers for this capability, and will build a further two *Aegis*-equipped warships.[137] Japan's missile-defence network also draws upon intelligence provided by two US-owned-and-operated X-band radars based at the Shariki radar site in Aomori Prefecture and Kyogamisaki Communications Site in Kyoto. These radars detect and track North Korean missile launches.[138]

China is working to develop its own missile-defence capabilities, further feeding the action–reaction dynamic. China already has one of the world's largest inventories of long-range SAMs, consisting both of Russian-sourced and indigenously developed missiles that potentially provide a limited capacity to engage ballistic and low-flying cruise missiles.[139] Beijing has also successfully tested an indigenous SAM (the HQ-19) against missiles in the 3,000 km range.[140] It is reportedly supported by indigenous Chinese radars; one, the JL-1A, may have the capacity to detect and track multiple ballistic missiles.[141] China has also begun testing the Russian S-400 long-range SAM system (SA-21), able to hit targets out to 400 km and to track a greater number of targets (including ballistic missiles).[142] In October 2019, Putin announced that Moscow would assist China with creating its own early-warning missile-defence system, a capability which only Russia and the US presently possess.[143]

Action–reaction in the cyber domain

Assessing action–reaction dynamics in the cyber realm is not straightforward. Many cyber capabilities are either dual-use (both commercial and military) or have no obvious military purpose, even if they may be able to generate economic and political consequences that could affect military capabilities and operations.[144] But the armed forces of China, Russia and the US, the most powerful actors in the cyber domain, are adopting and adapting cyber capabilities into their doctrines, strategies and planning processes.[145] Other Northeast Asian states are following suit.

China began to develop cyber capabilities in the mid-1990s, with the implementation of an IW plan in 1995.[146] Since 2008, all major PLA exercises have included cyber and IW elements.[147] A key turning point in developing those capabilities occurred in December 2015, when Beijing established the PLA Strategic Support Force (PLASSF). This consolidated China's cyber-, space-, electronic- and psychological-warfare capabilities into a single branch of the military. This step was driven by concerns over Chinese inferiorities relative to the US in the cyber domain.[148] Xi's stated objective is to establish China as a 'cyber superpower'.[149]

North Korea's cyber capabilities are considerable, especially for a country with such a small economy. They also contribute to the action–reaction dynamic in Northeast Asia. According to one recent estimate, illicit cyber operations have netted Pyongyang up to US$2bn in recent years.[150] South Korean estimates suggest that the North has a dedicated cyber-warfare unit of almost 7,000 personnel, although the opacity of the regime makes such assessments difficult.[151] Although global in scope, North Korea's cyber activities display a strong regional focus. Some are financially motivated – the October 2017 theft of US$60m from Taiwan's Far Eastern International

Bank, for example, has been attributed to the Lazarus Group, a North Korean cyber-crime ring which apparently answers to the regime's Reconnaissance General Bureau.[152] The group is also suspected of carrying out the 2017 *WannaCry* ransomware attack, which infected government, hospital and business computers in at least 150 countries.[153] Japan felt the brunt of North Korea's cyber activities in January 2018, when North Korean hackers apparently broke into its cryptocurrency exchange and stole digital coins worth US$520m.[154]

Japan has responded by bolstering its own cyber capabilities. In its December 2018 'National Defense Program Guidelines', for example, the Ministry of Defense signalled its intention to develop a 'Multi-domain Defense Force', which will include the cyber domain.[155] As part of this effort, the JSDF have established a 'Cyber Defense Group' (CDG), which 'coordinates cyber defence for the JGSDF, JMSDF and JASDF, and is charged with protecting the defence ministry's critical-information infrastructure'.[156] The CDG was expanded from 220 to 290 personnel in March 2021.[157] US–Japan cooperation is also deepening in the cyber domain. One of the most significant results of the April 2019 US–Japan 'two-plus-two' consultations, for instance, was an agreement between Washington and Tokyo that a cyber attack could 'in certain circumstances … constitute an armed attack for the purposes of Article V of the U.S.–Japan Security Treaty'.[158] This was a significant step up from the revised US–Japan defence-cooperation guidelines of April 2015, which stated that 'Japan will have primary responsibility to respond' to cyber incidents targeting Japan, with the US providing 'appropriate support'.[159]

Taiwan is subjected to an estimated 30m cyber attacks per month, with approximately 60% apparently originating from mainland China.[160] Chinese cyber attacks in the lead-up to the island's January 2020 elections were widely reported.

Significantly, Taipei alleged that Beijing took the unprecedented step of utilising artificial intelligence (AI) to interfere in those elections, employing AI-generated messaging to mimic the language of voters via social-media platforms.[161] Cyber operations are also expected to play a prominent role in any Chinese military offensive against Taiwan, with the PLASSF taking a central role.[162] In mid-2017, Taiwan established an 'Information, Communications and Electronic Warfare Command', with responsibility for coordinating the island's cyber defences. Like Japan, Taiwan is also working more closely with the US in the cyber domain. In November 2019, for example, Taipei for the first time co-hosted a multinational cyber-security exercise with the American Institute in Taiwan, which also involved officials from a range of other countries including Australia, Indonesia and Japan.[163]

CHAPTER THREE

Strategic outlooks and languishing institutions in Southeast Asia

Unlike Northeast or South Asia, where large-scale war between heavily armed neighbours is an ever-present possibility, Southeast Asia is not riven by intense adversarial relations between states. The main state-level security challenge emanates from outside, in the form of China's growing strategic extroversion, but there is little agreement within Southeast Asia on how serious that challenge is. To the extent that they are responding, Southeast Asian countries are mainly doing so diplomatically rather than militarily. Southeast Asian security is best assessed through the prism of politics and diplomacy, and only secondarily through a military lens.

Rivalries among Southeast Asian states are largely residual and, compared to other sub-regions, relatively muted. Accommodation within Southeast Asia permitted a regional entente in the form of ASEAN. Southeast Asian politicians, their dialogue partners and sympathetic observers have all, for diverse reasons, made much of the notion of the centrality of ASEAN to Asia's security order. But while ASEAN is the only regional institution in Asia able credibly to lay claim to a significant politico-security role, it provides only a weak basis for managing security in its own sub-region, let alone the wider Asia-Pacific or Indo-Pacific, for several reasons. Southeast Asia is highly complex politically; its states perceive the security challenges they face from distinctly national perspectives. They have thus had persistent difficulty in finding common ground in the external security sphere and, while there are sometimes similarities in their strategic outlooks, have responded in diverse ways to the changing regional distribution of power that has arisen primarily as a result of China's increased economic and military strength and assertiveness.

While ASEAN member states have regularly attempted to coordinate their diplomatic positions, they have not succeeded in staking out a clear collective position with respect to the arrival of China as a powerful and extroverted security actor. Although some Southeast Asian states have adopted diplomatic measures aimed at hedging their international security options, notably by reinforcing their security relations with the US, and in some cases by strengthening links with regional powers such as Australia, India and Japan, others have shown less concern over China's growing power and influence.

Their military responses to the evolving regional security environment have also varied considerably. Some have made serious efforts to improve their externally oriented defence capabilities, but these efforts have not always primarily been responses to the challenge from China. Others have not prioritised external defence to the same extent, and for some it has not even been a priority. Moreover, Southeast Asian states have generally not attempted to coordinate defence policies and planning in relation to external threats. Reflecting their diverse assessments of and responses to their security environment, as well as low-key bilateral tensions among them, ASEAN members' multilateral military cooperation has remained embryonic.

Tensions within Southeast Asia

The idea of Southeast Asia as a distinct sub-region is not natural or fixed; it only dates from the end of the Second World War. The establishment of the Southeast Asia Treaty Organization (SEATO) in 1954 and ASEAN in 1967, however, reified Southeast Asia as a coherent entity in the minds of policymakers and analysts. ASEAN's declaratory establishment in 2015 of a 'Community', including political-security as well as economic and socio-cultural dimensions, has at least for the time being reinforced that status. But it remains extraordinarily complex, subsuming as it does 11 states (the ten ASEAN members plus Timor-Leste) of diverse geographical extent, population size, ethnic and religious composition, level of economic development and political system, each with its own distinctly national outlook (sometimes contested domestically) on foreign, defence and security policy. Long-standing tensions among states have thus persisted, and there are important differences over the proper format for, and intensity of, relations with extra-regional powers.

ASEAN was formed in 1967, primarily on the basis of reconciliation among five non-communist states (Indonesia, Malaysia, the Philippines, Singapore and Thailand) following regime change in Indonesia that had a dramatic effect on Jakarta's foreign policy. In the period 1963–66, Indonesia had pursued a politico-military 'confrontation' against the newly formed federation of Malaysia, which it claimed was a neo-colonial entity that challenged its security, objecting particularly to the inclusion of the formerly British-controlled states of Sabah and Sarawak. Because of its own claim to Sabah, the Philippines also pursued a political campaign against Malaysia during the mid-1960s. A further significant development was Singapore's independence in 1965 following two unhappy years within the Malaysian federation.

Against the backdrop of the Vietnam War, Southeast Asian leaders intended ASEAN from its inception as not just a mechanism for economic cooperation but also as a political entente. They recognised that, in the interests of their own regime survival in the face of the politico-military challenge from communism, they needed greater certainty that they could develop their economies and maintain their existing political systems without the distractions and dangers inherent in the neighbourhood quarrels that had characterised the mid-1960s.

Overall, the subsequent success of ASEAN's original members (as well as Vietnam, which joined the association in 1995), in terms of economic development and promoting their peoples' overall welfare, has been striking. At the same time, while there has been significant political change in some member states (notably Indonesia, Malaysia, Myanmar, the Philippines and Thailand), this has stemmed largely from the evolution of these countries' own civil societies rather than because of external influence. Severe socio-economic inequalities persist, and several Southeast Asian states (Indonesia, Myanmar, the Philippines and Thailand) still face important internal-security challenges, largely rooted in the grievances of ethnic and religious minorities. Without the political accommodation embodied in ASEAN's norm of sub-regional non-interference, however, tensions and possibly even conflict in Southeast Asia would have prevented its members from attaining their present prosperity and security.

Nevertheless, though ASEAN's members have had a significant common interest in minimising their disputes with each other since the late 1960s, and have avoided major armed conflict among themselves, their success has been incomplete. In their contemporary forms, most of Southeast Asia's states are essentially legacies of Western colonialism. As a result, territorial boundaries often cut across ethnic and religious communities, and assertive nationalism has continued to play an important role in nation-building and in affirming governments' domestic legitimacy. Tensions linked to territorial disputes (for example, between Indonesia and Malaysia over the islands of Sipadan and Ligitan and nearby waters, and between Cambodia and Thailand over their land frontier) have sometimes disrupted bilateral relations. Conflict between armed ethnic-minority entities and Myanmar government forces has resulted in border tensions and even armed clashes with Thailand. Thailand's government and armed forces have remained wary of what they perceive as Malaysian interference in their country's Malay-populated southernmost provinces. Singapore is still acutely sensitive to the potential for political developments in Indonesia and Malaysia to threaten its own security. The Philippines has maintained its claim to Sabah state. Of particular contemporary significance, Brunei, Malaysia, the Philippines and Vietnam all claim features in the South China Sea, their claims overlapping not only with those of China and Taiwan, but in some cases with each other's. Meanwhile, illegal fishing in neighbours' EEZs has sometimes disrupted intra-ASEAN relations.

Between the US and China

The historical legacies and modern geopolitical circumstances of each Southeast Asian state have contributed to distinctly national outlooks on how to manage external security, particularly in terms of relations with the major powers involved in Southeast Asia. Even ASEAN's five original members did not hold uniform views, despite their common anti-communist policies at home and generally pro-Western dispositions during the Cold War. Since the 1990s, the expansion of ASEAN's membership to include Cambodia, Laos, Myanmar and

Vietnam has further complicated the organisation's efforts to find strong, common positions on the geopolitical challenges facing the sub-region.

China's rising power was evident even during the 1990s, but it has become much clearer and more threatening to the stability of the established Asian order, and to that of Southeast Asia, since Xi took power in 2012–13. From late 2013 China embarked on a major campaign using land-reclamation techniques to enlarge many of the features (islets, reefs, rocks and shoals) it occupies in the South China Sea and to build military installations on them. Other important indicators of China's growing strength include its large-scale naval modernisation; expanding deployments of maritime paramilitary vessels to coerce its neighbours, especially those in Southeast Asia; efforts to undermine ASEAN's unity; attempts to create an alternative regional security architecture excluding the US and other Western powers; and the use of economic instruments (including the BRI) as well as political-influence operations to gain sway over smaller powers.

Southeast Asian governments have also been anxious about US policy changes that have threatened to undermine America's vital role as a stabilising power in Southeast Asia and the wider region.[1] Nixon's 1969 Guam speech, in which he indicated limits on future US engagement in defending regional states, and subsequent reductions in America's military presence in the region (notably the withdrawal of naval and air forces from the Philippines in 1992) had previously provoked Southeast Asian governments to rethink their security and defence policies (see Chapter One). The Trump administration's approach was nevertheless a major shock for many in Southeast Asia. Of particular concern were Trump's indications while on the campaign trail that Washington might reduce its security commitments to Asian partners;

his announcement upon taking office that the US was with-drawing from the Trans-Pacific Partnership (of which Brunei, Malaysia, Singapore and Vietnam were members); his erratic leadership style; and his emphasis on correcting supposedly unfair trade balances not only with China but also with a number of American allies and partners including Indonesia, Malaysia, Thailand and Vietnam. During the Trump admin-istration the US developed mechanisms and policies – most notably the FOIP and a more assertive posture in the South China Sea – that indicated continuing commitment to main-taining Southeast Asia's security. While wishing for the US to remain closely involved in regional security, however, Southeast Asian governments have also felt decidedly uncomfortable with the intensifying economic and geopoliti-cal rivalry between the US and China. The fact that important structural factors underpin this intensifying Sino-American competition meant that the advent of the Biden administra-tion did not significantly mitigate this concern.

While some observers have attempted to classify contemporary Southeast Asian governments according to whether they 'lean' more towards China or the US,[2] such categorisation is difficult because most have attempted to maintain a balance in their relations with the two major powers that recognises the importance both of their economic ties with China and of the US maintaining its regional security role.

Singapore

This balancing phenomenon is most striking in the case of Singapore. Both during and after the Cold War, despite its non-aligned status and its lack of a formal alliance with the US, Singapore's view has been that its interests and those of Southeast Asia are best served by a regional balance of power maintained essentially by the US continuing to play an important role in East and Southeast Asian security.[3] Accordingly, since the late 1960s Singapore has moved gradually closer to the US in strategic terms, implementing over time a series of practical measures intended to facilitate continued American engagement.

In 1990, a bilateral Memorandum of Understanding (MoU) allowed expanded US use of facilities in Singapore for naval repairs and air-force training. In 2005, a confidential Strategic Framework Agreement codified the bilateral defence and security relationship, the most important elements of which encompass the long-term basing of Singapore Air Force training squadrons in the US and the location in Singapore of important US military facilities and units, including the naval task force that provides logistic support for the US 7th Fleet and organises the US Navy's cooperative activities throughout Southeast and South Asia. Since 2013, Singapore has hosted rotational deployments of US Navy Littoral Combat Ships. During 2019, several new agreements further bolstered long-term bilateral defence and security relations: in March, Singapore Minister of Defence Ng Eng Hen confirmed the city-state's first order for US-made F-35 Joint Strike Fighters; in September, Prime Minister Lee and Trump renewed the 1990 MoU, extending it to 2035; and in December, the two sides agreed that Singapore's air force could establish a fighter-training detachment on Guam.

Singapore has, however, been resolute in not acceding to a formal alliance with the US and has simultaneously developed its political, security and defence relations not only with US allies (most notably Australia and Japan) and partners (particularly India), but also with China, despite it being widely accepted that the latter is an emerging strategic peer competitor for the US. Singapore's refusal to be drawn into a formal alliance underscores that it remains determinedly neutral with respect to US–China differences. Lee underlined this in a keynote address to the 2019 IISS Shangri-La Dialogue Asian security summit, pointing to the need for the US to forge 'a new understanding that will integrate China's aspirations within the current system of rules and norms'.[4]

Singapore's relations with China are based primarily on a thriving economic relationship. The Chinese ethnicity of 76% of Singapore's permanent population has both facilitated economic relations and provided a solid base of support for closer ties with 'the mainland'. Indeed, Singapore's policy since the 1990s of encouraging large-scale immigration from China may ensure that strong domestic support for close relations with Beijing continues. However, Singapore has simultaneously and resolutely maintained close ties – including an important military-training arrangement – with Taiwan, and has only gradually and partially accommodated Beijing's pressure for even closer bilateral security coopera-tion. Although Singapore and China entered into an enhanced Agreement on Defence Exchanges and Security Cooperation in October 2019, what was envisaged did not approach the depth and breadth of collaboration evident between the Singapore and US defence establishments.[5]

Singapore would almost certainly make strenuous efforts to avoid being forced to take sides in the event of serious tensions, let alone conflict, between the US and China. This could be difficult in the event of hostilities between China and a US ally, such as the Philippines, particularly as Washington could wish to use Singapore as a base from which to support its operations. While Singapore might conceivably justify such support as a requirement under its long-standing security rela-tionship with America, it is virtually unthinkable that it could ever deploy any of its own forces as part of a US-led coalition opposed to China.

The Philippines

Perhaps surprisingly, although both the Philippines and Thailand are formal US allies, neither has expressed a strategic posture as consistently or as clearly as Singapore has since the end of the Cold War, nor has either unequivocally supported a continued American regional-security role. Indeed, both have at times appeared ambivalent regarding alignment with the US. In 1992, the Philippine Senate prevented then-president Corazon Aquino's administration from agreeing to extend the US military presence in the country, forcing the US to close its major Subic Bay naval base. Bilateral security relations subsequently diminished, and military ties only began to recover after a new Visiting Forces Agreement (VFA) was concluded in 1999. This facilitated the *Balikatan* exercises – a major annual bilateral military-training event – and, between 2002 and 2015, deployment of US troops to the southern Philippines in a counter-terrorism training role.

In 2012, a naval stand-off between the Philippines and China over the disputed Scarborough Shoal (a group of uninhabited rocks in the South China Sea, about 270 km west of Subic Bay) ended with China effectively controlling the area through a constant coastguard presence. Manila responded not only by going to the Permanent Court of Arbitration (PCA) in The Hague to file a case under the UN Convention on the Law of the Sea against China's extensive claims in the South China Sea in 2013, but also by moving to strengthen US–Philippine security relations. Nervous over the Philippines' lack of an effective external defence capability, then-president Benigno Aquino III's administration allowed US Navy ships to visit the former Subic Bay base more frequently. Joint exercises were stepped up, while the US also supplied additional surplus military equipment and helped establish a 'coast watch' centre intended to enhance maritime threat awareness.

Map 3.1: **South China Sea**

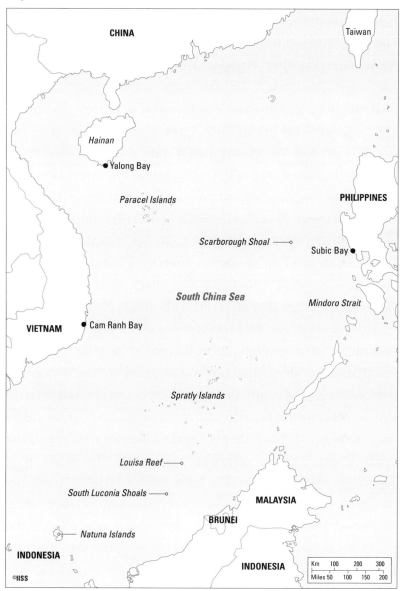

Although Manila was reluctant to accede to any arrangement that domestic political opponents might construe as involving new US bases,[6] the 2014 US–Philippine Enhanced Defense Cooperation Agreement (EDCA) provided a framework for even more intense collaboration, including US military operations from 'agreed locations' in the Philippines. A legal challenge, however, delayed implementation of the EDCA, which faced fresh obstacles after Rodrigo Duterte became president in June 2016. The Obama administration's criticism of Duterte's 'war on drugs' led the latter to threaten to review and possibly dispense with the defence agreement. Relations between Washington and Manila improved during the Trump administration, but the EDCA's implementation remained slow and its first major infrastructural project (a warehouse for humanitarian assistance and disaster relief (HADR) equipment) was not completed until January 2019.[7] In the meantime, though, US forces stepped up operations from the Philippines: in April 2016, for example, US Air Force A-10 attack aircraft from a rotational deployment flew close to Scarborough Shoal.[8]

Mutual ambivalence, however, has continued to cloud US–Philippine security cooperation. Crucially, the political context has changed under Duterte, who has promoted an 'independent foreign policy' which notably involves closer relations with China – despite the July 2016 PCA decision which overwhelmingly supported Manila's case against Beijing's claims in the South China Sea. The following December, Manila accepted a package of small arms and boats from China for use in its counter-terrorism and anti-narcotics campaigns.[9] And when Xi visited Manila in November 2018, China was already the Philippines' largest trading partner. During the visit, the two countries raised their relations to the level of 'comprehensive strategic cooperation' and finalised 29 documents on specific areas of collaboration, including infrastructural development in the Philippines through China's BRI. Importantly, a joint statement by Xi and Duterte also emphasised that their countries' differences in the South China Sea would not prevent cooperation in other fields, and that they would address their maritime disputes using peaceful means and expand their cooperation at sea including, potentially, on oil and gas exploration and exploitation.[10] In June 2019, Duterte's dismissal of a Chinese vessel's sinking of a Philippine fishing boat as 'a little maritime incident' provided further evidence of an accommodating posture towards Beijing.[11]

An assertive attitude towards the US has also characterised Duterte's 'independent foreign policy'. A focus for controversy has been whether the 1951 US–Philippines Mutual Defence Treaty would apply in the event of conflict over features that Manila claims in the South China Sea. As was also the case in relation to other potential Asian flashpoints – most notably Taiwan – the danger for Washington was that a clear-cut US guarantee that the treaty would indeed apply might embolden Manila to defend its claims more aggressively and risk entangling America in a dispute of questionable strategic importance. Making clear that the treaty would not apply, however, might encourage Chinese adventurism. In December 2018, Philippine Secretary of Defense Delfin Lorenzana openly criticised US ambivalence regarding its treaty obligations and called for a formal review of the alliance.[12] During 2019, American officials went out of their way to reaffirm that the US would come to the Philippines' defence if it faced external military aggression, while avoiding any specific commitment in relation to Scarborough Shoal. Visiting Manila in March 2019, for example, then-secretary of state Pompeo confirmed that 'as the South China Sea is part of the Pacific, any armed attack on Philippines forces, aircraft or public vessels in the South China Sea will trigger mutual defense obligations under Article 4 of our mutual defense treaty'.[13]

Underlining the instability of bilateral relations under Duterte, however, in February 2020 the Philippine president, angered by the US refusal to grant a visa to a political associate who had played a central role in the 'war on drugs', announced that Manila would terminate the VFA by August, severely undermining US capacity to support the Philippines militarily.[14] Although Duterte's government subsequently suspended the termination, it now seems unlikely that security relations between Washington and Manila will be normalised before the president's term ends in 2022.

Thailand

The US–Thailand alliance has become signally less important for both parties since 1976, when the US completed with-drawing from its Thai air bases following the communist victories throughout Indochina. Thailand's relations with China then intensified. Facilitated by the end of China's efforts to export communist revolution, close diplomatic and mili-tary cooperation following Vietnam's invasion of Cambodia in December 1978 revived bilateral ties between Bangkok and Beijing. These now include not only one of Thailand's most important trading relationships but also a high level of polit-ical consultation and a defence link codified in a Joint Action Plan on Thailand–China Strategic Cooperation in 2007. In 2012, then-prime minister Yingluck Shinawatra agreed a series of deals with China's then-premier Wen Jiabao which elevated bilateral relations to a 'comprehensive strategic cooperative partnership'.[15] Military cooperation involves not only frequent exercises, exchanges, visits and consultations, but also major arms sales by China to Thailand.

After a coup in May 2014, Thailand's relations with China became even closer as the US and other Western governments imposed sanctions on General Prayuth Chan-o-cha's military government. As the Obama administration cut finance for purchasing US military equipment, and cancelled or reduced the size of bilateral military exercises, Bangkok stepped up defence cooperation with Beijing, particularly in terms of equipment procurement. Most importantly, in 2017 Thailand ordered submarines and tanks from China. But while there have been signs of Thailand's traditional foreign-policy approach of 'bamboo bending in the wind'[16] asserting itself, with Bangkok effectively acquiescing in China's renaissance as a highly influential power in Southeast Asia, Thailand has nevertheless maintained at least the framework of its US alliance. Significantly, Thailand continues to host the annual *Cobra Gold* military exercise. Originally simply a bilateral US–Thai affair, since 1982 *Cobra Gold* has evolved to become a cornerstone of US efforts to engage on a more multilateral basis in Asian security and is now the largest set of regular multilateral war games in the region, with troops from Indonesia, Japan, Malaysia, Singapore and South Korea as well as Thailand and the US usually participating. Approximately 20 other countries send observers. Although the Obama administration slightly reduced US participation following the 2014 coup, by 2018 this was fully restored.

Indonesia
Ambivalence towards the US role in the region, however, has consistently been more pronounced in Indonesia and Malaysia. Since independence, the governments of these two non-aligned states have traditionally exploited populist nationalism in order to rally domestic political support. The overthrow in 1965–66 of Sukarno's vehemently anti-Western regime (which had become closely aligned with China and pursued aggressive regional policies, notably 'Confrontation' against Malaysia) and the installation of Suharto's military-backed government represented a strategic windfall for the US and the West in the midst of the challenges posed by the intensifying war in Vietnam. These developments also provided

the basis for the intra-regional reconciliation that allowed the formation of ASEAN.

Despite its generally pro-Western orientation, however, which was paralleled by an overt hostility towards China (with which diplomatic relations were suspended until 1990), Suharto's regime maintained the essence of Indonesia's 'active and non-aligned' foreign policy. A key aspect of this was Jakarta's promotion of regional solutions to regional problems, a stance encapsulated in ASEAN's declaration in 1971 of Southeast Asia as a Zone of Peace, Freedom and Neutrality (ZOPFAN) which would be 'free from any form or manner of interference by outside powers'.[17] A significant expression of Indonesia's regionalist foreign-policy orientation occurred in the 1980s, when Jakarta made clear its preference for a negotiated resolution of the diplomatic and military impasse created by Soviet-backed Vietnam's occupation of Cambodia. This contradicted the official ASEAN line, promoted by Singapore and Thailand and supported by the West (and China, keen as it was to circumscribe the influence of the Soviet Union and Vietnam), that it was necessary to reverse Hanoi's fait accompli.

Since Suharto's downfall in 1998, greater political freedom in Indonesia has allowed a substantial revival of Islamist politics and, in the context of the country's contemporary multi-party system, it has become normal for Islamist parties to form part of governing coalitions. This has provided an additional reason for Jakarta to emphasise its non-alignment, particularly in light of the widespread view among Indonesian Muslims that, as well as supporting Israel, the US and its Western partners have pursued wars of aggression against Muslims in Iraq, Afghanistan and elsewhere as part of their 'war on terror'. Nevertheless, relations with the US have formed an important part of Indonesia's increasingly confident international diplomacy that has developed in parallel with the domestic stability and prosperity under the successive presidencies of Susilo Bambang Yudhoyono (2004–14) and Joko Widodo ('Jokowi') (2014–). In 2010, Obama and Yudhoyono agreed a bilateral 'comprehensive partnership' involving enhanced cooperation on not only issues of democracy and civil society, education, environment and climate, energy, trade and investment, but also security. Building on links that have developed since Suharto's time, subsequent US–Indonesia security cooperation has been aimed at 'advancing Indonesia's defence modernisation efforts in order to enhance [its] role in regional and global security' and has included arms transfers and the establishment of a Defense Planning Dialogue.[18]

Despite these improvements in specific areas of bilateral defence relations, however, overall security collaboration with Indonesia has developed more slowly than Washington might have hoped. Crucially, the enduring strength of Indonesia's non-aligned impulse and resistance to external interference has limited both the intensity of the Indonesia–US entente and its strategic benefits for the US. The 'dynamic equilibrium' foreign-policy doctrine espoused by Yudhoyono's foreign minister, Marty Natalegawa, was essentially a contemporary manifestation of Indonesia's commitment to its long-established bebas aktif (active non-alignment) policy.[19] Under Jokowi since 2014, Jakarta's foreign policy has emphasised the ambition for Indonesia to become a 'global maritime fulcrum', the importance of 'ASEAN centrality', and the vision of an inclusive as well as 'stable, peaceful and prosperous' Indo-Pacific region built through dialogue and 'respect for international law'.[20] This vision, which provides the basis for the ASEAN 'Outlook', was in part a response to the United States' Indo-Pacific strategy that framed the Trump administration's policies in the region (see Chapter One).[21] Indonesia and ASEAN both made clear that they did not agree with Washington's more rigorous and potentially exclusive approach to the Indo-Pacific, which, in their view, risked alienating China.

While distancing itself from US policy, Indonesia has simultaneously continued to develop relations with China, with which it has had a 'strategic partnership' since 2005. The Yudhoyono administration even moved tentatively towards closer cooperation with China on defence and security.[22] Indonesian foreign policy under Jokowi has focused on 'down-to-earth diplomacy' and supporting economic development, and Jokowi's first administration (2014–18) emphasised China's role as the most important investor in the president's signature initiative, a national infrastructure-development programme.[23] At the start of his second term (2018–), however, escalating Chinese pressure on Indonesia's maritime interests around the Natuna Islands in December 2019 and January 2020 provoked an assertive and unprecedented response from Jakarta, which not only protested diplomatically but also dispatched frigates and combat aircraft to the area.[24] It seems unlikely, though, that Indonesian policy towards China will become tougher in a sustained way: the Jokowi administration's emphasis remains on economic development and for that reason stable relations with Beijing appear as necessary as ever.

Malaysia

Like Indonesia, Malaysia is a non-aligned state which has in the past had reason to fear Chinese subversion, and it has similarly attempted to steer a foreign-policy course that has precluded taking sides with any of the major powers. Political and military support from the UK, Australia and New Zealand was vital during Malaysia's formative years, and security relations based on the Five Power Defence Arrangements (FPDA) – involving Australia, New Zealand and the UK, as well as Malaysia and Singapore – have endured, as have important economic and cultural links with North America, Europe and Australasia. In 1984, amid concern over Vietnam's occupation of Cambodia, the government of then-prime minister Mahathir Mohamad entered into the low-profile but significant security agreement with Washington which allowed US naval ships to visit and use repair facilities in Malaysian dockyards, as well as bilateral intelligence-sharing and joint exercises. Bilateral defence and security relations subsequently expanded, particularly after the 11 September 2001 terrorist attacks, which brought closer cooperation on counter-terrorism and maritime security. The non-aligned posturing and anti-Western rhetoric that characterised Mahathir's leadership largely evaporated after he stepped down in 2003. Under Najib Tun Razak's premiership, from 2009–18 Malaysia often voted with the US in the UN General Assembly, sometimes supporting American positions on issues where it might previously have abstained (for example, sanctioning Iran). Mahathir's surprising return as prime minister from 2018–20, leading a coalition of parties opposed to the allegedly corrupt political establishment, led to a limited recalibration of relations with the US but no fundamental change in Malaysian policy.[25]

Yet Malaysia's cooperation with the US does not indicate that Kuala Lumpur has aligned itself with Washington. Non-alignment finds widespread support across Malaysia's multi-ethnic society and remains a foreign-policy keystone. Moreover, relations with China have intensified since Malaysia became the first ASEAN member to establish diplomatic ties with Beijing in 1974. Bilateral economic relations have boomed since the 1990s, with China becoming Malaysia's leading trading partner in 2009 and its leading source of investment in 2015.[26] Major Chinese BRI projects, focused on developing railways and ports, became politically contentious in advance of the 2018 general election, partly because of their links to the '1MDB' financial scandal in which Najib was implicated.[27] While the new government led by Mahathir promised, however, to renegotiate or cancel supposedly 'unfair' projects, within a year work restarted on the signature East Coast Rail Link. In 2019, then-finance minister Lim Guan Eng said that Malaysia would consider further BRI projects.[28] It was clear that the country's continuing prosperity was still closely linked to economic relations with China.

Economic imperatives may have moderated Malaysia's response to China's growing assertiveness, which has increasingly impinged on the smaller country's sovereignty. Individuals within Malaysia's security establishment, particularly senior military officers, sometimes privately express concern over China's growing projection of its power into Southeast Asia. Cabinet ministers have sometimes been more outspoken: in November 2015, then-deputy prime minister Zahid Hamidi warned that Malaysia would not stay silent on Chinese land-reclamation activities in the South China Sea and that Malaysians should 'rise to defend' their country's sovereignty if necessary.[29]

Najib's government, however, generally de-emphasised security concerns relating to China and appeared relatively accommodating of Beijing's South China Sea assertiveness. For example, in 2013 Najib argued that joint development of resources there should be seen as a means of avoiding conflict.[30] Soon afterwards, then-defence minister Hishammuddin Hussein said that his government had no objection to Chinese naval exercises close to Malaysian waters as long as Beijing's intent was peaceful.[31] This reflected the international legal reality, but many observers interpreted it as effective acquiescence to China's creeping domination of the South China Sea. Hishammuddin struck an accommodating note again in 2016 when contradicting a claim by the Malaysian Maritime Enforcement Agency that approximately 100 Chinese vessels had encroached into Malaysian waters near the South Luconia Shoals.[32]

After Mahathir became prime minister again in 2018, he appeared to equate the role of China in the South China Sea with that of the US when making the case that warships from neither of the great powers were welcome there.[33] However, renewed Chinese pressure, including the intrusion of the survey ship *Haiyang Dizhi 8* and accompanying CCG and militia vessels into Malaysia's EEZ in April 2020, continued to provoke concern among Malaysian defence and security officials.[34] Nevertheless, both governments which have followed Najib's administration since 2018 have apparently prioritised the stability of relations with China over their security concerns, primarily for economic reasons.[35]

Brunei

Superficially, Brunei's relations with China conform to a similar pattern. This mini-state comprising two semi-exclaves on the coast of the Malaysian state of Sabah only became fully independent in 1984 after almost a century as a British protectorate. It is a South China Sea claimant-state, though only with regard to a single feature, Louisa Reef. Though potential challenges from its much larger neighbours Indonesia and Malaysia were Brunei's principal external security concerns after achieving independence, it has found itself increasingly in a geopolitical predicament similar to those of the other Southeast Asian claimants as China's interest and activities in the South China Sea have grown.

The sultanate has remained broadly Western-aligned in security terms, notably continuing to host a 2,000-strong British military garrison under a bilateral agreement which in January 2020 was extended for a further five years.[36] However, the imperative to diversify its economy away from reliance on the oil and natural-gas resources that provide 90% of its exports by value has encouraged Brunei to strengthen economic relations with China substantially since the latter stepped up its drive to invest in and export infrastructure to Southeast Asia from 2013 onwards. Since then, economic cooperation has expanded to include creation of a bilateral 'economic corridor' and joint ventures for the construction of bridges, a crude-oil refinery and a port.[37] In November 2018 the two countries agreed an MoU on joint, cost-sharing oil and gas development in an area of Brunei's EEZ that they dispute.[38]

Despite escalating tensions in the South China Sea, and its own claim there, Brunei has maintained a notably low profile on the matter. In April 2016, Chinese Foreign Minister Wang Yi announced that Beijing had reached a four-point 'consensus' with Brunei, Cambodia and Laos on the South China Sea, in which they essentially agreed that the parties to disputes there should resolve their differences without outside interference.[39] Whether or not China has gained significant geopolitical advantage as a result of its heavy economic engagement with Brunei is unclear. While China has become its largest single source of foreign investment, Brunei is by no means economically dependent on its huge partner. Moreover, Brunei has not abandoned its claim to Louisa Reef, and its interest in potential joint development of maritime resources predates the expansion of economic ties with China.[40]

Vietnam

Vietnam has long been a 'front-line state' in the South China Sea, where it is in vehement dispute with China over not just all the Spratly Islands but also the Paracel Islands and other features. Historically, while subject to considerable Chinese cultural and political influence, Vietnam has fiercely resisted Chinese domination. It fought a major war with China as recently as

1979, and in 1988 there was a significant Sino-Vietnamese naval skirmish in the Spratlys, where bilateral tensions have again escalated sporadically since 2009. China has used maritime paramilitary forces rather than its navy to promote its South China Sea interests, but this 'grey zone' strategy has nonetheless provoked deep unease in Hanoi. Notably, in 2014 China precipitated a bilateral crisis by moving an exploratory oil rig, protected by coastguard and maritime-militia vessels, into Vietnam's EEZ. This threatened not only Hanoi's maritime interests but also domestic order as anti-Chinese protests up and down Vietnam escalated to attacks on Chinese-owned businesses.[41] More recently, in April 2020 a CCG ship rammed and sank a Vietnamese fishing boat near the Paracels.[42]

While Vietnam (like other countries challenged by China in the South China Sea) has evidently found it difficult to combat such 'grey zone' tactics, it has made determined efforts over the last decade to improve its naval and air capabilities, with a view to deterring any more direct Chinese use of force to change the status quo. Nevertheless, Vietnam evidently wishes to avoid armed conflict, having little choice but to coexist with its much larger and increasingly powerful northern neighbour, which has become an ever more important economic partner. China has been Vietnam's largest trading partner since 2004, and by 2019 was its fourth-largest source of foreign investment.[43] Moreover, Hanoi has been keen to strengthen bilateral economic relations further. In 2013, for example, Chinese Premier Li Keqiang visited Hanoi and signed agreements not only to expand bilateral trade and investment and create a cross-border economic cooperation zone, but also to resolve maritime disputes peacefully and to explore possible joint development of maritime resources.[44] Even as tensions at sea escalated in July 2020, bilateral channels of communication remained open and Vietnam's then-foreign minister, Pham Binh Minh, 'met' his Chinese counterpart, Wang Yi, via video-link and exchanged views on their South China Sea dispute.[45]

While Hanoi has sought to coexist peacefully with China, Vietnam's ruling Communist Party has also succeeded over the last decade in widening the country's foreign relations to provide it with additional economic and security options. Although Russia (as successor to Hanoi's Cold War sponsor, the Soviet Union) has remained Vietnam's primary supplier of military equipment, political and security relations with the US are now also substantial. Despite recent memory of the American War, during which the US was a bitter enemy, Hanoi evidently sees benefit from American interest in Southeast Asian security if this helps constrain China's behaviour in the South China Sea. Building on incremental improvements in bilateral ties, including tentative military-to-military links, since Washington and Hanoi established diplomatic relations in 1995, in 2013 Obama and his Vietnamese counterpart, Truong Tan Sang, launched a US–Vietnam Comprehensive Partnership. This involved not only an important economic dimension but also expanded maritime-security cooperation and an annual political-security dialogue. A Joint Vision Statement on Defense Relations followed in 2015.[46]

US emphasis on human-rights concerns meant that a ban on selling lethal weapons to Vietnam continued even under the Trump administration, but in 2017 and 2019 Washington nevertheless supplied two large ex-Coast Guard cutters to reinforce Hanoi's maritime capabilities, as well as a widening range of other non-lethal military equipment. Simultaneously, Hanoi showed more willingness to acknowledge closer security relations by allowing higher-profile US Navy port calls. Following a November 2017 joint statement by Trump and Vietnam's then-president Tran Dai Quang on strengthening and expanding the Comprehensive Partnership, in March 2018 a US Navy aircraft carrier visited communist Vietnam for the first time; another visited two years later. Also in 2018, Vietnamese ships joined the major, US-organised RIMPAC (*Rim of the Pacific*) multinational naval exercise for the first time. But despite these and other developments in bilateral security relations, Hanoi evidently remains reluctant to enter into a more formal security partnership with the US.

Cambodia

China's relations with the two smaller Indochinese countries, Cambodia and Laos, are less complicated than those with Vietnam, mainly because of the absence (at least so far) of major geopolitical contention with them. In Cambodia, Beijing has used economic instruments to gain considerable political influence. Vietnam had installed a sympathetic regime after invading the country in 1978 and deposing the Chinese-allied Khmer Rouge regime. But the success of a UN-sponsored peace process, followed by Vietnamese military withdrawal and elections in 1993, allowed Beijing to restore its relations with the country. In 1997, a pre-emptive *autogolpe* led by Senior Prime Minister Hun Sen deposed the Cambodian government's royalist second prime minister Prince Norodom Ranariddh and provided a diplomatic windfall for Beijing, which had been irritated by Ranariddh's efforts to develop ties with Taiwan. China's subsequent diplomatic and economic support for Hun Sen's government led him in 2003 to describe Beijing as his country's 'most trustworthy friend'.[47] In 2006 the two countries entered into a 'comprehensive partnership'; subsequently, China helped to cancel much of Cambodia's international debt, and provided fresh loans for building infrastructure, including government buildings. Chinese military assistance included substantial transfers of equipment.

US relations with Cambodia declined after 1997, when Washington severely cut its aid following Hun Sen's seizure of power. The US subsequently attempted to counterbalance Chinese influence by restoring its aid, including military assistance, and focusing greater diplomatic attention on the country, including a visit by then-secretary of state Hillary Clinton in 2010. However, by this time China's ties with Hun Sen's government were so profound that Beijing influenced Cambodia's role as ASEAN chair at the association's annual foreign ministers' meeting in July 2012.

Evidence that Cambodia's growing economic dependence on China has significantly undermined its foreign-policy independence has accumulated. Cambodia was an early recipient of large-scale Chinese BRI infrastructural investment, particularly in and around the port city of Sihanoukville, raising fears that the country would be caught in a 'debt trap'.[48] By early 2020, one-third of the foreign tourists visiting Cambodia came from China.[49] Western officials claim that in early 2019 Cambodia entered into a secret agreement with Beijing allowing the latter a 30-year lease on facilities at the Ream naval base; there were also reports that Chinese military aircraft would use a new airport being built 64 km from Ream.[50] Hun Sen's behaviour early in the COVID-19 crisis further highlighted Sino-Cambodian entente: he was the first foreign leader to visit China during the pandemic, and showed no qualms about visiting Cambodian students in Wuhan, then the COVID-19 epicentre. Moreover, as others closed their borders, Cambodia remained open to Chinese tourists.[51] Increasingly, it seems that Cambodia is becoming a quasi-ally of China.

Laos

During the 1980s, Laos was closely allied with Vietnam and the Soviet Union, and hostile to China. The end of the Cold War, however, changed sub-regional dynamics, making possible warmer relations with Beijing. Over the last three decades Vientiane has maintained political relations with Vietnam, but trade with China has expanded dramatically, as have Chinese investment and aid. Laos has also developed economic ties with Thailand, joined ASEAN (in 1997), and opened diplomatic and trading links with the US. Ties with China are important for economic development in Laos, one of the poorest countries in Asia. Current BRI projects include the China–Laos railway (a vital component of a route connecting China to Andaman Sea ports in Thailand), a major hydropower plant and rebuilding of a major road in northern Laos.[52] China has also replaced Russia as the major source of military equipment. These developments may yield long-term geopolitical benefits for China. Laos's ruling Communist Party, however, has employed deft diplomacy to avoid any undue submission to Beijing's influence over its foreign policy.[53]

Myanmar

After the military-controlled regime in Myanmar began a process of political reform, which saw a quasi-civilian administration in power from 2011, the country's international relations as well as domestic politics became more fluid. Myanmar's moves towards political and economic liberalisation, including the release of political prisoners, easing of press censorship and promise of elections in 2015, encouraged the US and other Western states to reduce or suspend economic sanctions imposed following the violent repression of pro-democracy activists in 1988 and the armed forces' refusal to honour the results of a general election in 1990. Hillary Clinton visited in late 2011 and an American ambassador was in place by July 2012 for the first time since 1988. Then-president Thein Sein visited the US in May 2013, and the two countries agreed

a bilateral Trade and Investment Framework. Myanmar's relations with other Western states made comparable progress.

These openings provided Myanmar with foreign-policy
alternatives to its previous heavy reliance on links with other
Asian states, particularly China. Following a period of equivo-
cal relations with Yangon (Beijing only ceased supporting the
insurgent Communist Party of Burma in 1986), China benefited from the West's diplomatic and economic ostracising of
Myanmar and from the late 1980s developed ties with Yangon
that ultimately appeared, to many Burmese as well as outside
observers, to threaten its autonomy.[54] In return for an economic
lifeline, and politico-military support which included compre-
hensively re-equipping Myanmar's armed forces, Beijing
gained not only access to a substantial market and natural
resources, but also geopolitical benefits such as a signals-
intelligence station on Great Coco Island and the prospect of
oil and gas pipelines through Myanmar that promised to allow
China to circumvent the vulnerability of its energy supplies to
interdiction in the Strait of Malacca. The growing intensity of
these relations caused unease not just in Western policy circles
but also within Myanmar's regime, where a degree of political
reform came to be seen as necessary in order to secure a relaxa-
tion of Western economic sanctions, which in turn would allow
a restoration of the foreign-policy neutrality that the armed
forces had idealised since independence.[55]

From 2011, greater balance appeared to return to Myanmar's
foreign policy. An indication of Beijing's weakening influence
was Myanmar's September 2011 suspension of the massive
Chinese-backed Myitsone dam-construction project in Kachin
State.[56] Closer security relations with the US also seemed to
be in prospect: speaking at the IISS Shangri-La Dialogue in
June 2012, then-secretary of defense Leon Panetta emphasised
that 'how we can improve our defense relationship' would be

'part and parcel' of Washington's efforts to develop links with Myanmar.[57] While the immediate US emphasis was on how military engagement might encourage political reform, there were clearly also important strategic undertones. Given the extent to which Myanmar was widely thought to have fallen into China's geopolitical orbit, the opportunity to develop significant security relations with the country following the 2015 general election promised Washington strategic benefits. However, developments inside Myanmar frustrated such hopes.

Although opposition leader and human-rights champion Aung San Suu Kyi became de facto head of government as a result of the party she led winning the November 2015 election with a landslide parliamentary majority, Myanmar's 2008 constitution allowed the armed forces autonomy through control of the home, border-affairs and defence ministries, as well as their allocation of 25% of parliamentary seats. This provided a permissive framework within which they could pursue their own agenda, regardless of whether this embarrassed Myanmar's new civilian government in its relations with Western countries. Under the new government, these relations initially prospered as the US and the European Union continued to lift sanctions and engaged with Myanmar economically, diplomatically and even, tentatively, in the security sphere.

Simultaneously, however, given the importance of Chinese trade, investment and aid, and also of maintaining foreign-policy balance, Myanmar did not abandon its close relations with Beijing.[58] Indeed, in August 2016 Aung San Suu Kyi's first foreign visit as national leader was to China; she and Xi signed wide-ranging agreements, and China expressed willingness to persuade recalcitrant ethnic-minority rebel groups with which it had links to join peace negotiations with Myanmar's government.[59] Over the next several years, relations with Beijing again proved to be a lifeline. Following attacks by insurgents in

2016–17, Myanmar's army launched large-scale operations targeting the Rohingya ethnic-minority population in Rakhine State in the country's west, leading to a major humanitarian crisis in late 2017 as 650–700,000 people fled across the border to Bangladesh. There was a fierce international reaction and from 2018 Myanmar found itself subject to renewed sanctions from Western countries, initially targeted mainly at its security forces.

In these circumstances, close relations with China, which provided diplomatic support over the Rohingya issue (notably by shielding Myanmar from criticism in the UN Security Council), became as important as ever for Myanmar's government and armed forces, despite tensions between the latter and Beijing over Chinese support for ethnic-minority rebel groups such as the United Wa State Army.[60] The armed forces' coup in February 2021, following a sweeping election victory by Aung San Suu Kyi's party, brought new condemnation from the West, accompanied by additional sanctions, and seemed likely to heighten Myanmar's dependence on Chinese diplomatic and economic support.

Other regional powers

Sino-US competition for influence in Southeast Asia, and Southeast Asian states' efforts to navigate that rivalry while maintaining their foreign-policy principles, have been central to the sub-region's geopolitics over the last decade and seem likely to remain so. It would, however, be misleading to portray the power equation in bipolar terms. Japan, India and Australia are all playing increasingly important roles. Indeed, one striking feature of Southeast Asia's international relations since 2012, when Abe Shinzo became Japan's prime minister for the second time, is what might be termed Tokyo's rebalance to Southeast Asia, involving a distinct emphasis on enhancing security relations with ASEAN member states.

Japan

Tokyo had evidently been interested since the early 1990s in bolstering the maritime-security capabilities of Southeast Asian states astride its vital sea lines of communication. However, this essentially reflected concern over low-intensity threats to shipping from pirates, and potentially terrorists, whereas the Abe government's policy towards Southeast Asia represented a strategic response to China's growing power and assertiveness in its littoral and envisaged Southeast Asian states as increasingly important, if still low-key, security partners for Japan. Central to Tokyo's new strategy was an effort to find common cause over China's maritime claims that affect Japan in the East China Sea as well as some Southeast Asian states in the South China Sea. This has involved not only practical measures, starting with a decision in 2013 to donate patrol vessels to the Philippine Coast Guard,[61] but also strenuous efforts to step up diplomatic coordination. This was evident in the closing joint statement at the 40th-anniversary ASEAN–Japan summit in December 2013, which emphasised the importance of resolving maritime disputes peacefully and in accordance with international law and, against the backdrop of China's announcement in November 2013 of an ADIZ over the East China Sea, of enhancing cooperation to ensure freedom of overflight.[62]

These efforts continued for the rest of the decade. Tokyo's proposal in 2014 for a Japan–ASEAN defence ministers' meeting failed to find comprehensive Southeast Asian support, indicating that there was no more unanimity within the sub-region over the desirability of closer strategic relations with Tokyo than there was over security ties with the US. Japan did enhance bilateral links with several Southeast Asian countries that it saw as strategically central. In August 2020, when the Philippines agreed to buy air-defence radars, it was Japan's first significant defence-equipment export contract since the relaxing of a ban on arms sales in 2014.[63] Underlining the importance for Japan of developing security as well as economic links with key Southeast Asian states, the first overseas visits by Suga Yoshihide as prime minister were to Indonesia and Vietnam in September 2020. According to Suga, Japan and Vietnam reached agreement in principle on the transfer of Japanese defence equipment and technology.[64]

India

Since 1991, India has pursued a 'Look East' policy that was envisaged as primarily economic in nature but has also, from the beginning, embodied an ambition to increase security coop- eration with selected Southeast Asian countries. The rationales for the policy have been reinforced by China's growing regional assertiveness (most importantly, from India's perspective, Chinese naval activities in the Indian Ocean and pressure along the Sino-Indian border, as will be detailed in Chapter Four). In 2008, the Indian Navy extended its annual Southeast Asian 'operational cruise', which includes joint exercises and port calls, into the South China Sea for the first time. These longer- range deployments paralleled India's intensifying strategic relations with Vietnam. This partnership with Hanoi, dating from 2007, includes the most important and comprehensive of India's Southeast Asian bilateral defence connections, in part reflecting New Delhi's uneasy relationship with China and its willingness to strengthen ties with other states feeling vulner- able in the face of Beijing's rising power. New Delhi also made efforts to foster defence relations with other Southeast Asian states. For Myanmar, tentative defence relations with India provided the military regime there with a partial alternative to reliance on China.

New Delhi's preoccupation with the demands of combative relations with Pakistan and, after the beginning of the US-led 'war on terror', concern over the stability of Afghanistan, together with concerns over stability in the Indian Ocean, all slowed the implementation of Look East.[65] However, the 'Act East' policy that the Modi government adopted in 2014, partly in reaction to China's enhanced strategic extroversion under Xi's leadership, provided a framework for more energetic efforts to develop strategic ties with Southeast Asia.[66] Most importantly, India's defence relations with Vietnam have expanded to include support for the latter's developing submarine capability based on *Kilo*-class boats, purchased from Russia, and assistance for Vietnam's establishment of a satellite-imagery centre.[67] Although an Indian shipyard began building a batch of patrol boats for Vietnam's coastguard in 2019, India's efforts to supply other defence equipment, such as *Brahmos* cruise missiles, had not come to fruition by early 2021 despite the promise of a line of credit. Possible reasons include Indian concern over China's potential reaction.[68]

Australia
Australia has been involved in Southeast Asia's security since the Second World War, contributing forces to successive conflicts in Malaya, Vietnam and Malaysia during the 1950s and 1960s, and subsequently maintaining or developing bilateral security relations of varying intensity with most states. The strongest of these have traditionally been with Malaysia and Singapore, to which Australia is also linked through the FPDA. But developing security ties with Indonesia has also been a priority, despite a history of bilateral suspicion.[69]

For much of the first two decades of the twenty-first century, Australia's external security and defence emphasis was primarily on supporting US-led counter-terrorism efforts in the Middle East and Afghanistan. But in response to the winding down of the war on terror, a perception that China posed a growing threat to regional stability and Australian security, and a calculation that Australia needed to support its US ally by assuming a greater share of the regional security burden, over the last half-decade Canberra has substantially refocused its diplomatic and defence attention on Southeast Asia. This has been particularly true since the publication in 2017 of a foreign-policy white paper which stressed the strategic importance of the South Pacific but equally emphasised Southeast Asia's significance as a major locus of great-power competition and promised that Australia would more than ever be a leading partner for ASEAN and its members.[70]

Canberra subsequently strengthened relations with Indonesia, Singapore and Vietnam, countries it identified as vital components of the regional strategic equation. Crucially, during 2020, Australia responded to the impact of COVID-19 on Southeast Asia with loans and aid in support of economic recovery, and succeeded in converting its hitherto biennial summit with ASEAN into an annual meeting.[71] At the same time, Canberra's defence strategy has increasingly emphasised deterrence and contingency planning in relation to Southeast Asia. The July 2020 *Defence Strategic Update* crystallised this thinking, stressing the need for a sharpened focus on Australia's 'immediate region', defined as 'from the north-eastern Indian Ocean through maritime and mainland Southeast Asia to Papua New Guinea and the South West Pacific'.[72]

Constraints

In each case there are important constraints on the extent to which it is feasible for Australia, India and Japan to play significant roles in Southeast Asia's security, and among the non-regional powers, other than China, it seems almost certain that the role of the US will remain pre-eminent for a long time. Apart from internal constraints on those three countries playing significantly more assertive roles, Southeast Asian governments are evidently as ambivalent about security links with Australia, India and Japan as they are towards intensified links with the US, essentially for the same reasons: fear of exacerbating tensions between major powers in the region, alienating China, and causing deeper divisions among themselves. From the perspective of the US and its allies Australia and Japan, close coordination bilaterally, trilaterally and even – if India can be persuaded of the strategic rationale – in quadrilateral format is important in response to China's economic, diplomatic and military advances across the region, including in Southeast Asia. However, in Southeast Asia itself there is little interest in joining any moves that could lay the foundations for a harder-edged confrontation with Beijing. Indeed, Singapore's Prime Minister Lee spoke for many in Southeast Asia in his keynote address to the 2019 Shangri-La Dialogue when he expressed the hope that China and the US would 'find a constructive way forward'.[73]

Defence priorities

Southeast Asian states' evolving relations with the larger Asia-Pacific countries (including the US) highlight the complexity of their political responses to the geopolitical predicament of their sub-region being a locus for major-power competition. At the same time, most Southeast Asian states emphasise the importance of continuously modernising their armed forces. Some observers assume not only that Southeast Asian political and military leaders are intent on building up their countries' external-defence capabilities, but also that these efforts are responses to perceived threats from China. The reality, though, is that Southeast Asian governments' national defence priorities differ widely, reflecting their diverse national circumstances and threat perceptions.

Three levels of ambition for national military capability can, broadly speaking, be distinguished in Southeast Asia. Firstly, there are those countries (Singapore and Vietnam) that have built their armed forces to face potential external threats and have dedicated substantial resources to developing relevant capabilities. Secondly, there are those countries (Brunei, Indonesia, Malaysia and the Philippines) that have traditionally focused more on responding to internal-security challenges than to external threats but which, given their changing geopolitical environment and evolving threat perceptions, are in the process of transitioning to a wider vision of defence. Finally, there are countries where, because of long-standing emphases on maintaining regime stability or internal security, or both, the armed forces remain largely inward-looking. In practice, of course, defence establishments may operate in a wide variety of roles, but this categorisation attempts to reflect the overarching priority of each country's armed forces.

Response to external threats

Singapore and, since the late 1970s, Vietnam have developed their military capabilities primarily to deter and, if necessary, defend against external threats. Their security perspectives, though, have been quite distinct. Singapore has focused the development of its military capabilities against potentially existential threats from larger countries in its immediate region. The city-state's small size and its reliance on maritime trade, which passes through neighbouring states' territorial waters, have engendered a sense of vulnerability which has led Singapore's government to direct considerable resources over more than five decades to developing particularly well-equipped and well-trained armed forces.[74] As a result, Singapore has become one of the world's most densely defended territories. Following the 11 September 2001 attacks in the US and the subsequent discovery of regional terrorist plots directed against Singapore, the Singapore Armed Forces (SAF) took on an additional domestic counter-terrorism role while also making small-scale contributions to US-led coalition operations in the Middle East and Afghanistan. This reflected not only Singapore's perceived vulnerability to international terrorism, but also the need to maintain close security relations with Washington in the interest of bolstering the long-term engagement of the US in Southeast Asian and wider regional security. These diversifying roles required the SAF to widen its capability spectrum to include potential low-end as well as high-end operations.

Vietnam also has an acute sense of external security challenges, but unlike Singapore it is highly focused on China. Although the Vietnam People's Army (VPA) was originally a revolutionary insurgent force, it has developed since the 1970s into a fully fledged conventional armed force, reflecting Hanoi's concern over what it perceives as a long-term threat from China, particularly in the South China Sea. Vietnam's 2019 defence white paper emphasised rising tensions in the 'East Sea' (as Hanoi calls the South China Sea), implicitly referring to Chinese assertiveness there.[75] The stress on defending national maritime claims and interests has necessitated particularly strong efforts to develop the VPA's naval and air capabilities. As part of a broadening of Vietnam's foreign-policy and international-security options over the last decade, the VPA has engaged in exercises with international partners and made initially minor contributions to UN international peace-support missions. While Singapore and Vietnam face quite different geopolitical predicaments, in each case an emphasis on countering external threats implies that, in the absence of any significant changes in their threat perceptions, they are both likely to continue to make strenuous efforts to develop their armed forces' capabilities for conventional warfare with state-level adversaries.

From internal to external security

The armed forces of the three large maritime Southeast Asian countries – Indonesia, Malaysia and the Philippines – have diverse origins, primarily from a revolutionary movement in the case of Indonesia, and from an original focus on internal security in Malaysia and the Philippines. Much smaller Brunei's armed forces have always had a dual focus on external defence and internal security. While these origins have provided significant contexts for their development, all four countries' armed forces are undergoing long-term transformations that involve broadening their missions to take greater account of external challenges.

In Indonesia, military reforms since 1998 have had only limited success in moving the Indonesian armed forces (Tentara Nasional Indonesia, or TNI) towards a more externally oriented, conventional role, involving less emphasis on army-based territorial defence and greater focus on maritime and air capabilities and on joint operations. The TNI's doctrinal outlook is still influenced by its origins and the legacy of its 'dual function role' under the military-dominated New Order regime from 1966–98, and it performs domestic roles that in many countries would be outside the armed forces' remit. Since 2009, however, the 15-year 'Minimum Essential Force' defence-policy framework has underpinned a shift towards better-funded, reconfigured and better-equipped armed forces, more oriented towards external security challenges.[76] Over the last decade, Indonesia's political leaders and senior TNI officers alike have become increasingly concerned over the implications for Indonesia's security of intensifying great-power competition in the region. Together with Jokowi's announcement in 2014 that Indonesia would become a 'respected maritime power' in its region, and increasingly focused concern in Jakarta over Chinese pressure on

Indonesia's maritime interests, this broader geopolitical thinking seems certain to encourage the TNI to continue to refocus on external deterrence and defence, despite the evident interest of military (and particularly army) leaders in maintaining and even sometimes reinforcing residual domestic roles, notably in counter-terrorism and disaster relief.[77]

Since the end of the Communist Party of Malaya's rebellion in 1989, the Malaysian Armed Forces (MAF), which were traditionally army-dominated and focused on internal security, have developed more effective conventional-warfare capabilities, with a stronger air force and navy as well as a better-equipped and more mechanised army. However, constraints on Malaysia's defence budget against the backdrop of a deteriorating regional security environment, particularly in the South China Sea, have raised questions about the MAF's capacity to defend national interests effectively. Following domestic political upheaval in May 2018 which brought to power a radically different political coalition, the new government tabled a defence white paper in December 2019.[78] It characterised Malaysia as a 'maritime nation with continental roots' and set out an aspiration to be a 'middle power' in security terms. While not accusing China directly, it pointed to foreign encroachments on Malaysia's maritime interests as a challenge, and also to the need to provide better security for the eastern states of Sabah and Sarawak. Although the white paper reinforced the case for modernising the MAF's conventional-warfare capabilities, it was clear that resources for defence will probably remain stagnant unless stronger economic growth is achieved.[79]

Despite rising tensions in the South China Sea, the Philippines' defence policy remains heavily focused on long-running counter-insurgency campaigns against communist and Muslim-separatist rebels, particularly in the south of the country. The five-month-long battle for the city of Marawi, large parts of which were seized by groups affiliated to the Islamic State (also known as ISIS or ISIL) in May 2017, only strengthened this orientation. Overall, the Philippines' military-modernisation programme – which began as long ago as 1995, partly with the aim of equipping the armed forces to face external challenges more effectively – has been slow to improve the country's military capabilities, largely owing to consistently inadequate defence funding. However, the second phase of a revised modernisation programme, running from 2018–22, is bringing limited improvements in naval and air capabilities relevant to the defence of maritime interests.[80]

Indonesia, Malaysia and the Philippines face broadly comparable mixes of high- and low-intensity defence challenges, and all three countries are tentatively moving towards stronger emphases on deterring external threats. Their assessments of the seriousness (or otherwise) of the threat posed by China to their maritime interests will be an important influence on the commitment that each makes to this transition.

The defence policy and military effort of Brunei, Southeast Asia's smallest state in terms of population and second smallest by area, do not fit neatly into any of the three categories identified here. However, they have most in common with those of the second group. While Brunei's primary defence focus was originally (from the 1960s to the 1990s) on perceived threats from the country's much larger neighbours (Indonesia and Malaysia), its small professional armed forces were also well suited to internal-security duties, though they never needed to operate in that role. However, Brunei's vision of defence has expanded to include the protection of maritime interests, reflecting the country's extensive South China Sea EEZ and its claim to an atoll there, and despite budgetary constraints it also aims to better equip its army for conventional warfare.[81]

Looking inward

The armed forces of mainland Southeast Asian countries other than Vietnam (that is, Cambodia, Laos, Myanmar and Thailand) continue to prioritise their domestic roles, which include a central place in national politics in the cases of Myanmar and Thailand, despite having developed significant conventional-warfare capabilities in the case of the latter. Thailand's armed forces, and particularly the Royal Thai Army, have retained a substantial internal-security role, especially in the far south of the country where the army and marines have engaged in a counter-insurgency campaign against ethnic-Malay separatist groups since 2004.[82] At the same time, they have remained a central political actor: their takeover of national government in 2014 led to almost five years of military rule, after which a military-supported party led by coup leader General Prayuth Chan-o-cha won elections in 2019. Nevertheless, over the last 40 years Thailand's armed forces have developed substantial capacities for deterring and, if necessary, defending the country against state-level adversaries. Since the late 1980s there have been border clashes with Laos (1987–88), Myanmar (2001) and Cambodia (2008–11). Thailand has no claims in the South China Sea and does not see any direct security challenges in China's rise. However, its long coastline, extensive EEZ, interest in protecting fisheries and developing undersea resources, and its need to protect maritime trade help to explain its evident interest in developing its naval capabilities.[83]

Myanmar's armed forces, the Tatmadaw, evolved from an anti-colonial force into one focused on dealing with the numerous ethnic-minority insurgencies that broke out following independence – a primary role that continues to this day. Peace processes, including the most recent, have largely failed, with the result that counter-insurgency has remained the armed forces' long-term operational priority. The Tatmadaw has also had an enduring, direct involvement in domestic politics. While there have been limited efforts to develop external defence capabilities, mainly in response to tensions with neighbouring Bangladesh and Thailand, as well as somewhat unrealistic fears about the possibility of major-power intervention, the twin domestic roles of counter-insurgency and direct political involvement seem likely to continue shaping the Tatmadaw's role and capability ambitions.

In Cambodia and Laos, the primary role of the armed forces is to support regime security and manage domestic threats. In Cambodia, the regime led by Hun Sen depends for its survival in part on a close alliance with senior military officers. But while the Royal Cambodian Armed Forces ensure regime security, they also have a border-defence role. In Laos, the armed forces are linked closely to the party-state system: high-ranking officers are members of the Lao People's Revolutionary Party Central Committee[84] and also occupy senior posts in the government.[85] As well as supporting the communist regime, the Lao People's Armed Forces (which are mainly an infantry-based army) also perform an internal-security role.

Diversity vs coordination

The diversity of Southeast Asian states' approaches to developing their armed forces helps to explain, along with their uncoordinated responses to their changing strategic environment and the continuing existence of suspicions and rivalries within the sub-region, why they have not coordinated their defence policies to any strategically significant degree. Since 2006, the ASEAN Defence Ministers' Meeting (ADMM) has aimed 'to promote mutual trust and confidence through greater understanding of defence and security challenges as well as enhancement of transparency and openness'.[86] While the ADMM has provided a framework for cooperation among

ASEAN member states' defence establishments, this has mainly involved serving as a mechanism for confidence-building through regular procedural meetings involving senior defence officials and military officers and as the core of the ADMM+, a broader grouping which involves ASEAN Dialogue Partner countries and has similar objectives but on a wider scale. The ADMM could provide the basis for closer collaboration on operational defence planning and mutual support, but such cooperation is highly unlikely without broader agreement among ASEAN member states on their geopolitical objectives.

Defence spending

Southeast Asia's defence-spending pattern is also characterised by national diversity in terms of scale and details. Annual defence spending in 2020 ranged from Brunei's US$437m to Singapore's US$10.9bn; Vietnam's budget was estimated at US$5.7bn, and those of Indonesia and Thailand at around US$8.4bn and US$7bn respectively. While compiling accurate estimates of defence spending in the region is far from straightforward, owing to a widespread lack of transparency and in some cases the vagaries of party-state systems' budgeting and the defence sector's use of 'off-budget' funding, it is nevertheless evident that Southeast Asia accounts for around 10% of Asia's total defence spending. However, growth in Southeast Asia's aggregated defence spending has broadly matched that of the wider region (see Figure 3.1).[87] Southeast Asian defence spending has not, overall, increased more quickly than the size of the sub-region's economy; the jump in defence budgets since 2010 may have been due as much to generally increased prosperity as to a greater allocation of resources to defence. Indeed, as a proportion of GDP, aggregate Southeast Asian defence spending declined slightly from 1.47% in 2008 to 1.38% in 2020 (see Table 3.1).

Figure 3.1: **Annual defence-spending growth in real terms, Asia and Southeast Asia, 2010–20**

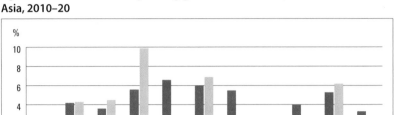

Source: IISS, Military Balance+, https://milbalplus.iiss.org, accessed July 2021   ©IISS

In Cambodia and Myanmar, where armed forces focus primarily on internal security and regime protection, defence-funding allocations as a proportion of GDP are higher than the Southeast Asian average. Thailand spends a relatively low proportion of GDP on defence, while at the same time developing some external defence capacity, and thus does not fit into the same pattern. In Singapore and Vietnam, with their more acute threat perceptions and high levels of military ambition, defence also absorbs a relatively high portion of national wealth (see Table 3.1). However, in those countries which are moving

Table 3.1: **Southeast Asian defence spending as a proportion of countries' GDP, 2020**

Brunei	3.66%
Cambodia	3.98%
Indonesia	0.79%
Malaysia	1.10%
Myanmar	2.94%
Philippines	1.01%
Singapore	2.91%
Thailand	1.36%
Vietnam	1.68%

Source: IISS, Military Balance+, https://milbalplus.iiss.org, accessed July 2021

Figure 3.2: **Defence spending in real terms, Indonesia and Malaysia, 2015–20**

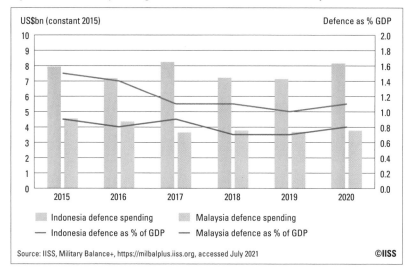

from an inward to an outward defence focus (Indonesia, Malaysia and the Philippines), and where major funding allocations might be expected, the numbers remain well below the Southeast Asian average.

Although Southeast Asia's aggregate defence spending rose in the decade to 2020, this trend was not uniform. In particular, defence spending by Indonesia and Malaysia has declined as a proportion of GDP since 2015 (see Figure 3.2). Economic constraints played a role here: low commodity prices since 2014 have undermined government revenue in both countries. At the same time, domestic political imperatives have encouraged them to prioritise social and other spending. Consequently, Indonesia and Malaysia have each found difficulty in paying for current and future military procurement. In 2019 Malaysia's government started discussions with at least six countries about paying for future defence equipment using palm oil.[88] Similarly, in 2020 Indonesia opened talks to renegotiate with South Korea its 20% financial support for joint development of the KFX/IFX fifth-generation combat aircraft.[89]

Resources for investment in new military equipment, let alone research and development in support of domestic innovation and production, are limited throughout Southeast Asia. Indonesia, Malaysia, the Philippines and Vietnam are each estimated to spend less than US$1bn per year on defence procurement. Thailand may spend slightly more, while Singapore is the only country in the sub-region estimated to spend more than US$2bn on procurement.

Major weapons acquisitions

Despite these limitations, increased defence spending has allowed the gradual modernisation of Southeast Asian armed forces' equipment holdings, regardless of their governments' specific defence-policy priorities. Increased funding has also underwritten an expansion of military roles, allowing those countries' armed forces to respond to a wider range of challenges. But varying national aspirations and funding levels have led to diverse choices in terms of the type of military equipment procured.[90]

In Singapore, recent and planned procurement of defence equipment highlights the continuing drive by the city-state's government to ensure that all elements of the SAF are modernised. This is in line with the ambition for the SAF to maintain a technology-based capability advantage within its immediate region. In the air domain, Singapore's force of combat aircraft is being upgraded, though from 2026 they will be replaced by fifth-generation F-35 combat aircraft, which Singapore will almost certainly be the only Southeast Asian state to operate.[91] The city-state began replacing its KC-135R tanker aircraft with A330 MRTT tankers in 2018, and H225M and CH-47F transport helicopters are replacing the current fleet. In 2018, the SAF confirmed the SAMP/T air-defence system had entered service, significantly enhancing

Singapore's ground-based capabilities. At sea, Type-218SG submarines will replace older, Swedish-built boats by 2025.[92] A new class of locally built Multi-Role Combat Vessels (MRCVs) is set to replace existing missile corvettes during the period 2025–30, and from around 2030 Joint Multi Mission Ships will replace existing amphibious vessels.[93] On land, the Next-Generation Armoured Fighting Vehicle (NGAFV) will replace the SAF's armoured personnel carriers (APCs).[94]

Vietnam's military-procurement pattern is also consistent with its focus on deterring China. In particular, Hanoi is purchasing weapons systems that provide building blocks for an A2/AD capability. Between 2010 and 2016, Vietnam's air force took delivery of 35 Su-30 combat aircraft, which it operates alongside similar but older Su-27s. Over the last decade, Vietnam's navy has developed a submarine capability, bringing into service six *Kilo*-class submarines. The navy has also enhanced its limited anti-submarine, surface-warfare and air-defence capabilities with two additional frigates commissioned in 2018. Another crucial element of Vietnam's growing A2/AD capability is advanced intelligence, surveillance and reconnaissance. While a long-expected order for maritime-patrol aircraft has failed to materialise (probably due to funding shortfalls), in 2020 Hanoi ordered a Japanese-produced satellite-based surveillance system.[95] In addition, Vietnam has purchased *ScanEagle* uninhabited aerial vehicles (UAVs) under the United States' Foreign Military Sales programme, and has also been developing UAVs indigenously.[96]

Indonesia's defence establishment is moving incrementally towards establishing the capabilities necessary to respond effectively to a widening array of security challenges across the entirety of its massive archipelago and related seas. Over the last decade, new equipment has provided a basis for enhanced high-intensity maritime capabilities, notably through commissioning two Dutch-built *Sigma*-class frigates in 2017–18. In 2020, a contract was signed for upgrading an older frigate's mission system to the same standard as these new ships.[97] Indonesia is also procuring less expensive vessels, such as missile-armed fast-attack craft, suitable for a wide range of maritime-security operations.[98] Defence-spending constraints have, however, limited major military procurement, notably undermining cooperation with South Korea on the KFX/IFX combat aircraft.[99] Nevertheless, from late 2019 Defence Minister Prabowo Subianto travelled extensively to more than a dozen countries to discuss potential defence-procurement and defence-technology cooperation, including the potential acquisition of various types of combat aircraft.[100] Meanwhile, Indonesia's air force has developed its mobility capabilities, buying locally built aircraft and transport helicopters. Army procurement has increasingly involved acquisition of equipment suitable for conventional warfare, including modernised second-hand *Leopard* 2 main battle tanks, locally built *Harimau* medium tanks, *Marder* and *Pandur* II infantry fighting vehicles (IFVs) and AH-64E attack helicopters.

Malaysia is also procuring equipment that can fulfil a variety of missions, such as A400M transport aircraft and H225M helicopters that could be used to support a wide spectrum of operations, ranging from internal security and HADR to defence against external threats. As in Indonesia, there have been delays in ordering new combat aircraft.[101] The defence minister announced in 2019 that existing fighter types would not be replaced until 2030; the focus would instead be on acquiring light combat aircraft, as well as maritime-patrol aircraft and UAVs.[102] The reconnaissance elements of this procurement would potentially help to expand Malaysia's maritime-security capabilities, which the purchase of patrol boats from both China and Japan, and six domestically produced *Gowind*-class frigates, is already boosting.[103] Again, growing maritime capabilities could support a range of missions, from peacetime maritime surveillance, aimed mainly at low-intensity challenges, to deterrence of, and defence against, state-level external threats.

The Philippines' armed forces appear to be further from a transition from an inward- to an outward-looking defence posture. Compared with Malaysia and Indonesia, not only are the Philippines' defence resources more constrained, but it is less clear that the country's political leaders have the ambition and drive to establish a more credible capacity to face external security challenges. The second phase (2018–22) of a revived modernisation programme for the Armed Forces of the Philippines (AFP) includes plans to acquire relevant equipment, but it is clear that progress towards widening AFP capabilities will be slow.

While there is growing awareness in Manila that the Philippines faces a serious challenge from China in the South China Sea, and there are questions over the future of the alliance with the US, internal-security challenges remain the day-to-day operational priority for the armed forces. Even the air force's new FA-50 light attack aircraft, purchased primarily with a view to providing a limited air-defence capability, were used for ground-attack missions against Islamist insurgents during the siege of Marawi in 2017.[104] Subsequently, A-29 light combat aircraft were ordered to bolster air-force counterinsurgency capabilities, along with AH-1F attack helicopters.

The modernisation of the Philippine Army is strongly geared towards meeting internal-security challenges, as demonstrated by the delivery in 2015, from multiple suppliers, of modernised second-hand M113 APCs. In November 2020 the Philippines' defence secretary announced that a programme to acquire land-based cruise missiles from India (which would be for coastal defence and army-operated) was 'moving forward but the challenge now is funding'.[105] Within the AFP, the navy has made the greatest progress towards a more outward-looking posture, with two Korean-built frigates commissioned in 2020–21. These vessels should significantly boost the navy's anti-air, anti-surface and anti-submarine defences, along with its electronic-warfare capabilities.[106] Two AW159 helicopters that entered service in 2019 should also strengthen anti-submarine and anti-surface capabilities. However, even in the navy's case, some new equipment has multiple potential roles: for example, two new amphibious ships, commissioned in 2017, could support HADR missions as well as internal-security and external defence operations.

While the arbitrating political role of Thailand's armed forces highlights the centrality of domestic concerns in the country's defence policy and the military's operational roles, it also ensured strong growth in defence spending and the availability of substantial procurement funding, at least until the COVID-19 pandemic undermined Thailand's economy during 2020. Despite the absence of a clearly identified major external threat, all three services are making efforts to develop capabilities for external defence as well as internal security. Thailand's air force took a major step towards developing a modern air-defence capability during the 2010s when it brought into service a squadron of *Gripen* combat aircraft. Crucially, these are part of a larger system that also includes airborne early-warning and control aircraft and the data link which connects the aircraft to Thai navy frigates employing Saab combat-management systems, creating an integrated air-defence network.[107] The air force has also upgraded its larger force of older combat aircraft and brought into service equipment such as H225M helicopters, which could support HADR as well as combat search and rescue (CSAR) operations.

Thailand's navy is also developing its conventional-warfare capabilities, above all through establishing a submarine force based initially on three Chinese-provided S26T boats, the first of which is due for delivery in 2024. However, the economic downturn, combined with popular criticism of the purchase, led Thailand's government to delay ordering the others until 2022.[108] In 2019 the Thai navy also ordered new ships from China – including a Type-071 landing platform dock, which should strengthen its HADR capability. Meanwhile, major equipment procurement for the army over the last decade, including main battle tanks from Ukraine and China, and artillery systems from Israel, means that it will be better equipped to defend the country's borders. However, other new army equipment, such as Chinese- and US-made IFVs acquired in 2019–20, are as relevant to counter-insurgency operations in Thailand's southern provinces as they are to contingencies involving state adversaries.

Myanmar's major weapons purchases have been limited compared with those of other large Southeast Asian states, reflecting the fact that defence spending has been primarily directed towards maintaining a large, infantry-based army that is engaged in numerous counter-insurgency campaigns. Nevertheless, the Tatmadaw has made some efforts to develop a limited capacity for conventional warfare, mainly with neighbouring countries in mind as potential adversaries. In 2017–19, Myanmar's air force brought into service a small number of JF-17 light combat aircraft, developed by China and Pakistan, and ordered Russian-made Su-30 fighters in 2018.[109] The navy's most significant procurement has involved a *Kilo*-class submarine donated by India in late 2020, signalling Myanmar's intention to start building a more convincing offensive maritime capability. Some other procurement programmes, such as those for advanced trainer and light

122 | Asia's New Geopolitics: Military Power and Regional Order

attack aircraft, attack helicopters and a large amphibious ship, will help to strengthen capabilities for counter-insurgency and (in the case of the ship) HADR.[110] Armoured vehicles purchased from Russia were seen on Myanmar's streets during the February 2021 coup, demonstrating their relevance to the armed forces' domestic political role.[111]

Southeast Asia's arms-procurement pattern thus clearly reflects the diverse defence priorities of its various countries. Singapore and Vietnam are both purchasing weapons systems intended to bolster their conventional military capabilities, with a view to deterring potential state adversaries. While maintaining and even developing their armed forces' capacities for internal security and HADR, Indonesia, Malaysia and the Philippines are all – at varying rhythms and with differing degrees of success – attempting to widen the scope of their capabilities so that these provide more effective deterrents against external aggressors. Overall, compared to Indonesia and Malaysia, the Philippines is acquiring less advanced, cheaper platforms and remains focused primarily on internal security, although the Philippine Navy is progressing more quickly towards an externally oriented posture. In mainland Southeast Asia, Myanmar and Thailand are on different paths. While the armed forces play central political roles in both countries, Myanmar's are much more heavily involved in counter-insurgency than their Thai counterparts, and at the same time have much smaller resources for procurement.

Several other things are clear. Firstly, except in the case of Vietnam, there has been no determined effort to develop capabilities focused clearly on deterring China. Notwithstanding occasional attempts to demonstrate sovereignty militarily,[112] most Southeast Asian states lack the resources for direct military confrontation with China and are likely to avoid this at all costs. Secondly, there is scant evidence of arms racing within

Southeast Asia. While some Southeast Asian governments and defence establishments certainly watch their neighbours' defence policies and military procurement closely, there is no strong evidence of action–reaction dynamics among the sub-region's countries in terms of their efforts to develop their military capabilities. In fact, the evidence suggests that levels of defence spending are strongly influenced simply by the resources available. Any claim that there is an 'arms race' in Southeast Asia should be treated with caution.[113] Thirdly, Southeast Asian states' diverse strategic outlooks, widely varying levels of resources for defence, and divergent approaches to capability development, along with the residual suspicions that exist between them, mean that coordination of defence policies has been limited.

CHAPTER FOUR

Geopolitical evolution in South Asia

Undivided India under the British Raj made enormous military contributions to the imperial defence system of Great Britain, particularly during the first and second world wars. After the decolonisation and partition of India in 1947, however, the subcontinent was marginalised in terms of great-power contestation and the larger security politics of Asia and the Indian Ocean. Unresolved territorial and other disputes between India and Pakistan, including frequent wars, meant that the military energies of the subcontinent turned inwards. Jawaharlal Nehru, India's prime minister from 1947 to 1964, emphasised non-alignment and opposition to military alliances, and New Delhi became extraneous to regional military equations. Islamabad, in contrast, joined the Western military alliances in the region, the Central Treaty Organization (CENTO) and SEATO, but Pakistan's military importance to the West waxed and waned over the years. The Sino-Indian war of 1962 and the frequent conflicts between India and Pakistan drew great-power interest, but the region never reacquired the importance that it had enjoyed up to the middle of the twentieth century. That might, however, be changing. Several factors, including persistent conflict in Afghanistan, China's rise, the gradual emergence of India, the introduction of nuclear weapons, the return of great-power rivalry, and the dynamic interaction between South Asia and its neighbours are pulling the subcontinent back to centre stage in Asian geopolitics.

The growing military sophistication of India and Pakistan, coupled with China's substantial military modernisation, lends a special edge to conflicts in South Asia. The introduction of nuclear weapons has created a paradox: they have dampened any propensity for a conventional military conflict, but opened space for hybrid warfare, involving a combination of regular and irregular instruments and techniques, including terrorism, insurgency, criminality and information operations, that has destabilised the sub-region.[1] China's rise has also begun to alter both the economic geography and security politics of South Asia. While India's own emergence as a power raises its potential contribution to securing Northeast and Southeast Asia, its deepening conflict with Pakistan limits its regional role beyond its own neighbourhood.

The shadow of Afghanistan

The importance of Afghanistan, a landlocked nation on the subcontinent's northwestern marches, has often been overlooked. However, in the past few decades there has been no denying the centrality of Afghanistan in shaping South Asian geopolitics. Two extended military occupations (by the Soviet Union in the 1980s and then by the US beginning in 2001) have had a profound impact upon the military affairs of this subregion, shaping the direction of its international relations and altering internal politics in both Pakistan and India.

Historians have long pointed to the dynamic relationship between the trans-Indus territories that might now be called the 'Af–Pak' region and the rest of the subcontinent.

K.M. Panikkar, one of modern India's most influential strategic thinkers, observed that developments in the Kabul valley have had profound strategic significance for several thousand years.[2] Defence of the northwestern frontiers, the main invasion route into the subcontinent, was the principal preoccupation of every major Indian empire from the Maurya to the Raj, culminating in the nineteenth-century competition between the Raj and the European powers known as 'the Great Game'.[3] Fears of a Russian invasion of India through Afghanistan eased after the Anglo-Russian entente of 1907, however, and the country avoided being caught up in the Soviet–American rivalry for much of the Cold War. In the 1980s, following the Soviet invasion, Afghanistan again became a focal point of East–West conflict. The strategy used to defeat the Soviet occupation would ultimately return to haunt the US on 11 September 2001.

The Afghan strategy employed by Pakistan's Inter-Services Intelligence service (ISI) and the United States' CIA involved arming extremist militias and the deliberate use of radical Islam to bleed the Soviet bear.[4] This period of Western support for religious extremism also coincided with General Muhammad Zia-ul-Haq's injection of conservative Islam into the body politic of Pakistan. Islamabad would subsequently use the same template against both India and Afghanistan from the 1990s. The period of US–Pakistan collaboration in Afghanistan was also the moment when Washington decided to tacitly acquiesce to Islamabad's nuclear-weapons programme, a strategic development that would fundamentally alter the structure of South Asia's geopolitics.[5]

The US turned its back on Afghanistan after the Soviets withdrew, but returned after 9/11. Defeating, disrupting and dismantling the bases of religious extremism in the Af–Pak region became, ironically, the main American objective in response to the terrorist attacks. Although victory initially seemed easy with the rather quick routing of the Taliban at the end of 2001 and the establishment of a new government in Kabul, the US ultimately struggled to achieve its objectives. The Taliban turned out to be highly resilient, frustrating US efforts to stabilise Afghanistan from its sanctuaries in Pakistan.

Washington's approach to Afghanistan was also undermined by shifting objectives and deep internal divisions.[6] As the war dragged on, political support in Washington declined. Barack Obama, who came to office calling the Afghan intervention a 'war of necessity' rather than a 'war of choice', decided in 2009 to increase the US troop presence beyond 100,000 but to also end America's military presence by 2014.[7] In the event, a near total drawdown was delayed until 2016, with 8,400 US troops remaining in the country by the time Obama left the White House. Donald Trump was even more sceptical than Obama about 'winning' the war in Afghanistan. In the summer of 2017 he announced a small expansion of the military presence to give US armed forces one more chance to stabilise the country. But his impatience eventually led to a serious negotiation with the Taliban and the signing of a peace settlement on 29 February 2020.[8] The agreement allowed the US to withdraw most of its forces from Afghanistan in return for assurances that the Taliban would prevent attacks from Afghan territory on America and its allies. The agreement also called for intra-Afghan talks and an agreed transition to a new political arrangement in Kabul. By 18 June US troop numbers were back down to 8,600. Any hopes that the agreement might bring peace, however, quickly evaporated amid the Taliban's continuing violence and Trump's impatience for an early exit. In October 2020, for example, the Taliban attempted to seize Lashkar Gah (the capital of Helmand province), only to be denied by US airstrikes. When Trump left office, troop numbers were officially down to 2,500 and the Taliban dominated the Afghan countryside and controlled the country's highways, which it used to raise revenue.[9]

Full American withdrawal from Afghanistan in 2021 will inevitably affect the security dynamic between India and Pakistan. Two decades of US military presence has helped India expand its influence in Kabul, especially in the economic arena. India has generally had good relations with Afghanistan, with the exception of the period of Taliban rule (1996–2001), when New Delhi severed ties and had to contend with Pakistan's increased weight in Kabul. Since 2001, successive Afghan governments have been more than friendly to India and deeply suspicious of the Taliban and Pakistan. Since 2009, when the Obama administration announced its surge and exit policy, New Delhi has been deeply concerned about the consequences of eventual US withdrawal. Its anxieties include Pakistan's use of Afghan territory to train terrorist groups for deployment against India, Islamabad's perception of Afghanistan as a potential form of 'strategic depth' against India and, more broadly, its political and diplomatic shadow over Kabul.

Pakistan, by contrast, viewed the agreement between the Trump administration and the Taliban as a vindication of its long-standing positions on Afghanistan and as a triumph for its diplomacy in facilitating the peace settlement. Throughout the previous two decades, Islamabad had chafed at India's expanding diplomatic presence in Afghanistan and the burgeoning economic, political and security ties between its two neighbours.[10] Yet while Pakistan might be pleased with any potential setback to the Indian presence in Afghanistan, it remains acutely aware of the dangers of instability across its western border in the post-American era, and alert to the meddling of other regional actors, including India, in Afghanistan. The Taliban's new weight in Kabul, moreover, is not entirely reassuring for Pakistan, since Islamabad's ability to control the Taliban, and

Afghan nationalism more broadly, is far from guaranteed.[11] A long border with Pakistan and the Pashtun population across it – Pakistan itself has a large and restive Pashtun minority numbering approximately 35m, or 15% of the population – has both given Islamabad a significant ability to intervene in Afghan affairs and made inevitable the spillover of the Afghan conflict into Pakistan.

There is little symmetry in the relative influence of New Delhi and Islamabad over Afghanistan. India's salience in Afghanistan has always been constrained by a lack of direct geographic access, compounded by the fact that India needs to keep its own relationship with Pakistan in mind. New Delhi must continually balance its interests in normalising relations with Islamabad and raising the intensity of its involvement in Afghanistan. India has thus refused to be drawn into the disputes between Kabul and Islamabad; it has, for example, been reluctant to support Kabul's rejection of the Durand Line (agreed between Britain and Afghanistan in 1893) as the border with Pakistan.[12] For its part, since 2002 Kabul has been eager for stronger military support from India. Despite its commitments under a 2011 strategic-partnership agreement, New Delhi has been quite cautious in the kind of support it has extended.[13]

The Trump administration's calls for India to play a larger security role in Afghanistan did not, unsurprisingly, meet a favourable response. Such urgings appear to have been motivated less by India's record in Afghanistan than the political conviction in Washington that America's friends must assume more of the burden for regional security. A small section of the Indian strategic community has been enthusiastic about deploying a military force in Afghanistan, but others have strongly cautioned against it. History suggests that India's well-known caution and prudence should prevail.[14]

Yet many of the traditional assumptions about Indian strategic policy have weakened under Prime Minister Modi (2014–present). He has stepped up military assistance to Afghanistan and is believed to have authorised more active intelligence operations on Pakistan's western frontier. He has also publicly taken up the cause of Balochi resistance against Pakistan.[15] If Pakistan turns Afghanistan into a terror base against India, New Delhi is bound to react in some manner, setting the stage for an escalation in their long-standing conflict. India could well join hands with other regional powers, as it did in the late 1990s, to support Afghan forces that might confront the Taliban and Pakistan. Modi also has the option of seeking reconciliation with the Taliban (which has always remained open to engagement with India), thereby reclaiming its traditional good relations with Kabul irrespective of the nature of the regime. As India's power continues to grow, its options to challenge Pakistan in Afghanistan are bound to widen. That, in turn, might sharpen Pakistan's own instincts to use the Afghan theatre against New Delhi.

Changing terms of the India–Pakistan conflict

India and Pakistan fought three wars in the 25 years after the partition, in 1947, 1965 and 1971, and since the late 1980s there have been frequent military crises and conflicts, including in 1987, 1990, 1999, 2001–02, 2008, 2016 and 2019.[16] Most of these latter crises saw international diplomatic intervention to prevent escalation into a fully fledged conventional war that could have turned nuclear. The source of the problem was undoubtedly the nuclearisation of South Asia. Pakistan's acquisition of nuclear weapons had, by the late 1980s, reversed the military equilibrium established after the 1971 war. The independence of Bangladesh (formerly East Pakistan) and the signing of the 1972 Shimla Agreement, which offered a framework to negotiate the fraught territorial dispute over Jammu and Kashmir, initially seemed to establish New Delhi's military primacy vis-à-vis Islamabad.[17] But the period of relative stability was short-lived. Pakistan saw the Shimla Agreement as an imposed peace,[18] convinced itself that the US was not a reliable ally, and from 1972 determinedly pursued a clandestine nuclear-weapons programme to restore the balance with India. China, concerned about Indian hegemony over South Asia, extended assistance to Pakistan's nuclear and missile programmes, and the US, which needed Pakistan's support against the Soviet intervention in Afghanistan, acquiesced.[19]

Once it acquired nuclear weapons, Pakistan explicitly rejected the Shimla Agreement, reopened the Kashmir question, supported political movements demanding the separation of Kashmir from India, and nurtured militant groups to foment insurgency in Indian-controlled Kashmir and beyond. India's own mismanagement of the Kashmir situation played into the hands of Pakistan, forcing New Delhi to contend with the new asymmetric strategy that Pakistan began to pursue. Pakistan's nuclear weapons served to neutralise India's conventional superiority, substantially limiting New Delhi's options for dealing with Islamabad's support for cross-border terrorism. If the 1987 crisis heralded the dawn of a new nuclear age in South Asia, the crises that followed underlined an explosive mix of terrorism, nuclear weapons and conventional military mobilisation. This was alongside the intractability of the dispute over Jammu and Kashmir.

The 1999 crisis came about after New Delhi discovered that irregular Pakistani forces had occupied mountainous areas in the Kargil district on India's side of the Line of Control (LoC) in Jammu and Kashmir, and involved limited military conflict under the nuclear shadow. India responded with conventional military force on its own side of the LoC, with a view to expelling the Pakistani intruders.[20] The 2001–02 crisis involved a significantly larger military mobilisation by New Delhi following a December 2001 terrorist attack on the Indian parliament, accompanied by demands that Pakistan end its support for cross-border terrorism. Renewed terrorist attacks in May 2002 saw the two sides come close to war. International diplomatic intervention elicited assurances from Pakistan that its territory would not be used for terror attacks against India.[21] When another terrorist attack occurred in Mumbai in November 2008, India once again contemplated the use of military force, but did not follow through.[22]

India used military force in 2016 in response to a major militant attack against security forces in the town of Uri in Jammu and Kashmir, announcing that its troops had conducted operations across the LoC, striking several terrorist camps in Pakistan-controlled Kashmir.[23] While New Delhi presented this as a major change in its approach towards terrorism originating from the LoC, Islamabad simply denied that such attacks had taken place. In 2019, the Indian Air Force (IAF) bombed a terrorist camp at Balakot in Pakistan's Khyber Pakhtunkhwa province in response to a terrorist attack on Indian security forces at Pulwama in Kashmir. In an aerial skirmish, Pakistan shot down an Indian fighter aircraft and captured its pilot, who landed on the Pakistani side of the LoC. As the threat of escalation loomed large and attracted international attention, Pakistan defused the crisis by releasing the pilot.[24]

The events of 2016 and 2019 marked an important shift in the pattern of crises since 1987. Central to that shift has been India's refusal, under Modi's leadership, to be held back from military retaliation in response to major terror attacks. His decisions to send the army across the LoC in 2016 and fighter aircraft into Pakistan in 2019 have underlined New Delhi's new determination to deter Pakistan's use of cross-border terrorism under the shadow of nuclear weapons. While analysts differ on the success of this approach, there is no question that Modi has been willing to test the limits of nuclear constraint when responding to provocations from Pakistan.[25]

Yet the incident at Balakot revealed weaknesses in the capabilities of the IAF. There was widespread scepticism as to whether the IAF had actually hit the terror camp in Balakot. A claim that an IAF pilot shot down a Pakistani F-16 went unproven. India lost not only its own fighter aircraft, but also a helicopter, brought down by friendly fire. The Pakistan Air Force emerged from the encounter looking much better, even though its retaliation was relatively restrained.[26]

Pakistan's diplomatic weakness was equally unmistakable. India leveraged pressure from third parties, including the US, to get Islamabad to release the captured pilot in 2019 and, more broadly, to acquiesce to India's attempts to change the terms of engagement. The roots of Islamabad's weaker diplomatic position lie in the increasing economic differentiation between India and Pakistan, as the former's economy is on a high growth trajectory while the latter's continues on a downward spiral. India's economic reforms, initiated amid a deep economic crisis that engulfed the nation in 1990, began to gain traction in the 2000s. These reforms, which are still by no means complete, were sufficient to generate expansive growth during the 2000s. Shrugging off its historic underperformance, the Indian economy achieved a growth rate of 9% per year by the middle of the 2000s, and averaged around 8% per year across the decade as a whole despite the 2008–09 global financial crisis. As a result, India had the fifth-largest economy in the world by 2019.[27] Pakistan's economy, by contrast, lagged with growth rates of approximately 3–4% as its population grew rapidly, so the economic gap between Pakistan and India steadily increased.[28] In 2019 India's GDP stood at around US$2.8 trillion, while Pakistan's was only US$278.2bn.[29]

Figure 4.1: **Military expenditure in China, India and Pakistan as a percentage of their GDP, 2000–20**

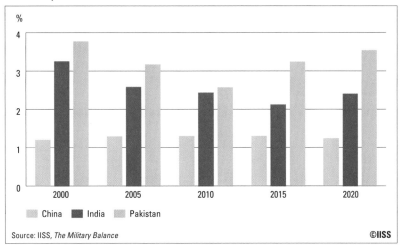

Source: IISS, *The Military Balance*   ©IISS

Military spending in both India and Pakistan has steadily declined as a percentage of GDP. The reduction has been larger for India, from 3.26% in 2000 to 2.41% in 2020. Pakistan's defence expenditure fell from 3.78% to 3.55% of GDP over the same period (see Figure 4.1). Since India's GDP grew more rapidly than Pakistan's during this period, however, the gap has widened in absolute terms. India's defence expenditure rose from US$28.9bn in 2000 to US$70bn in 2019, while Pakistan's grew from US$5bn to US$11.7bn.

This has not, however, translated into effective conventional deterrence for India. Pakistan's nuclear equaliser appears to have limited India's ability to use its conventional military edge to deter its neighbour. Yet the crux of India's problem here, according to some commentators, is not in the nuclear domain. Much of India's defence spending is directed towards salaries and pensions, with capital expenditure as a proportion of the defence budget declining in recent years. Critics also point to India's failure to adequately secure its forces in Kashmir and to the absence of a credible strategy for modernising its military.[30]

Pakistan has traditionally relied on its great-power friends – especially the US and its Western allies, as well as China – to offset India's larger economy, armed forces and diplomatic influence. New Delhi's tilt towards the Soviet Union during the final decades of the Cold War, along with India's policy of non-alignment, helped by introducing distance between New Delhi and the West. India's economic dynamism and Pakistan's concomitant slowdown have, however, begun to test this traditional framework. The end of the Cold War freed India to pursue more purposeful engagement with other powers, and its economic reforms provided a new basis for commercial engagement with China, Europe, Japan and the US. This, in turn, provided a basis for the major powers to recalibrate their approaches towards India and Pakistan.

While all of these powers have exhibited concern about the series of crises between India and Pakistan, they have been willing to afford India greater leeway and to acknowledge a sensitivity to New Delhi's concerns. As India's economic weight and political importance have risen, new incentives have emerged for the major powers to expand engagement with India on its own merits. The idea of separating, or 'de-hyphenating', US relations with India and Pakistan was expressed most clearly by the George W. Bush administration in 2001, and other Western powers have taken the same approach.[31] The 9/11 attacks and the resulting need for Pakistani support did not lead to a return to Washington's traditional zero-sum approach to South Asia. Instead, for the first time since the emergence of India and Pakistan as independent nations, the US and the West began to enjoy good relations simultaneously with both.

A more self-confident India certainly found it less important to object continually to US support for Pakistan in the 'war on terror'. Indeed, for the first time since 1954, when the US and

Pakistan signed a Mutual Defense Assistance Agreement, New Delhi became significantly less vehement in its objections. In March 2005, when the Bush administration announced a major package of military assistance to Pakistan, New Delhi both restrained its criticism and took up Washington's offer to initiate a strategic-partnership agreement. The changed approach towards the US led to two landmark agreements, on bilateral defence cooperation in June 2005 and civilian nuclear cooperation in 2008, which together transformed the basis of India–US military and political relations.[32] This shift in New Delhi's attitude stemmed from the recognition that the primary threat from Pakistan lay not in the conventional military equipment it might acquire but in its ability to unleash sub-conventional conflict through supporting cross-border terrorism. India thus began to focus less on dissuading the West from selling arms to Pakistan and more on persuading it to exert pressure on Pakistan to stop hosting anti-India terrorist groups. The question of terrorism also acquired a prominent place in India's own political engagement with Pakistan following the nuclear tests conducted by both countries in 1998.

The US policy of de-hyphenation that began under Bush continued under Obama and Trump. Although de-hyphenation sounds even-handed, it actually favoured India. Obama visited India twice during his time in office (in 2010 and 2015) but did not include Pakistan in either trip, although travelling to both South Asian countries had been an unstated presidential policy for decades. Besides India's growing economic weight, frustration steadily grew in Washington with a Pakistan that was seen as playing both sides of the street in Afghanistan. Meanwhile, India increasingly came to be seen as integral to constructing a stable balance of power in a region that was coming under Chinese influence. What seemed like an abstract concept during the Bush era gained greater currency in both the Obama and the Trump years.[33] Whether it was Obama's 'pivot' to Asia or Trump's FOIP strategy, New Delhi's growing strategic importance to the US started generating significant concerns in Pakistan.[34]

Washington's response to the 2019 crisis confirmed Islamabad's worst fears. As one Pakistani analyst observed, a US which had seemingly played the role of 'reliable and neutral third party' in all crises since 1987 appeared now to be tilting towards New Delhi by calling India's attack on Balakot a 'counterterrorism action', and by underlining India's right to self-defence.[35] And as India threatened to escalate after the capture of its pilot, the US reportedly intervened to pressure Pakistan into releasing him. To make matters worse, two of Pakistan's closest traditional allies, the United Arab Emirates and Saudi Arabia, also leant on Islamabad to release the pilot.[36] Beyond the tilt towards New Delhi in crisis management, the US and the West increasingly joined India in exerting pressure against Islamabad on the question of terrorism originating from Pakistani soil. What began as affirmations in bilateral statements eventually moved to a range of multilateral institutions including the UN, the International Monetary Fund and the Financial Action Task Force (FATF). Pressure at the FATF turned out to be particularly significant, given its impact on Pakistan's already difficult financial situation.[37] Although the level of support from the West might still have been less than New Delhi would have liked, there is no question that it began to complicate Pakistan's calculus on the benefits and risks of waging low-intensity conflict against India.

The shift in international attitudes also appears to extend to global perspectives on Kashmir and the India–Pakistan peace process. In August 2019, soon after his re-election with an increased mandate, Modi altered the constitutional status of Kashmir within the Indian Union.[38] Pakistan reacted with outrage, and liberal opinion worldwide criticised Modi's move as reckless. In practical terms, however, governmental responses were rather muted. Washington was more concerned about the lockdown that India imposed on Kashmir after the constitutional change than about the change in the region's status itself. Pakistani efforts to get the United Nations Security Council (UNSC), which has been involved in the dispute since 1948, to deal with the matter were blocked by France and the US on India's behalf.[39]

Pakistan was certainly right in accusing Modi of trying to change the legal and political framework that has traditionally shaped India's internal approach to the Kashmir question and its negotiating position with Islamabad. The Indian prime minister had clearly come to the view that the approach of his predecessors (which involved reconciling internally with Kashmiri dissident and militant groups, while externally seeking a compromise with Islamabad on Kashmir) was unsustainable amid Pakistan's continued support for terrorism and, more importantly, its ability to exercise political leverage with a coalition of Kashmiri separatist groups called the Hurriyat. Determined to overcome these constraints, Modi's alternative approach consisted of three elements: developing military deterrent capabilities against Pakistan-supported cross-border terrorism; putting the peace process on hold until Islamabad ceased supporting terror; and refusing to negotiate with militant groups while changing the internal political framework so as to remove any ambiguities surrounding Kashmir's integration with India.[40] While it is by no means assured that Modi will succeed in his ambition to change the structure of New Delhi's engagement with Pakistan over Kashmir, he does appear willing to invest considerable political capital in this effort and has the requisite domestic support, at least for now.[41]

India and China: eroding tranquility

In contrast to the India–Pakistan conflict, India and China enjoyed an extended period of peace and tranquility on their border from the late 1980s until the mid-2000s. That relatively benign phase yielded to a more complex dynamic by the late 2000s, in which the long and contested border became increasingly volatile in military terms. The differences between the two Asian giants on a range of issues, from the economic to the political, became sharper. Their competition for influence in South Asia has steadily grown, and the new dynamic has become increasingly enmeshed in the larger contest to define Asia's new security order.[42]

The normalisation of Sino-Indian relations after their 1962 border war had to wait until 1988, when then-prime minister Rajiv Gandhi visited China. The two sides agreed to expand bilateral relations while simultaneously pursuing negotiations on resolving their boundary disputes. During the 1990s, Beijing and New Delhi affirmed their commitment to maintain peace and tranquility on the border and, in 1993 and 1996, signed two agreements on military confidence-building measures.[43] India's June 2003 recognition of Tibet as part of China eased a bitter dispute that had been at the root of the Sino-Indian conflict since the middle of the twentieth century.[44] While China's special relationship with Pakistan, including collaboration on nuclear and missile programmes, continued during the 1990s, Beijing took a more nuanced position on the Kashmir dispute between New Delhi and Islamabad, encouraging them to resolve their differences peacefully and to set them aside if necessary, focusing instead on building economic and other forms of cooperation.[45]

From the early 2000s, Sino-Indian trade burgeoned from approximately US$3bn in 2000 to US$55bn in 2008, and to an all-time high of US$95bn in 2018. India faced a widening deficit in favour of China,[46] yet broadening economic and commercial ties also provided a good foundation for a more stable partnership. In 2003 the two sides agreed to renew boundary negotiations at a higher political level and from a political perspective, rather than emphasising historical claims and legal arguments. This, in turn, led to an agreement in 2005 on the political parameters and guiding principles for the settlement of the boundary disputes. This agreement on principles was to be followed by a second negotiating phase defining mutual territorial compromises, leading to a third phase where a new boundary would be delineated on the map and demarcated on the ground.[47]

Hopes for a transformation of the bilateral relationship and an early resolution of the boundary dispute were, however, short-lived. As the two sides argued over interpretations of the 2005 agreement, political arguments over Kashmir, Tibet and the state of Arunachal Pradesh intensified, and there was a steady escalation of tensions between Chinese and Indian forces along the boundary. From the mid-2000s, Beijing began to make more strident claims to Arunachal Pradesh, publicly describing it as 'southern Tibet', and became increasingly vocal in its objections to New Delhi's exercise of territorial sovereignty there. China also began blocking multilateral development assistance to Indian projects in the state. As Tibet became restive once again in the early years of the twenty-first century, China pressured New Delhi to crack down on Tibetan refugees in India and to curtail the activities and movements of the Dalai Lama.[48] On Kashmir, China ended its more balanced position between India and Pakistan. As Beijing's interests grew in the China–Pakistan Economic Corridor, which enters Pakistan through the part of Kashmir controlled by Islamabad, it tilted further away from India. Beijing objected furiously to the change in the constitutional status of Jammu and Kashmir in August 2019, and actively sought a UNSC debate. As China sought to internationalise the Kashmir question, New Delhi's wariness about Beijing deepened.

Several other factors contributed to the deterioration in Sino-Indian relations. One was the improvement in military and civilian infrastructure in Tibet. While China's construction of a major rail link to Tibet drew considerable attention, it was the overall development of transport infrastructure that began to alter the military balance in this region. The comprehensive expansion of road and rail networks, building of new airports and construction of almost 200 logistics hubs in the Tibet Autonomous Region significantly improved the PLA's operational capacity on the Sino-Indian border. Although difficult terrain and logistical challenges had previously constrained PLA operations in Tibet, these limitations appear to have been overcome. Accordingly, the PLA's mobilisation capacities and its operational readiness on the border with India have improved substantially, posing significant challenges to Indian armed forces.[49]

Another factor was the new Chinese military doctrine of 'active defence', which has meant a more aggressive PLA posture on the border. Rather than conducting a 'people's war', 'active defence' calls for forward positioning, frontier defence, engagement of the enemy at or beyond the border, and potential engagement in conflict beyond China's immediate periphery. As Indian defence analyst Gurmeet Kanwal has noted, 'compared with China's historically reactive stance of luring the adversary deep inside and destroying him through strategic defence, this doctrine is essentially pro-active and seeks to take the battle into enemy territory'.[50] What seemed an abstract approach in the 1980s has now been translated into a muscular military stance.[51]

New Delhi began to respond to this challenge. For decades, India consciously avoided the development of modern infrastructure in areas bordering China. During the 2000s, however, it unveiled an ambitious programme for development of road, rail and air connectivity, including construction of nearly 6,000 km of border roads, bridges and helipads. While progress was slow under Manmohan Singh's United Progressive Alliance government (2004–14), the Modi administration has sought to increase the pace of military-infrastructure modernisation. Beginning in 2005, the IAF also reactivated numerous landing strips along the border. India has also raised additional army divisions for deployment on the border.[52]

Until the 2000s, the frontier was contested but not intensely militarised. This relative tranquility, which had lasted since the late 1980s, began to erode as the resources and capabilities of both countries' armed forces increased and political solutions remained elusive. The attempt in the early 2000s to resolve the boundary disputes actually added incentives for more aggressive patrolling in order to reinforce claims. Since the late 2000s, both armies have patrolled along the border with increasing vigour and there have been far more incursions into territory claimed by the other side, resulting in frequent face-offs.[53]

This erosion of tranquility manifested in three major crises during the 2010s. Each was defused through high-level political intervention from New Delhi and Beijing, but without resolving any of the underlying problems. In early 2013, soldiers from both sides pitched tents in a disputed area at Daulat Beg Oldi in northern Ladakh. This was a significant departure from past practice, where both sides had made formal claims at a disputed part of the boundary and then departed. A similar incident occurred a few weeks later at Chumar in another part of Ladakh. On both occasions the traditional confidence-building measures appeared inadequate. Instead, high-level diplomatic intervention was required to restore the status quo ante, with the May 2013 visit of Chinese Premier Li Keqiang to New Delhi providing the political incentive to address the crisis.[54]

In September 2014, Xi's first visit to India as Chinese leader also coincided with a major flare-up in border tensions, this time at Demchok in Ladakh. On a regular patrol, Indian border forces found that Chinese troops were building a road on territory claimed by India. Having failed to persuade the Chinese troops to leave, the Indian forces set up camp directly opposite them. Despite the cloud this incident cast over Xi's visit, and reports that Modi raised the issue directly with him, the crisis continued throughout his stay. Xi reportedly promised Modi that he would sort out the issue once he was back in Beijing; a few days after his return, the Chinese troops pulled back.[55]

A 2017 crisis on the disputed Doklam Plateau, on the frontier between Bhutan and China, was far more serious and more difficult to resolve. It began when Bhutan discovered a significant Chinese effort to build roads through the disputed area. The Indian Army intervened to stop the Chinese construction activity, leading to occasional physical confrontation between troops from the two sides. They gradually settled into a military stand-off that lasted 73 days. In the end the Chinese agreed to step back, but while the stand-off at the point of contact was defused, the Chinese presence on the plateau continued. The PLA was able to consolidate its position, essentially enabling it to shape its boundary dispute with Bhutan by changing the facts on the ground.[56]

India initially responded by returning to the diplomatic route, engaging with China at the highest level. Xi and Modi met twice, at Wuhan in 2018 and Chennai in 2019, to try to develop a better framework to address the boundary dispute along with other contentious bilateral issues. They achieved no breakthroughs, but for India these meetings nonetheless appear to have served the main purpose of preventing the relationship from breaking down into conflict and maintaining a high-level channel of engagement.[57]

But 2020 was an especially tense year in Sino-Indian relations, significantly dampening New Delhi's enthusiasm for diplomacy and possibly prompting a significant shift in the Modi government's approach to its dealings with Beijing. In June 2020, hundreds of Chinese and Indian troops engaged in hand-to-hand combat (using stones and clubs, some reportedly wrapped in barbed wire) at Pangong Lake on the Ladakh–Tibet border, leading to the deaths of 21 Indian soldiers and an unconfirmed number on the Chinese side.[58] Both sides responded by pouring in tens of thousands of troops along the notional Line of Actual Control that separates Indian-controlled from Chinese-controlled territory, supported by fighter aircraft, tanks and heavy artillery. In late August, tensions increased further when Indian special forces seized a strategically significant peak in Chushul, prompting the first exchange of gunfire along the border since 1975.[59] Indian Minister of External Affairs Subrahmanyam Jaishankar and his Chinese counterpart Wang Yi met in Moscow in September for a lengthy meeting on the sidelines of the SCO. Although they were able to agree a five-point statement for easing tensions, the underlying causes remained unresolved.[60] The deadlock was finally broken in February 2021, when the two sides agreed to disengage their forces at Pangong Lake. A 6.5 km buffer zone was created from which each side agreed to withdraw permanent bases and cease military patrols to reduce the risk of further clashes.[61]

China's growing military muscle and political will, combined with advantages over India in comprehensive national power that continue to widen in Beijing's favour, have meant that there is no giving way to India on the boundary dispute. Just as a substantial economic gap has opened up between Pakistan and India over the last decade, the difference in GDP between New Delhi and Beijing has increased

Figure 4.2: **Military expenditure in China, India and Pakistan, 2000–20**

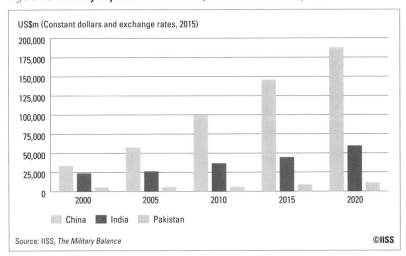

US$m (Constant dollars and exchange rates, 2015)

China India Pakistan

Source: IISS, *The Military Balance*   ©IISS

in favour of the latter. The impact is visible in their military expenditures, with China's defence spending now more than three times that of India (see Figure 4.2). China's armed forces also far outweigh India's in numerical terms. China does have a multitude of strategic challenges to contend with on its eastern frontiers (see Chapter Two), however, which renders a straightforward comparison of military strengths unrealistic. And while India's weapons inventory is clearly smaller, the quality of some of its weaponry – and of its soldiers, especially when operating in mountainous terrain – is far superior. But China is steadily closing the gap in weapons quality, while the modernisation of the PLA has improved the skills of its military personnel. Although China's primary military focus remains the Western Pacific, where it confronts the military might of the US and its allies, securing Tibet has been a key priority for Beijing since 1949–50. The hopes of part of the Indian establishment that the demands of managing its eastern front lines against the US would lead to China easing up on its southern frontier with India have continuously been dashed.

Nuclear calculus

The introduction of nuclear weapons in South Asia in the 1990s has done more than give Pakistan increased freedom to pursue sub-conventional conflict against India. As the gap in comprehensive national power between India and Pakistan has widened, Islamabad has responded by investing in its nuclear arsenal. From the Pakistani perspective, the logic of deterring an increasingly stronger India demands a doctrine that calls for full-spectrum, rather than minimum, deterrence. This, in turn, requires the development of a broad range of nuclear weapons and delivery systems.[62] Pakistan has also continued to expand its capacity to produce fissile material, especially plutonium (see Table 4.1). In 2019, Pakistan's nuclear arsenal comprised up to 160 warheads (up from 90 in 2010) and India's up to 150 (see Figure 4.3).[63]

The pace at which Pakistan's stockpile has grown, including the development of tactical nuclear weapons, has drawn worldwide attention, and there is even speculation that it might overtake that of the UK. While not denying this growth, Pakistani analysts argue that it has been driven by developments on the Indian side. For example, one stated concern is that the US–India Civil Nuclear Cooperation Initiative permits India to keep eight of its civilian reactors outside International Atomic Energy Agency safeguards.[64] This gives New Delhi the option to dramatically increase production of fissile material and therefore the size of its nuclear arsenal. Pakistan

Table 4.1: **Fissile-material inventories, 2010 and 2020**

	Highly enriched uranium (tonnes)		Plutonium (tonnes)	
	2010	2020	2010	2020
China	16	14	1.8	2.9
India	1.3	5.2	4.24	8.8
Pakistan	2.6	3.9	0.1	0.41

Note: 20% uncertainty is assumed for China's total military stockpile of highly enriched uranium, 30% for Pakistan's, and 40% for India's. Uncertainty of 10–30% is assumed for the countries' military stockpiles of plutonium.

Source: International Panel on Fissile Materials

Figure 4.3: **Nuclear-warhead stockpiles – China, India and Pakistan**

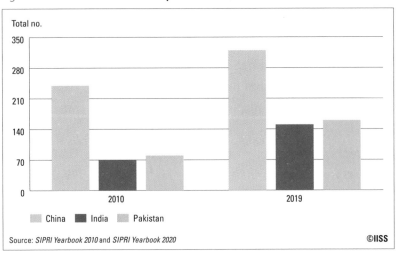

Source: *SIPRI Yearbook 2010* and *SIPRI Yearbook 2020*   ©IISS

is particularly worried that India might be abandoning its minimum-deterrence posture based on a retaliatory-strike capability in favour of counterforce options. Hints from the Modi government that it might be departing from its no-first-use doctrine, including during the Pulwama–Balakot crisis, have reinforced Islamabad's fears.[65]

Pakistan also cites concerns about India's 'Cold Start' doctrine as a further rationale for the rapid expansion of its nuclear arsenal.[66] This was New Delhi's response to the crises of 1999 and 2001–02, which shook the Indian strategic community's assumption that the introduction of nuclear weapons in South Asia had significantly reduced the prospect of a conventional military conflict. Cold Start envisaged a swift conventional military response to cross-border terrorism that would enable New Delhi to achieve its political and military objectives in a short war without running the risk of crossing Pakistan's nuclear red lines. It had two conceptual components: use of the 'Pivot' corps, traditionally meant to hold ground, to launch quick offensive operations from a cold start; and developing integrated battle groups to launch limited offensive operations to a shallow depth, capturing a long swathe of territory across the international boundary to use as a bargaining chip. Although New Delhi saw the doctrine as an answer to Pakistan's support for cross-border terrorism and an attempt to break out from the constraints of the nuclear shadow, from Pakistan's perspective it was nothing more than a translation of India's growing military capabilities into an offensive approach along the border.[67] This argument became central to Pakistani propaganda against India, while New Delhi soon realised that translating the concept into practice would be too costly and difficult.[68]

A third reason was India's declared interest in developing missile-defence capabilities. New Delhi first signalled its interest in missile defence in the wake of the Bush administration's 2001 decision to withdraw from the Anti-Ballistic Missile (ABM) Treaty and to accelerate the US deployment of missile defences. India's support for the Bush initiative surprised analysts both at home and abroad.[69] However, the subsequent India–US dialogue on potential missile-defence cooperation failed to produce any major breakthroughs, leading India's Defence Research and Development Organisation to launch its own programme. After a series of interceptor tests between 2006 and 2019, there were claims that a multi-layered defence system had been developed to protect high-value targets in New Delhi and Mumbai. The system reportedly includes indigenously developed interceptors, missiles acquired from Israel, the planned purchase of S-400 missiles from Russia, and an advanced air-defence system from the US.[70] These developments raised concerns in Islamabad over their potential to degrade the credibility of Pakistan's nuclear deterrent. Pakistan responded by testing multiple independent re-entry vehicle (MIRV) technology on its missiles in the late 2010s.[71] Whether or not the Indian Ballistic Missile Defence system is ultimately credible and deployable in the short term, both countries now have a significant array of missiles in their inventories (see Table 4.2), further deepening the instability of deterrence in South Asia.

The US has been another important source of concern for Islamabad's nuclear posture. Since 9/11 there has been much debate in the US about the security and safety of Pakistan's nuclear arsenal.[72] The American security establishment fears that parts of Pakistan's stockpile could fall into the hands of jihadi groups, whose strength and influence in the country have been on the rise. According to this line of thinking, in trying to keep its nuclear weapons from the prying eyes of the US, Pakistan has inadvertently rendered them more vulnerable to seizure by terrorists. One element of the US policy debate has thus been about expanding American assistance to Pakistan to help with securing its nuclear arsenal. Any suggestion of American assistance beyond the provision of funds, however, feeds into Pakistani concerns regarding the dangers of external penetration and sabotage of its nuclear programme.[73] This paranoia is heightened by Pakistani apprehensions about unilateral American military actions to forcibly 'take out' its arsenal.[74] While contingency plans for such an action might well have been contemplated, Washington remains acutely aware of the limited prospects for success of such a mission and the dangerous consequences of failure.[75] Publicly at least, Washington has sought to assure its own people and the world that the Pakistani arsenal remains secure.[76] But even the remote possibility of external intervention has strengthened Islamabad's incentive to expand and disperse its nuclear-weapons infrastructure.

Superficially, the nuclear dynamics in South Asia look like a traditional arms race. Upon closer inspection, however, the reality is not so straightforward, as those dynamics are shaped by many factors. India's main challenge is not the expanding

Table 4.2: **Selected cruise- and ballistic-missile programmes – China, India and Pakistan**

Type	Country	System Name	Status	Range (km)
Cruise missiles	China	CJ-10	Operational	1,500+
		CJ-10A	Operational	1,500+
		YJ-63	Operational	n/k
		CJ-20	Operational	1,500+
		CJ-100	Entering service	n/k
		YJ-18	Development	500
	India	Brahmos I	Operational	300
		Brahmos II	Development	n/k
		Nirbhay	Development	n/k
	Pakistan	Babur I	Operational	350
		Babur IA	Operational	450
		Ra'ad I	Operational	350
		Babur IB/II	Development	700
		Babur III	Development	450
		Ra'ad II	Uncertain	500
Hypersonic-glide-vehicle systems	China	DF-17 (MRBM)	Entering service	2,000
		DF-5C (ICBM)	Development	12,000+
Short-range ballistic missiles	China	DF-11	Operational	300
		DF-11A	Operational	600
		DF-15A	Operational	850+
		DF-15B	Operational	725+
		DF-16	Operational	700+
	India	Prithvi II	Operational	250
		Agni I	Operational	700
		Pranash	Development	200
		Pralay	Development	n/k
	Pakistan	Hatf-1	Operational	50
		Nasr	Operational	60
		Abdali	Operational	200
		Ghaznavi	Operational	300
		Shaheen-1	Operational	750
		Shaheen-1A	Uncertain	n/k
Medium-range ballistic missiles	China	DF-21A	Operational	1,750+
		DF-21C	Operational	1,500+
		DF-21D	Operational	1,500+
	India	Agni II	Operational	2,000+
	Pakistan	Ghauri I	Operational	1,250
		Ghauri II	Operational	1,500+
		Shaheen-2	Operational	2,000
		Shaheen-3	Development	2,750
		Ababeel	Development	2,200
Intermediate-range ballistic missiles	China	DF-26	Operational	3,000+
	India	Agni III	Operational	3,200+
		Agni IV	Development	3,500+
Intercontinental ballistic missiles	China	DF-4	Operational	5,500+
		DF-5A	Operational	12,000+
		DF-5B	Operational	12,000+
		DF-31	Operational	7,000+
		DF-31A	Operational	13,000+
		DF-31A(G)	Operational	n/k
		DF-41	Operational	n/k
	India	Agni V	Development	5,000+
		Agni VI	Development	8,000+
Submarine-launched ballistic missiles	China	JL-2	Operational	7,000+
		JL-3	Development	10,000+
	India	K-15	Operational	700
		K-4	Development	3,500
		K-5	Development	5,000+

Source: IISS, Military Balance+, https://milbalplus.iiss.org, accessed July 2021

size and sophistication of Pakistan's nuclear arsenal, but Pakistan's ability to support cross-border terrorism in India without the fear of punitive retaliation. And even as it struggles to cope with the Pakistani challenge, India is also focused on acquiring a credible nuclear-deterrent capability against China. The two countries may indeed be pursuing their respective national-security aims with growing alacrity, but as two US analysts put it, 'they are running on different tracks and chasing vastly different goals', and the dynamic is not confined to South Asia.[77]

India's initial explorations into a nuclear-weapons capability were in fact triggered by China's first nuclear test in 1964.[78] Its response eventually came in May 1974, with the testing of a 'peaceful nuclear device'.[79] But India's nuclear-weapons programme then went into cold storage and was not revived until evidence of Pakistan's nuclear-weapons programme came to light in the 1980s. India ordered the weaponisation of its nuclear programme in 1988 and conducted five underground nuclear tests in May 1998.[80] In coming out of the nuclear closet, India cited the threat from China rather than the one from Pakistan; but it also pointed to Beijing's support for Islamabad's nuclear and missile programmes.[81] Since that time, developing a credible deterrent capability against China has become an important priority. In addition to its bombers, which can reach Tibet and southwest China, India has focused on developing longer-range missiles that can strike deeper into Chinese territory. It has also focused on developing SLBMs, giving New Delhi a secure second-strike capability (see Table 4.2).[82]

Nuclear parity with China has been a long-standing Indian strategic objective, but it is unlikely to contribute to nuclear stability. Until very recently, China did not have to factor India's nuclear weapons into its deterrent calculus. Beijing was comfortable letting the Pakistani nuclear arsenal, built with China's support, balance India's limited nuclear capabilities. With India acquiring a credible deterrent against China, however, Beijing might start factoring India's long-range missile capability into its nuclear-force planning, creating pressure on India to keep pace. China also now regularly deploys its nuclear submarines in the Indian Ocean and there is speculation that Pakistan has hosted them at the Port of Karachi.[83] Pakistan has reportedly been pressing China to lease it a nuclear submarine, in much the same manner as Moscow did with India in 2012.[84]

New developments in military space technology, hypersonic missiles and underwater drones, and in the cyber domain, will almost certainly have an impact on the nuclear calculus in South Asia, as well as an indirect effect on the sub-region's development, by compelling changes in global arms-control frameworks. The United States' withdrawal from the ABM Treaty and its embrace of missile defence and conventional prompt global strike (CPGS) weapons have created a permissive environment for the development not only of ballistic-missile defences but also of space weapons.[85] These developments have been emulated in China and South Asia, and it might also be necessary to include Russia as part of the complex South Asian nuclear calculus. The collapse of the INF Treaty between the US and Russia in 2019 is likely to draw all of Asia deeper into the unfolding competitive dynamic between China and the US.

China's support for Pakistan's nuclear and missile programmes met with little American opposition in the 1980s, when Washington was focused on the Russian occupation of Afghanistan, and only weak resistance in the 1990s. As the Bush administration's geopolitical calculus altered radically in the 2000s, however, it offered an exclusive civil-nuclear deal to India that ended New Delhi's prolonged nuclear isolation. When the US refused to extend a similar deal to Pakistan, Beijing lost no time in providing diplomatic, political and programmatic support for Islamabad's nuclear aspirations. The Soviet Union and later Russia also supported India's nuclear and missile development, to strengthen its strategic ties with New Delhi amid Moscow's own contests with Washington and Beijing. As post-Soviet Russia's embrace of China becomes tighter, however, the five-way play between China, India, Pakistan, Russia and the US is likely to become even more turbulent.

The return of great-power rivalry

The US–India civil-nuclear initiative was part of an effort to transform Washington's bilateral relations with New Delhi and to support India's rise as a great power. This, in turn, was based on the proposition that India could not be viewed simply through the prism of South Asia, but that it needed to be seen as a potential partner in stabilising the Asian balance of power. This meant decoupling US policies towards New Delhi and Islamabad, and entailed viewing India in the context of the challenges posed by a rising China.[86] This shift set the stage for a slow but definitive transformation of great-power politics on the subcontinent. The new US tilt towards India ended a period of prolonged stasis in the South Asian balance of power, but the emergence of new great-power rivalries was also fuelled by China's rapid economic and military rise, along with India's slower evolution into a major power.

From the early 1970s, when Sino-US rapprochement began, South Asian policymakers operated with certain assumptions about the regional balance of power. Both the US–Soviet and Sino-Soviet rivalries were seen as fundamental to that balance. At the sub-regional level, this saw China, Pakistan and the US drawing together on one side, and India joining the Soviet Union on the other.[87] The collapse of the Soviet Union two decades later led to the unravelling of this framework, opening the door for new alignments.[88] Yet the dominant feature of the post-Cold War world was the absence of great-power rivalry, with attempts made in the 1990s to integrate both Russia and China deeper into Western-led structures. The emergence of the so-called 'Washington consensus' on liberalisation and globalisation meant that all major powers had a strong incentive to expand economic cooperation. Through the 1990s and beyond, the US and China developed tighter economic interdependence. The two sides declared a 'strategic partnership' in 1998 when then-president Bill Clinton travelled to Beijing. Clinton and Jiang Zemin also talked about working together to 'stabilise' South Asia, much to the chagrin of New Delhi and the delight of Islamabad.

US–India relations continued to warm considerably following the Bush administration's historic shift, and Obama continued to invest in stronger strategic ties with India.[89] But the Trump administration set the stage for a very different American approach to South Asian geopolitics. By emphasising the return of great-power rivalry as the central theme in international politics, and by enunciating the FOIP concept as its preferred vision for regional order, Washington highlighted the new importance of India in its strategy to secure the vast 'Indo-Pacific' littoral zone.

Moscow had warily watched the rapid growth of India–US military engagement since the Bush administration's first term. Washington and New Delhi signed a ten-year defence framework agreement in June 2005, which seemed to take their bilateral defence engagement to a higher level. Under this framework, India and the US agreed to expand bilateral defence-industrial cooperation and identified common military missions that they could each participate in. Significantly, this was the first such agreement that independent India had ever signed.[90] The scale and intensity of bilateral exercises has grown steadily over time; by 2020 the US was conducting

Table 4.3: **Major US arms sales to India, 2001–21**

Equipment type	Year of order/ deliveries	Number delivered	Comments
Austin-class amphibious transport dock	2006/07	1	USS *Trenton*, purchased for US$48m (incl. modernisation); Indian name INS *Jalashwa*
SH-3 *Sea King* helicopter	2006/07	6	Ex-US Navy UH-3H versions, purchased for US$39m
C-130 J-30 *Hercules* transport aircraft	2008	6	US$962m deal (US$596m for the aircraft, the rest for special equipment) for India's special forces
P-8A *Poseidon* anti-submarine-warfare (ASW) aircraft	2009/2013–16	8	US$2bn deal with 30% offset including production of components in India; P-8I *Neptune* version
C-17A *Globemaster* III transport aircraft	2011/2013–14	10	US$4.1bn deal with offset valued at US$1.1bn
C-130 J-30 *Hercules* transport aircraft	2013/2017	6	US$1.1bn deal with 30% offset including production of components in India; for India's special forces
M777 155mm lightweight towed howitzers	2013/2017	145	US$542m deal
CH-47F *Chinook* transport helicopter	2015/2019–23	15	US$1bn deal; CF-47F version
AH-64E *Apache* attack helicopter	2015/2019–20	22	US$1.4bn deal includes production of components in India
P-8A *Poseidon* ASW aircraft	2016/2020–21	4	US$1bn deal
AH-64E *Apache* attack helicopter	2017	6	US$800m deal including production of components in India; delivery planned from 2023
C-17A *Globemaster* III transport aircraft	2018	1	US$262m deal
MH-60R *Seahawk* ASW helicopter	2019	24	US$2.6bn deal
P-8A *Poseidon* ASW aircraft	2019	6	Selected but not ordered by end of April 2021
RQ-1 *Predator* UAV	2020	2	One-year lease

Sources: *SIPRI Arms Transfers Database 2001–20*; IISS, *The Military Balance*; Defense Security Cooperation Agency, United States Department of Defense

more such exercises with India than with any other non-NATO country.[91] Also, since 2001, India's purchases of military equipment from the US have steadily expanded (see Table 4.3). The total value of US military sales to India in the period 2005–19 reached nearly US$15bn.[92] India has not yet participated in joint military operations with the US.

India's growing arms imports from the US mark a definitive evolution of its military procurement. The shift has been a source of concern for Russia, which has long been New Delhi's dominant arms supplier. India does, to be sure, continue to pursue deals with Moscow for some sophisticated conventional weapons, such as S-400 missiles, and for special arrangements that are not on offer from other major powers, such as the lease of nuclear attack submarines.[93] But its freedom to pick and choose between suppliers is beginning to shrink amid increasing tensions between the US and Russia. For example, the US has threatened sanctions if India decides to proceed with the purchase of S-400s. Moscow, meanwhile, continues to signal its displeasure with New Delhi by talking up the prospects for arms sales to Pakistan. As it consolidated its strategic partnership with India in the 1970s, the Soviet Union consciously abjured any defence ties with Pakistan. However, as fissures emerge between New Delhi and Moscow, Pakistan is eager to enhance its political engagement and cooperation with Russia.[94] Russia's alliance-like relationship with China casts a further shadow over its close bonds with an India that is increasingly at odds with Beijing.[95]

Beyond concerns about preserving its dominant role in India's arms market, Russia is worried that New Delhi's drift towards Washington undermines Moscow's efforts to build a global coalition against the US. Moscow has seen India as an important part of this coalition since the 1990s, when it drew New Delhi into a triangular relationship with China. The forum expanded to include Brazil and later South Africa, to form the so-called BRICS group.[96] Russia also actively backed full Indian membership of the SCO. Beijing, in turn, supported Pakistan's full SCO membership. For Russia and China, this was about drawing the two South Asian rivals into a framework for a multipolar world, one designed to limit the dominance of the US in Eurasia and beyond.[97]

Charting a course between the US and this Eurasian alliance has been challenging for India. Even as it expanded its engagement with the US in the 1990s, New Delhi remained deeply worried about US policies on Kashmir and non-proliferation. It thus continued to hedge, holding on to the Russian relationship and finding new ways to deepen ties with China. Two decades on, however, India under Modi finds itself an enthusiastic US partner. The previous government was torn between an enduring legacy of anti-Americanism in the Congress party and left-of-centre political formations, on the one hand, and the new opportunities to transform relations with the US on the other. It found it difficult to sell the virtues of the civil-nuclear initiative, expanded defence cooperation and more substantive political cooperation with the US to its core political base. Modi, by contrast, has declared that India's 'historic hesitations' with the US are over and that New Delhi is ready to take strategic cooperation with the US to a new level.[98]

Modi's critics contend that abandoning non-alignment and embracing the US have aroused Chinese hostility. An opposing perspective, however, suggests it is the mounting threat from China that has actually served to nudge New Delhi towards Washington.[99] Across South Asia there is ample evidence to support the view that China is seeking to expand its position at India's expense. The Doklam confrontation is a vivid example. The fact that the frontier in question was between China and Bhutan, not between China and India, gave Beijing a potential basis for driving a wedge between New Delhi and Thimphu.[100] One element of the vitriolic Chinese media campaign against India during the crisis was the claim that India had unnecessarily and unhelpfully interjected itself into the dispute.

China has long chafed at India's special relationship with Bhutan, which had previously been a protectorate of the British Raj. The ending of British rule over Bhutan coincided with India's independence in 1947, and Thimphu and New Delhi have maintained a very close relationship. Moreover, it continues to irk Beijing that Bhutan is the only country in

Table 4.4: **Chinese and Indian two-way trade (in goods) with South Asia, 2010 and 2019 ($US millions)**

	China		India	
	2010	2019	2010	2019
Afghanistan	178.9	630.3	536.2	1,385.9
Bangladesh	7,058.0	18,371.6	3,374.5	9,456.7
Bhutan	1.6	10.9	344.9	943.6
Maldives	63.5	375.7	132.0	232.2
Nepal	742.7	1,516.9	2,410.6	7,758.3
Pakistan	8,668.7	17,991.4	2,556.5	1,253.5
Sri Lanka	2,097.1	4,484.6	3,823.2	5,220.8

Source: *UN Comtrade Database*

South Asia with which it does not have diplomatic relations. It has become increasingly difficult for Bhutan to ignore Beijing's efforts to establish a more normal relationship. For example, Beijing has been offering Bhutan a boundary settlement and significant economic assistance in the hope of gaining advantage over India.[101]

The rest of South Asia is increasingly open to a significant Chinese economic and security presence. Much of this appears inevitable in retrospect. As its economic weight and military power have rapidly expanded, China has become an increasingly important external actor on the subcontinent. On the commercial front, China is now the largest trading partner for Bangladesh, the Maldives and Pakistan (see Table 4.4). Its new, high-profile investments in South Asian infrastructure development had begun well before the BRI was unveiled in 2013. Some of the dual-use infrastructure – for example, Gwadar Port in Pakistan and Hambantota Port in Sri Lanka – has created deep anxiety in New Delhi. Of even greater concern is China's emergence as a major supplier of arms to most of India's South Asian neighbours (see Table 4.5).

Although the expansion of economic and strategic influence in South Asia would seem a natural consequence of China's rise, New Delhi's seemingly intractable rivalry with Beijing makes it hard for India to simply acquiesce. New Delhi has attempted to push back by expanding its own economic and

Table 4.5: **Arms exports to South Asia, 2001–20 (trend-indicator values)**

	China			US			Russia		
	2000–10	2011–20	Total	2000–10	2011–20	Total	2000–10	2011–20	Total
Afghanistan	0	1	1	644	2,478	3,122	145	442	587
Bangladesh	284	2,594	2,878	0	115	115	94	447	541
Bhutan	0	0	0	0	0	0	0	0	0
India	0	0	0	247	4,166	4,413	14,887	20,365	35,252
Maldives	0	0	0	0	0	0	0	0	0
Nepal	2	23	25	0	2	2	7	14	21
Pakistan	3,004	5,738	8,715	2,308	1,068	3,376	245	406	651
Sri Lanka	245	60	305	30	64	94	63	20	83
Total	3,535	8,416	11,924	3,229	7,829	11,028	15,441	21,694	37,135

Note: SIPRI trend-indicator values are calculated figures intended to reflect military capabilities rather than financial values. For a detailed explanation of SIPRI sources and methods, see https://www.sipri.org/databases/armstransfers/sources-and-methods. The totals have been rounded up and thus may differ slightly from the SIPRI totals, which are rounded down.

Source: *SIPRI Arms Transfers Database*

security cooperation with all its South Asian neighbours except Pakistan. But it is difficult for India to match China on either the economic or military front. One consequence has been New Delhi's openness to work with the US and Japan in generating an effective response to China. New Delhi emerged early as a major critic of the BRI, voicing concerns that were later echoed by the US and others. But for India's smaller neighbours the BRI was a welcome opportunity, and all except Bhutan have formally endorsed it.

India's difficult relations with many of its smaller neighbours mean that they have long looked for cooperation with other powers to limit New Delhi's dominance.[102] The Himalayan states (Nepal and Bhutan) and island republics (Sri Lanka and Maldives) are enjoying the new attention paid to them by Beijing and are acutely aware of the economic benefits that come from strengthening ties with China. Beijing has also become a useful card for these small states to play in warding off political pressure from India and the US. Afghanistan, which has relied entirely on the West for economic and military sustenance, is now seeking a more productive relationship with China in the hope that Beijing can convince Islamabad to change its attitude towards Kabul.[103]

Regional asymmetries

One broad theme underlies the many conflicts that have enveloped South Asia: the security imperatives of asymmetry. In the northwest, a vast and long-standing gap exists between the military capabilities and, more broadly, the state capacities of Afghanistan and Pakistan. Pakistan's attempts to create a friendly, if not pliable, regime in Kabul have been a persistent cause of conflict. Even a large-scale foreign-military presence by the Soviet Union or the US has not been sufficient to reverse this conflict dynamic between Afghanistan and Pakistan.

As the US withdraws its military from Afghanistan, this asymmetry will reassert itself. Preventing Pakistani interference in the internal affairs of Afghanistan will become more challenging. If the current military structures fail to hold in Afghanistan, Afghan factions opposed to Pakistan and the Taliban are likely to engage in asymmetric war against the new rulers in Kabul and to look for external supporters in the neighbourhood and beyond. There is no indication that the Taliban has any interest in promoting a sustainable political reconciliation with the non-Pashtun ethnic population and the non-Sunni communities in Afghanistan. Although Pakistan has the power to disrupt the political order in Afghanistan, it is yet to demonstrate the capacity to promote order and stability that is conducive to regional harmony and international security.

The conjunction of terrorism, insurgency, military modernisation and nuclear weapons has produced a unique set of challenges for India and Pakistan since the beginning of the twenty-first century. The current situation no longer fits the arms-race model that characterised the India–Pakistan dynamic in the pre-nuclear era. Pakistan has adopted an asymmetric strategy towards India, including nurturing anti-India terror groups and expanding its nuclear arsenal to cope with the growing economic and conventional military gap between the two countries. From a purely military perspective, the future of India–Pakistan relations is likely to be plagued by ongoing instability and to be continually at risk of fresh strategic crises that could escalate to the nuclear level.

Optimists point to the progress made by the two countries on trade and economic cooperation, as well as people-to-people contact, since the introduction of nuclear weapons. Pessimists, however, contend that deep-seated tensions between New Delhi and Islamabad are likely to persist. As the asymmetry between India and Pakistan grows in favour of the former, however, the latter is likely to rely increasingly on hybrid warfare. This trend prevents India from accepting reasonable compromises. Any Indian efforts to change the terms of engagement – on the questions of restraint and deterrence as well as the Kashmir question – might also have the paradoxical effect of pushing Pakistan into doubling down on asymmetric warfare. The current stalemate, then, is likely to continue. Pakistan has the capacity to hurt India through its hybrid warfare, but not enough to force India to concede to its main political demands. New Delhi's relative power vis-à-vis Islamabad has grown, but the gap is not sufficient to allow India to force a decisive change in Pakistan's policies. The only way out of this stalemate seems to be significant internal political change in India, Pakistan or both.

Asymmetry has also become the dominant feature of Sino-Indian military relations. New Delhi has had to drop the sense of parity that had long characterised its relationship with Beijing and to begin to address the growing power gap between the two nations. Three features of India's new strategy stand out. Firstly, New Delhi has sought to match improvements in Chinese civil and military boundary infrastructure. India is also close to acquiring a measure of nuclear deterrence vis-à-vis Beijing with the development of long-range missiles, as well as a sea-based capability. New Delhi still has a long way to go, however, to match China's overall conventional military capabilities. Secondly, India has opted to sustain an uneasy political engagement with China, despite growing difficulty in getting Beijing to satisfy any of its core interests. Thirdly, India has simultaneously chosen to search for a measure of external balancing by strengthening military cooperation with the US and its allies in Asia. On all of these fronts, however, China retains powerful advantages, both in terms of the resources it can bring to bear and in the potential leverage it can exert against countries such as Australia, Japan, the US and European powers. New Delhi does, however, appear to have sufficient capabilities, for the time being, to ensure a stalemate, as it did in the 2017 Doklam confrontation and its 2020–21 border stand-off with China.

Asymmetries also mark the relationships between the smaller South Asian states and the major powers. Bhutan, the Maldives, Nepal and Sri Lanka were once seen as largely irrelevant geopolitically, but all the major powers now recognise their strategic geographical importance and are wooing them with growing intensity. This has opened unprecedented possibilities for the elites of these countries to bargain with the major powers, but this new leverage has not been an unmixed blessing. The growing importance of these smaller states has significantly increased the prospects for external interference in their internal affairs. Here too the interests of China and those of India and its Western partners are asymmetric. Whereas China might benefit from military-access arrangements in Sri Lanka and the Maldives, India gains little by having military facilities in those two countries. New Delhi's strategy is therefore largely one of denying such arrangements to Beijing. In Nepal and Bhutan, the situation is the opposite. China wants to loosen the strategic bonds between these Himalayan states and India, while New Delhi is struggling to maintain its traditional influence. South Asia's deepening asymmetries have set the stage for a very different geopolitics of the subcontinent.

CHAPTER FIVE

Prospects for Asian order

The intensifying geopolitical rivalries, rising defence spending and proliferation of the latest military technology in Northeast, Southeast and South Asia analysed in the preceding chapters, and their interactions across Asia as a whole, suggest that the region is set for a prolonged period of strategic contestation. None of the three competing visions for the future of Asian order – a US-led 'Free and Open Indo-Pacific', a Chinese-centred order, or the ASEAN-inspired 'Indo-Pacific Outlook' – is likely to prevail in the short to medium term. In the absence of a new framework, the risk of open conflict is heightened, and along with it the need for effective mechanisms to maintain peace and stability.

Geopolitical futures

Northeast Asia has been involved in a sustained build-up of defence capabilities for three decades, scarcely affected by economic troubles. While acquisitions in the 1990s could be explained by and large in terms of modernisation, over the following two decades they have been increasingly driven by competition. This combination of increasing capabilities and action–reaction is the essence of arms racing.[1] Over the next ten or 20 years, arms racing will increasingly drive the military build-up. Northeast Asia's missile and missile-defence action–reaction dynamic is likely to intensify, with potentially severe ramifications for strategic stability. China's stockpile of nuclear warheads will almost certainly grow over the coming decade, as US missile defences improve and Beijing strives to retain the ability to penetrate them.

There are no arms-control regimes in Northeast Asia to constrain or constrict acquisitions. Regional security dynamics, including arms racing, will also be much more complex than those which obtained in the bipolar world of the Cold War. None of the distinctive categories, milestones and firebreaks that were carefully constructed during the Cold War to constrain escalatory processes and promote crisis stability are present. Conventional-weapons acquisition programmes will also interact with developments in WMD and long-range delivery systems. In this environment, with many parties and many levels and directions of interaction, the possibility of calamity is high.

In Southeast Asia, despite China's specific and serious challenges to littoral states' interests in the South China Sea, and potentially to freedom of navigation and overflight, as well as its broader strategic behaviour, most countries have failed to develop credible capabilities for defending themselves against external threats. At the same time, the absence of security and defence cooperation means that Southeast Asian states will remain vulnerable to significant pressure from external powers.

China's growing power is also threatening the cohesion of ASEAN, with some member states unwilling, to greater or lesser degrees, to antagonise Beijing by supporting measures to challenge its apparent attempts to control the South China Sea. In response to Beijing's strategic extroversion, the US and other interested powers are stepping up their efforts to balance not only China's growing assertiveness in Southeast Asian waters, but also the capacity it is exercising through the BRI to meet regional states' infrastructural needs. Yet Southeast Asian states are generally also reluctant to support these efforts.

Southeast Asian governments will increasingly face crucial foreign-policy challenges. These will not involve the spurious choice of 'siding with China or siding with the US'. Most Southeast Asian states have shown clearly that they want to maintain multidirectional foreign policies, open to strengthening economic, political and security relations with, among others, Australia, India, Japan, South Korea, the US and European states, as well as with China. They want to avoid their foreign policies becoming increasingly unidirectional and have already chosen to remain open to stronger relations with all comers where there can be mutual benefit. Barring the almost inconceivable scenario of the implosion of CCP rule, however, Beijing's role in the sub-region is likely to grow, narrowing foreign-policy options and ultimately undermining the national sovereignty and capacity for self-determination of Southeast Asian countries.

Depending on external powers to maintain a favourable regional balance will probably be insufficient on its own to ensure a future where Southeast Asian countries can maintain their security and autonomy. It makes sense in the absence of alternatives, but as a permanent strategy it could make Southeast Asia unduly dependent for its security on decisions made in distant capitals. And it would be naive to assume that recent enthusiasm in the US, its allies and partners for playing more active security roles in the 'Indo-Pacific' will necessarily persist in the long term in the face of inevitable changes of government and the distraction of other domestic and foreign challenges. Southeast Asia has seen a succession of extra-regional powers come and go over the last 500 years, and major changes in their roles within living memory. There can be little doubt that this will continue.

If Southeast Asian states ultimately wish to deal with external security challenges from a position of strength, they must enhance ASEAN's politico-security role. This would mean not only much closer foreign-policy coordination, but also a greater ASEAN-wide approach to defence policy in the long term. There will be many obstacles: ASEAN's slow progress in strengthening its political cohesion since the 1990s has shown the difficulty of community-building in the absence of a strongly held common perception of external threat. Many will argue that ASEAN was never intended to have a major security role. Others will point to the diversity of Southeast Asian states' cultures, political systems and levels of development – and to continuing bilateral disputes among them. Some naysayers will highlight the European Union's current multidimensional distress as evidence of the limitations of regional groupings.

It may indeed prove too difficult for ASEAN to develop into a geopolitical bloc that could provide more effectively for its member states' security against external challenges. But deciding not even to try could have important consequences for the extent to which Southeast Asian states are able to protect their national interests. There is, of course, a near-infinite array of possibilities for how Southeast Asia's security dynamics might evolve, but most will likely be variants of two scenarios. In the first, Southeast Asian states will rely on a balance between external powers to guarantee their region's security, but may find that their powerful immediate neighbour, China, ultimately has the greatest staying power and thereby comes increasingly to be the dominant force, with negative implications for the autonomy of Southeast Asian governments. In the second, while remaining open to partnerships with extra-regional players, Southeast Asian states will have collectively taken significantly greater responsibility for their own sub-region's security, providing considerable long-term stability and a degree of insulation from major-power pressures.

In South Asia, the traditional dyads of conflict (India–Pakistan and China–India) are no longer completely self-contained. They have become increasingly fused, for example, in the Kashmir conflict, where each of the three states has control over parts of the disputed territory. There is greater alignment between Islamabad and Beijing in challenging New Delhi's efforts to change the structure of the conflict, and China's long-standing assistance to Pakistan's nuclear and missile development serves to reinforce this triangular dynamic. The fact that the US was reluctant to criticise India's move to change the constitutional status of Kashmir in August 2019 underscores Washington's tilt towards India and represents an important recalibration of US policy towards the region. This, of course, had much to do with the perceived importance of India in the emerging US strategy of more actively balancing China.

India's emerging tilt towards the US is likely to become an enduring feature. While economic engagement is an important dimension of this new relationship, military cooperation has also emerged as a critical element of the new India–US partnership. It is important, however, to remember that India is not a treaty ally of the US and that it is developing its own terms of engagement. New Delhi is acutely aware of the increasing unpredictability of US policies and has looked to develop ties with other powers, both in Europe and Asia, as insurance. Even as it draws a line under its historic distrust of the West, New Delhi has sought to avoid a premature confrontation with China and will sustain its cooperation with Russia for as long as possible. While the return of great-power rivalry will complicate this balancing act, already in some trouble in the face of Beijing's aggressive posture towards New Delhi, India's own emergence as a major power gives it some room for manoeuvre.

While India's strategic import to the West has risen due to China's growing power and assertiveness, Pakistan's leverage may be diminishing in Washington and other Western capitals. The withdrawal of international forces from Afghanistan is likely to further limit Western interest in Pakistan, despite ongoing concerns about nuclear proliferation and terrorism. This, in turn, could push Pakistan even closer towards China. This might not be an entirely comforting situation for Islamabad, which has always valued close ties with the US and the West. While China is celebrated as an all-weather friend, the Pakistani elite has strong connections with the West and will find it hard to abandon these completely. Islamabad played a part in facilitating Sino-US rapprochement in the 1970s, and benefited from it. But as Sino-American relations deteriorate, Pakistan will struggle to find an appropriate balance between the two. Meanwhile, the smaller countries in South Asia have welcomed China's rise because it has afforded them greater bargaining leverage with India and will limit New Delhi's dominance over their polities; yet few of them are prepared for a full-blown rivalry between China and the US, and an India aligned more closely with the latter.

A distinctive new naval dimension is also beginning to unfold in South Asia's geopolitics. Unlike in the Western Pacific, where conflict manifests through maritime territorial disputes, the source of this new maritime dynamic is China's growing power projection into the Indian Ocean and its expanding naval cooperation with India's neighbours, including Bangladesh, the Maldives, Pakistan and Sri Lanka. China's ability to project military power into the Indian Ocean is likely to remain shaky for quite some time, giving New Delhi a window of opportunity to put pressure on Beijing's growing naval presence. For India, this will involve investing a lot more in its naval forces than it does today (only 15% of India's defence spending presently goes to the navy)[2] and an acceleration in its maritime coalition-building with Australia, Japan, the US and other regional partners. The Indian Ocean is one area where New Delhi can use geographic proximity to its strategic advantage.

The COVID-19 crisis will probably serve to sharpen South Asia's asymmetries. The Indian economy is likely to be slow to recover, making New Delhi's ability to achieve its GDP target of US$5trn by 2024 increasingly unrealistic. Pakistan's economy, which has also been struggling in recent years, will continue to contract in 2021.[3] These trends are likely to further widen the power gaps between China and India, and between India and Pakistan.

Less predictable are the domestic political dynamics in China, India, Pakistan and the US. Although China appears stable for now, the prospect of political upheaval cannot be dismissed. Ongoing political volatility in the US will continue to fuel uncertainty about Washington's international orientation. Meanwhile, the massive economic and social disruption occasioned by the COVID-19 pandemic will test the ability of the leaders in India and Pakistan to sustain internal political stability. India's domestic politics have entered a turbulent phase and it is by no means clear that Modi's nationalism and Hindu assertiveness will overcome India's most important vulnerability in the shape of its ethnic and religious diversity. Pakistan, for example, has found it hard to sustain unity in a nation created in the name of a religion; it certainly did not learn from the break-up with Bangladesh in 1971. Its attempts to instrumentalise Islamic radicalism to win the secular objective of a friendly regime in Kabul have failed spectacularly as Islamism engulfs Pakistan's own polity, creating fertile conditions for the spillover of the Afghan war into Pakistani territory. These increasingly uncertain politics among each of the major players are likely to have a profound impact on South Asian geopolitics.

Which vision?

It seems clear that each of the three visions for a new Asian order discussed in Chapter One is fraught with internal weaknesses and contradictions, and that none of these frameworks look set to triumph in the contest to replace the fading US-led system that has prevailed since 1945. This implies that the region will face a protracted, potentially decades-long strategic interregnum.

Free and Open Indo-Pacific

The divergences in strategic outlook between the Quad members – the four countries who have adopted versions of the FOIP – are arguably as great as, if not greater than, the similarities. Each defines the Indo-Pacific differently in terms of its geographic scope, and their respective definitions have evolved.[4] Washington sees the region as 'spanning a vast stretch of the globe from the West Coast of the United States to the western shores of India'.[5] Tokyo's vision is even more expansive, conceiving of the Indo-Pacific as a 'region stretching from eastern Africa to the western Americas, covering the entire Indian Ocean and Pacific Ocean'.[6] Canberra's understanding sits somewhere in between, defining the Indo-Pacific as 'the region ranging from the eastern Indian Ocean to the Pacific Ocean, connected by Southeast Asia, including India, North Asia and the United States'.[7] As this characterisation implies, Canberra has put greatest emphasis on the Southeast Asian portion of the Indo-Pacific and, increasingly, on the South Pacific as part of the Australian government's signature 'Pacific step-up'.[8]

A central difference between the four capitals concerns the role of China. Washington sees 'inter-state strategic competition, defined by geopolitical rivalry between free and repressive world order visions [as] the primary concern for US national security'. Beijing, Washington asserts, 'seeks Indo-Pacific regional hegemony in the near-term and ultimately global pre-eminence in the long-term'.[9] In stark contrast, New Delhi officially maintains that 'India does not see the Indo-Pacific region as a strategy or as a club of limited members. Nor as a grouping that seeks to dominate. And by no means do we consider it as directed against any country.'[10] Japan's FOIP concept differs from those of the US and India, embodying a mixture of competitive and cooperative strategies towards China that Japanese scholar Koga Kei calls 'tactical hedging'.[11]

These disparities have clearly affected collaborative endeavours. In February 2018, for example, there was speculation that the Quad countries might collaborate on joint Indo-Pacific infrastructure development to counter China's BRI.[12] A trilateral agreement along such lines was announced in July 2018, with India opting out, reportedly to avoid antagonising Beijing.[13] New Delhi similarly turned down repeated requests from Canberra for Australia to rejoin India's normally trilateral *Malabar* naval exercises with the US and Japan, begun bilaterally with the US in 1992 and held annually since 2002. (Australia had participated once previously, in 2007, in an expanded version of *Malabar* that also included Singapore and, for the first time, Japan.) In February 2008, Australia's withdrawal from the Quad, announced by then-foreign minister Stephen Smith alongside his Chinese counterpart Yang Jiechi, reportedly antagonised New Delhi.[14] More recently, India's continued refusal to extend a *Malabar* invitation to Australia has been linked to its desire to reset relations with Beijing following the 2017 Doklam stand-off (see Chapter Four).[15] However, following the latest eruption of Sino-Indian border tensions, in early June 2020 Australia and India declared a new 'Comprehensive Strategic Partnership'.[16] Soon afterwards Chinese and Indian troops clashed violently, and in early September they exchanged gunfire for the first time in 45 years. Apparently reflecting New Delhi's lessening propensity to avoid annoying Beijing, in mid-October India revealed that Australia's navy would participate in the following month's *Malabar* exercise.[17]

In contrast to its eagerness to participate in annual *Malabar* exercises, however, Canberra has displayed considerably greater reserve in response to repeated US requests that it conduct freedom-of-navigation operations challenging the legality of Beijing's artificial features in the South China Sea.[18] Australian Foreign Minister Marise Payne publicly distanced herself from confrontational comments made in July 2020 by the United States' then-secretary of state Pompeo: 'the Secretary's positions are his own … Australia's position is our own … Yes, the US and Australia have shared values and a longstanding military alliance … But most importantly from our perspective, we make our own decisions, our own judgements in the Australian national interest.'[19] Payne's comments were particularly significant coming at the Australia–US Ministerial (AUSMIN) talks, which she had flown to Washington to attend at the height of the COVID-19 pandemic and in the face of considerable domestic opposition.

Such cleavages have led some analysts to speculate regarding the limits to cooperation among Quad countries in the event of conflict. For example, during the 2017 Doklam confrontation, Japan was the only Quad member to publicly express support for India.[20] India's 'Act East' policy notwithstanding, it seems just as unlikely that Delhi would commit forces to a contingency east of the Malacca Strait.

China-led order

There are at least three major obstacles to overcome for Xi to realise his vision for a Chinese-led order, even one limited geographically to Asia. Firstly, notwithstanding impressive gains since embarking upon a programme of military modernisation during the mid-1990s, the PLA's ability to project power across the region and to enforce and defend a Chinese-led order remains questionable.[21] Although China's armed forces are undoubtedly growing stronger, they are not without vulnerabilities and have not been tested in modern, high-intensity combat. The last time China engaged in inter-state military hostilities was during the short Sino-Vietnamese War of 1979, and the result of even that limited conflict was far from a triumph for the PLA. China's leaders are certainly aware of the PLA's limitations, especially in relation to the US, and are taking steps to address them. In 2018, for example, the PLA produced a new 'Outline of Training and Evaluation', emphasising joint military training across all warfare domains and in realistic scenarios.[22] Yet while it is difficult to say with certainty how long it will take for China's military-modernisation efforts to bring the PLA to a level of capability close to that of the US armed forces, it could be as long as two decades.[23]

Secondly, formidable domestic challenges will continue to constrain Beijing's ability to implement Xi's vision of a China-centred Asia, even though a crucial domestic motive – regime preservation – underlies that vision. These challenges include managing the growing gap between rich and poor, rooting out endemic corruption, coping with a rapidly ageing population, reversing severe environmental degradation and keeping rising nationalist sentiment in check. China's economic growth had slowed down even before the COVID-19 pandemic: in 2019, according to official figures, GDP grew by 6.1%, the lowest rate in almost three decades. In May 2020, in an address to the National People's Congress, Prime Minister Li took an unprecedented (since the practice began in 1994) step by not setting an annual growth target. China's economy subsequently contracted for the first time in four decades.[24]

Although the economy rebounded quickly, the inability of numerous other crisis-riven countries to meet their BRI repayments may trigger China's first overseas debt crisis. Overseas-development lending from two of China's largest state-controlled banks – the China Development Bank and the Export–Import Bank of China – had already plummeted from US$75bn in 2016 to a mere US$4bn in 2019.[25] Methodological questions have been raised in some quarters regarding the data underpinning this assessment, with one prominent critique suggesting that Beijing's banks are simply structuring their BRI lending to favour projects involving Chinese firms, rather than lending less.[26]

Finally, Xi's vision lacks ideational appeal beyond China. China's leaders have long recognised this shortcoming, and since at least the mid-2000s they have made efforts to augment the country's reputational or 'soft' power.[27] Through its so-called 'mask diplomacy', for example, Beijing has sought to enhance its image by offering medical supplies to European countries during the COVID-19 pandemic.[28] In Southeast Asia, in particular, it has also tried to assuage fears by giving countries a central place in the BRI and by resurrecting negotiations with ASEAN to establish a 'Code of Conduct' for the South China Sea. Recurrent tensions in these waters, however, such as the April 2020 *West Capella* incident – in which Australian, Malaysian, US and Vietnamese vessels faced off against an assortment of Chinese craft that had sought to disrupt the operations of a Malaysian drillship operating near the outer limits of Malaysia's claimed EEZ – have undermined these efforts.[29] China is still placed towards the lower end of global 'soft power' rankings.[30]

ASEAN's outlook

ASEAN-led institutions have failed to show that they are up to the task of mediating the challenges of a more contested Asia; they have been absent during virtually every major regional crisis of the past three decades, and the organisation's struggles to forge a coherent approach to South China Sea disputes have called into question its viability as a leading politico-security actor. In July 2012, for example, ASEAN was unable to agree a joint communiqué at the end of its annual summit for the first time in its history, over the question of whether to mention a stand-off between Chinese and Philippine vessels which had occurred earlier in the year at the disputed Scarborough Shoal.[31] Similar scenes played out at subsequent ASEAN gatherings, such as a May 2016 Special ASEAN–China Foreign Ministers' meeting, when a joint statement was retracted for 'urgent amendments' only hours after it had been issued.[32] Moreover, ASEAN-led forums have increasingly become venues for major-power competition, for example when disagreement between the US and China prevented the November 2015 meeting of the ADMM+ from issuing its customary joint declaration.[33] These trends suggest that unless ASEAN members apply substantial thought and effort to revitalising the group's role, the prospects for an ASEAN-centred security order may be no better than for a US-led or Chinese-centred alternative.

Maintaining peace

As Asia's geopolitical rivalries intensify, so too do the risks of strategic crises and even possibly armed conflict. Given the unimaginable costs involved, conventional wisdom suggests that most, if not all, contemporary leaders would much prefer geopolitical competition not to spill over into full-blown conflict, especially one involving nuclear weapons. But such a preference is by no means absolute, and few leaders today are willing to accept 'peace at any price'. The Munich analogy still resonates strongly.[34]

China's willingness to use its growing power to achieve geopolitical gains is the single most important change in the region's geopolitical circumstances since the 1990s. This has become increasingly salient since Xi came to power in 2012. Responses by other Asian states have varied, but overall have been characterised by efforts to integrate China into regional institutions (including security institutions such as ARF and ADMM+) and to find common ground with Beijing wherever possible; to maintain a regional balance of power that includes the US as a way of offsetting China's growing strength; to strengthen diplomatic and security ties among themselves; and in many cases to reinforce their own national military capabilities. But while China's status and behaviour as a rapidly growing power, and the reactions this has provoked, are central to Asia's militarisation and an increased risk of inter-state conflict, they have not been the only influences. The region is replete with other rivalries deriving from intense nationalism and territorial disputes.

In these circumstances, there is a danger that constraints on the application of military power will weaken. The Indian government under Modi has, for example, displayed a greater willingness to threaten, and even to use, limited military force against its nuclear-armed neighbour Pakistan, despite the danger of escalation. China, meanwhile, has adopted a more forward-leaning 'active defence' military posture along the Sino-Indian border, leading to the outbreak of hostilities there for the first time in decades. Elsewhere in Asia, the number and scope of large-scale military exercises, which are often used as messages to deter potential adversaries, are increasing.[35] These sometimes result in rival armed forces coming into close proximity. On at least one occasion in July 2019, South Korean aircraft fired warning shots at their Russian counterparts. The skies around Taiwan are increasingly ripe for such exchanges, as Chinese aircraft penetrate the island's ADIZ and Taipei pledges to 'forcibly expel' these incursions.

The conventional wisdom is that such encounters almost never escalate into full-blown conflict. Writing nearly half a century ago, Australian historian Geoffrey Blainey argued that the idea of 'accidental war' is conceptually misleading and near impossible to substantiate. Although not suggesting that inadvertent conflict has never occurred or could never happen again, Blainey maintained that war is more typically the product of 'determined and intentional' government decisions.[36] In the latest iteration of this argument, the American strategic observer Hal Brands suggests that although a contemporary US–China conflict is possible, it would not be the product of an accident or inadvertence: 'when countries really do want to avert a showdown, they are generally willing to tack or retreat even at the cost of some embarrassment'.[37]

But asymmetries in Asia's regional and sub-regional balances of power could influence the prospects for conflict or peace. For instance, while China continues to gain ground on the US militarily, and although it enjoys geographical advantages in Northeast and Southeast Asia (particularly in the South China Sea and with respect to Taiwan), US superiority in critical areas of military capability, notably C4ISR and cyber, remains impressive. Moreover, a strong focus on China as a peer competitor by the US Department of Defense under the Biden administration seems likely to ensure that the US will continue efforts to offset the PLA's growing capabilities for years to come. According to Deputy Secretary of Defense Kathleen Hicks in February

2021, the top issue was 'advancing the capabilities needed to deter, and if needed, to compete and win in the face of Chinese military modernization'.[38] Such determination stands a good chance of ensuring that China is deterred from taking decisive military action – such as invading Taiwan – which might risk major war. Even a small probability of being defeated in a war with the US, which could have calamitous results for the CCP, would almost certainly dissuade Beijing from major military adventurism. As China's military capabilities grow, however, it does not seem unreasonable to expect that the military balance with the US could eventually shift in Beijing's favour, making the direct use of military force less unattractive.

At the sub-regional level, China's growing military strength may already be making an impact on the way that policymakers in Beijing see disputes with less powerful Asian states. China continues to pull ahead of India in both economic and military power, giving Beijing an advantage it can increasingly bring to bear in its long-standing geopolitical contest with Asia's other emerging giant. Similarly, the growing strategic imbalance between China and Taiwan, reflecting not just the former's accretion of capabilities but also the decay of the latter's military power, is increasingly provoking the question of whether Beijing might in the medium term feel more confident about using intimidatory military options such as blockades or selective missile strikes, calculated to not provoke direct US intervention. In the South China Sea, the implications of the PLA's growing strength are relatively oblique, but nevertheless it has already contributed to an overall pattern in which, in the absence of direct US military commitments, Southeast Asian states are cautious about standing up to China. In the medium term, a growing capacity to project military power into maritime Southeast Asia could embolden China to use force more directly in support of its maritime interests there. Meanwhile, although the US has multidimensional military superiority over North Korea, this has not deterred Pyongyang from continuing to develop its nuclear and missile capabilities, which may ultimately embolden it to undertake risky strategic behaviour in relation to both the US and its own regional neighbours.

In these circumstances, the US and regional states are making efforts to maintain sub-regional and regional stability through measures intended to enhance deterrence. This has been true under successive US administrations, whatever their political inclination or the descriptive labels they attach to American security policy in the region. In different ways and with varying intensity, Australia, India and Japan are all making efforts to strengthen their national military capabilities; they are also attempting to synergise their capabilities among themselves and with the US. In Southeast Asia, the same is happening on a smaller scale and with complexities unique to that sub-region.

Yet power balancing on its own, even when combined with the common sense and self-restraint of politicians and policy-makers, will almost certainly be insufficient to ensure peace in Asia. Three important aspects of Asia's unfolding geopolitics strongly suggest that other measures will be necessary to protect the region from future inter-state conflict. Firstly, although the so-called 'East Asian Peace' – the period since 1979, marked by an absence of major inter-state conflict – has been subject to some analysis,[39] it should not be assumed that supposedly distinctive cultural factors that may have had a role in sustaining the present era of relative stability will prevent war in the future. Northeast Asia, in particular, remains rife with virulent and deep-seated nationalist sentiments that stretch back centuries and are never far beneath the surface of Asia's geopolitical rivalries; and rising nationalism has long been recognised as a powerful driver of major-power conflict.[40] Simultaneously, Southeast and South Asia are home to many nation-states that are relatively new in their present forms, with domestic political dynamics that are often inherently fragile and unpredictable. The pressure of domestic political instability and continuing bilateral mistrust within Southeast Asia, in particular, coupled with the impact of growing major-power rivalry, make it impossible to discount the possibility of this sub-region reverting to its more fractious, crisis-prone past.

Secondly, the escalation pathways to major-power conflict – particularly in Northeast and South Asia – may be neither as linear nor as predictable as those of previous eras, due to the deployment of advanced military technologies and the influence these have on doctrine and operational practice. The firebreaks between conventional and nuclear capabilities that were key to maintaining strategic stability during the Cold War are increasingly blurred due to proliferating dual-use (nuclear and conventional) missile systems. Advances in developing hypersonic-missile systems, the speed and manoeuvrability of which could confound currently deployed anti-missile defences, hold the potential to exponentially increase the pace of warfare in the near future.[41] Advances in the cyber domain – which some analysts suggest is emerging as the *sine qua non* of military capability – potentially provide the opportunity to eliminate an opponent's ability to fight before a shot is fired.[42] The vulnerability of the complex network of systems – radars, sonars and satellites – that contemporary armed forces employ to track opponents' military deployments and readiness only heightens the pressures to escalate rapidly in a crisis or conflict scenario.[43]

Established conceptions of crisis, such as Herman Kahn's famous 44-rung 'ladder of escalation',[44] look increasingly outdated for the present era when conflict is more likely to emanate from what American strategic analyst Rebecca Hersman calls 'wormhole escalation', in which 'holes may suddenly open in the fabric of deterrence through which competing states could inadvertently enter and suddenly traverse between sub-conventional and strategic levels of conflict in accelerated and decidedly non-linear ways'.[45]

Finally, history is replete with examples of decision-makers – often by their own admission – genuinely losing control of events in the heat of a crisis. Just because most such instances have not escalated into full-blown conflict in the past does not guarantee that this will be the case in future. The October 1962 Cuban Missile Crisis is a salient example: the US and Soviet leaders were not always in full control, and serendipity as much as adept crisis management played a role in averting nuclear catastrophe. In that well-documented case, a string of mishaps occurred – a pre-scheduled ICBM test, a mistaken report of a Soviet missile launch, an accidental violation of Soviet airspace by a US spy plane – which could easily have led to inadvertent conflict and escalation.[46] As the US defense secretary at that time, Robert McNamara, put it in 2003, 'it was luck that prevented war. We came that close to nuclear war at the end. Rational individuals: Kennedy was rational; Khrushchev was rational; Castro was rational. Rational individuals came that close to total destruction of their societies. And that danger exists today.'[47]

During the Cold War, the US and the Soviet Union studiously respected the dividing line between coercion and conflict. This was especially so in the immediate aftermath of the Cuban Missile Crisis, when a hotline was established to facilitate crisis management by allowing direct communication between the two sides' leaders.[48] In May 1972, the US and Soviet Union signed an 'Incidents at Sea Agreement' (INCSEA) intended to reduce the risks of dangerous interactions when their navies were operating in close proximity. Provocative actions, such as pointing guns, low flyovers by aircraft with their bomb doors open and the illumination of fire-control radars, were all to be avoided. Special 'flag signals' were developed to facilitate better communication. Annual discussions were to be held where representatives from the two superpowers' navies would meet to review the agreement. The INCSEA directly inspired similar mechanisms elsewhere, such as the 1998 US–China agreement on establishing 'a consultation mechanism to strengthen military maritime safety'.[49]

Yet precisely when such mechanisms are needed most in Asia, they are either atrophying or no longer fit for purpose. The military confidence-building measures agreed by Beijing and New Delhi during the 1990s were insufficient to prevent violent clashes along the Sino-Indian border in 2020. The cross-strait hotline agreed by Beijing and Taipei in November 2015 now lies dormant. As emphasised by its demolition of the Kaesong liaison office in June 2020, North Korea has walked away from many of the crisis-management and -avoidance mechanisms to which it agreed during the brief inter-Korean peace process of 2018–19. Questions continue to be raised over whether Beijing is adhering faithfully to the risk-reduction measures that it has signed up to, such as the 2014 'Code for Unplanned Encounters at Sea' (or CUES), or if Sino-American agreements reached the same year on the avoidance and management of air and naval collisions remain operative given the increasingly hostile state of US–China relations.[50] Meanwhile, there seems little prospect that the protracted negotiations between Beijing and ASEAN to develop a South China Sea 'Code of Conduct' will produce a worthwhile agreement with significant potential to constrain provocative actions.[51]

These worrying trends suggest that the time is ripe for a serious reinvigoration, and even some re-imagining, of crisis-management and -avoidance mechanisms in Asia. Such efforts are especially needed in the cyber domain, where potentially destabilising action–reaction dynamics are increasingly apparent but where very little crisis-management machinery exists.[52] It is easy to take the pessimistic view that China's presumed disregard for such measures would inevitably render this a futile exercise. Yet the Cold War experience shows that even ideologically disparate governments can be convinced to forge and then adhere to such arrangements when these are perceived to be in their self-interest. An initially unwilling Moscow, for instance, responded to long-standing American entreaties for an INCSEA after a spate of hazardous incidents at sea during the 1960s. It is also worth bearing in mind that Chinese thinking about crisis-management theory and practice has only begun in earnest over the past two decades, whereas Western thinking and practice in this field dates back more than half a century. As in the case of the Soviet Union, China's seeming ambivalence towards crisis-management and -avoidance mechanisms could shift as Chinese thinking and practice evolve.[53]

These arguments emphasise that power balancing and national self-restraint are unlikely to be sufficient guarantors of Asia's peace, particularly as regional states and extra-regional powers alike continue to enhance their capabilities, adding new and potentially dangerous complexity to the regional military equation. More robust crisis-management and -avoidance mechanisms will be difficult to establish, and might not work perfectly, but they potentially have a crucial role to play in ameliorating the increasingly complex and dangerous action–reaction dynamics in Northeast and South Asia.

Crisis-management and -avoidance measures are both forms of arms control. But the intensifying militarisation of Asia raises the question of whether broader arms-control measures, aimed at controlling the types and scale of weapons systems deployed across the region, are also desirable. So far there have only been tentative and limited efforts in this direction. The limited scope of the UN Register of Conventional Arms has in the past led to discussion about a more detailed regional arms register.[54] The secondary reason (after allegations of Russian non-compliance) for the demise of the INF Treaty in 2019 was Washington's concern that it did not deal with the challenge posed by China's growing missile force, which led to calls from Japan (rejected by Beijing) for China to be included in a new, multilateral version of the treaty. But given that continuing efforts by regional states and the US to improve their military capabilities across Asia are likely to remain a prominent feature of the strategic environment, there is a strong case for at least starting to contemplate and discuss a regional arms-control regime. Given the large number of states involved in Asian security, and the lack of a clear-cut division similar to that which characterised the Cold War, establishing such a regime would necessarily be a complex, long-term process. However, that does not detract from the case that it might be vital for regional security in the long term.

Conclusion

The year 2020 will be long remembered as the point when 'non-traditional' security challenges came into their own. Concern among strategic analysts and policymakers focused on current and future pandemics, but the security implications of climate change also received greater attention. However, as severe as the human and financial tolls of the COVID-19 crisis have been, and those of climate change may be in the future, the costs of a modern major-power conflict could be at least as large – and would be even larger if that conflict involved nuclear weapons.

The immense potential destructiveness of military power continues to make it particularly salient for Asian security.

While policymakers in Asia were preoccupied by the pandemic over the course of 2020, simmering territorial tensions flared dramatically across the region. China may have simply been taking advantage of a chaotic situation, but there is reason to believe that this was symptomatic of a deeper and more lasting transformation. The growing geopolitical rivalries and developing military capabilities in Asia, the present ill-equipped regional security architecture and the prospect of an extended period of strategic contestation all point to a post-COVID-19 world that is a significantly darker, disconnected and, ultimately, dangerous place.

As Asia's (and the world's) leaders seek to rebuild their economies and their societies in the wake of the havoc wrought by COVID-19, they would do well to reflect upon some of the lessons offered by the pandemic and their potential applicability in the strategic realm. If they could step back in time, for instance, many would probably wish that they had acted earlier to contain the pandemic when they had the chance. Further, those societies that have navigated the COVID-19 crisis most effectively have been able to do so by putting in place stringent protective measures such as mask-wearing, rigorous testing-and-tracing regimes, and social-distancing regulations. To the extent that crisis-management and -avoidance mechanisms and even, in the longer term, wider arms control can be seen as the strategic equivalent of such measures, there is a strong case that they should be pursued with urgency in Asia to reduce the risks of an even greater calamity.

NOTES

Chapter One

1 See Robert J. Art, 'The Fungibility of Force', in Robert J. Art and Kelly M. Greenhill (eds), *The Use of Force: Military Power and International Politics* (Lanham, MD: Rowman & Littlefield, 2015), pp. 3–18.

2 See, for example, Zbigniew Brzezinski, *The Grand Chessboard: American Primacy and its Geostrategic Imperatives* (New York: Basic Books, 1997).

3 For a useful summary of these arguments, see Richard A. Bitzinger and Barry Desker, 'Why East Asian War Is Unlikely', *Survival: Global Politics and Strategy*, vol. 50, no. 6, December 2008–January 2009, pp. 105–28.

4 See, for example, Ron Huisken, 'ADMM+8: An Acronym to Watch', East Asia Forum, 8 October 2010, https://www.eastasiaforum.org/2010/10/08/admm8-an-acronym-to-watch.

5 Choe Sang-Hun, 'North Korea Cuts Off All Communications Lines to South Korea', *New York Times*, 8 June 2020, https://www.nytimes.com/2020/06/08/world/asia/north-korea-south-korea-communications.html; and Laura Bicker, 'North Korea Blows Up Joint Liaison Office with South in Kaesong', BBC, 16 June 2020, https://www.bbc.com/news/world-asia-53060620.

6 Zeeshan Shaikh, 'India, China Working on Hotline for Their Defence Ministries', *Indian Express*, 31 August 2018, https://indianexpress.com/article/india/india-china-hotline-defence-ministries-modi-jinping-doklam-5333474.

7 See, for example, Allan Gyngell, 'Australia's Response to Changing Global Orders', Australian Outlook, Australian Institute of International Affairs, 6 July 2018, https://www.internationalaffairs.org.au/australianoutlook/australias-response-to-changing-global-orders.

8 Vietnam, Ministry of National Defence, '2019 Viet Nam National Defence', October 2019, p. 11, http://news.chinhphu.vn/Uploaded_VGP/phamvanthua/20191220/2019VietnamNationalDefence.pdf.

9   Japan, Ministry of Defense, 'Defense of Japan 2020', https://www.mod.go.jp/en/publ/w_paper/wp2020/DOJ2020_EN_Full.pdf.

10 Australia, Department of Defence, '2020 Defence Strategic Update', July 2020, p. 14, https://www1.defence.gov.au/sites/default/files/2020-11/2020_Defence_Strategic_Update.pdf.

11 See Henry Kissinger, *World Order* (New York: Penguin Press, 2014), p. 9.

12 Allan Gyngell, 'The World We Knew Before the Coronavirus Will Not Return', *Australian Financial Review*, 31 March 2020, https://www.afr.com/policy/foreign-affairs/the-world-we-knew-before-the-coronavirus-will-not-return-20200330-p54f62.

13 Demetri Sevastopulo, 'Donald Trump Open to Japan and South Korea Having Nuclear Weapons', *Financial Times*, 27 March 2016, https://www.ft.com/content/c927017c-f398-11e5-9afe-dd2472ea263d.

14 Joe Gould and Leo Shane III, 'Trump's Proposed Troop Moves in South Korea Raise Concerns for Lawmakers', *Defense News*, 12 June 2018, https://www.defensenews.com/news/pentagon-congress/2018/06/12/trumps-proposed-troop-moves-in-south-korea-raise-concerns-for-lawmakers.

15 Lara Seligman and Robbie Gramer, 'Trump Asks Tokyo to Quadruple Payments for U.S. Troops in Japan', *Foreign Policy*, 15 November 2019, https://foreignpolicy.com/2019/11/15/trump-asks-tokyo-quadruple-payments-us-troops-japan.

16 See, for example, Simon Denyer and Eva Dou, 'Biden Vows to Defend U.S. Allies as China Asserts Power in Asia', *Washington Post*, 12 November 2020, https://www.washingtonpost.com/world/asia_pacific/biden-china-japan-korea-allies/2020/11/12/6cf6e212-24af-11eb-9c4a-0dc6242c4814_story.html. On the Obama administration's call for its Asian allies to increase their defence contributions, see Zack Cooper, 'Pacific Power: America's Asian Alliances Beyond Burden-sharing', War on the Rocks, 14 December 2016, https://warontherocks.com/2016/12/pacific-power-americas-asian-alliances-beyond-burden-sharing.

17 For further reading, see Thomas J. Christensen, *Worse Than a Monolith: Alliance Politics and Problems of Coercive Diplomacy in Asia* (Princeton, NJ: Princeton University Press, 2011), pp. 211, 215.

18 Clint Work, 'U.S. Soldiers Might Be Stuck in Korea Forever', *Foreign Policy*, 1 May 2018, https://foreignpolicy.com/2018/05/01/u-s-soldiers-might-be-stuck-in-korea-forever.

19 US, Department of Defense, Office of International Security Affairs, 'United States Security Strategy for the East Asia-Pacific Region', February 1995, https://nautilus.org/global-problem-solving/us-security-strategy-for-the-east-asia-pacific-region. This document is known as the 'Nye Report' after its lead author, Joseph Nye.

20 See Margaret MacMillan, *Nixon and Mao: The Week That Changed the World* (New York: Random House Trade, 2007).

21 Aaron L. Friedberg and Charles W. Boustany, Jr, 'Partial Disengagement: A New US Strategy for Economic Competition with China', *Washington Quarterly*, vol. 43, no. 1, Spring 2020, pp. 23–40, especially p. 23.

22 For further reading, see Aaron L. Friedberg, 'Competing with China', *Survival: Global Politics and Strategy*, vol. 60, no. 3, June–July 2018, pp. 7–64.

23 See White House, 'National Security Strategy of the United States of America', December 2017, https://trumpwhitehouse.archives.gov/wp-content/uploads/2017/12/NSS-Final-12-18-2017-0905.pdf; US, Department of Defense, 'Summary of the 2018 National Defense Strategy of the United States of America', January 2018, https://dod.defense.gov/Portals/1/Documents/pubs/2018-National-Defense-Strategy-Summary.pdf; and US, Department of Defense, 'Indo-Pacific Strategy Report: Preparedness, Partnerships, and Promoting a Networked Region', June 2019, https://media.defense.gov/2019/Jul/01/2002152311/-1/-1/1/department-of-defense-indo-pacific-strategy-report-2019.pdf.

24 See, for example, Robert D. Kaplan, 'A New Cold War Has Begun', *Foreign Policy*, 7 January 2019, https://foreignpolicy.com/2019/01/07/a-new-cold-war-has-begun.

25 Thomas J. Christensen, 'A Modern Tragedy? COVID-19 and US–China Relations', Brookings Institution, May 2020, https://www.brookings.edu/research/a-modern-tragedy-covid-19-and-us-china-relations.

26 Minxin Pei, 'COVID-19 Is Finishing Off the Sino-American Relationship', The Strategist, Australian Strategic Policy Institute, 30 April 2020, https://www.aspistrategist.org.au/covid-19-is-finishing-off-the-sino-american-relationship.

27 *Ibid.*

28 Robert Delaney, 'China Shaping Up to Be Central Campaign Theme for Both Donald Trump and Joe Biden', *South China Morning Post*, 1 May 2020, https://www.scmp.com/news/world/united-states-canada/article/3082401/china-shaping-be-central-campaign-theme-both-donald.

29 C. Fred Bergsten, 'Two's Company', *Foreign Affairs*, vol. 88, no. 5, September–October 2009, pp. 169–70, https://www.foreignaffairs.com/articles/americas/2009-09-01/twos-company.

30 Steps towards decoupling have included long-standing Chinese internet restrictions and, more recently, limits placed by the US and some of its allies (notably Australia) on the use of Chinese-made IT components and on Chinese investment in strategically important industries. See Joseph S. Nye, Jr, 'Power and Interdependence with China', *Washington Quarterly*, vol. 43, no. 1, Spring 2020, pp. 7–21, especially pp. 9–11.

31 According to Nye, for example, 'the overall financial relationship is over US$5 trillion, including nearly two trillion in Chinese listings on US stock exchanges and US$1.3 trillion in Chinese official holdings of US government bonds'. See *ibid.*, p. 10.

32 Desmond Ball, 'Implications of the East Asian Economic Recession for Regional Security Cooperation', Working Paper No. 331, Strategic and Defence Studies Centre, December 1999.

33 J. Berkshire Miller, 'China–U.S. Tensions Loom Large as Shangri-La Dialogue Addresses Asian Security Issues', *Japan Times*, 30 May 2019, https://www.japantimes,co.jp/news/2019/05/30/asia-pacific/politics-diplomacy-asia-pacific/u-s-china-tensions-loom-large-shangri-la-dialogue-addresses-asian-security-issues.

34 Michael R. Pompeo, 'Taiwan's Exclusion from the World Health Assembly', 18 May 2020, https://geneva.usmission.gov/2020/05/18/taiwans-exclusion-from-the-world-health-assembly.

35 Carl Bildt, 'The Post-American World Is Now on Full Display', *Washington*

Post, 19 May 2020, https://www.wash-ingtonpost.com/opinions/2020/05/19/post-american-world-is-now-full-display; and Stephanie Nebehay and Emma Farge, 'U.S. Savages WHO As It Promises Pandemic Review, But China Pledges $2 Billion', Reuters, 18 May 2020, https://www.reuters.com/article/us-health-coronavirus-who-idUSKBN22U111.

36 See Kurt M. Campbell and Rush Doshi, 'The Coronavirus Could Reshape Global Order', *Foreign Affairs*, 18 March 2020, https://www.foreignaffairs.com/articles/china/2020-03-18/coronavirus-could-reshape-global-order.

37 For further reading, see Desmond Ball, 'Improving Communications Links Between Moscow and Washington', *Journal of Peace Research*, vol. 28, no. 2, May 1991, pp. 135–59.

38 See, for example, Barry R. Posen, 'Do Pandemics Promote Peace?', *Foreign Affairs*, 23 April 2020, https://www.foreignaffairs.com/articles/china/2020-04-23/do-pandemics-promote-peace.

39 Michael Howard, 'Military Power and International Order', *International Affairs*, vol. 85, no. 1, January 2009, pp. 145–55, especially p. 153.

40 See Hugh White, 'War and Order: Thinking About Military Force in International Affairs', in Nicholas Farrelly et al. (eds), *Muddy Boots and Smart Suits: Researching Asia-Pacific Affairs* (Singapore: ISEAS–Yusof Ishak Institute, 2017), pp. 127–40, especially p. 128.

41 Art, 'The Fungibility of Force', p. 13. Art notes that a by-product of this balance was 'the creation of an open and interdependent economic order among the United States, Western Europe, and Japan'.

42 George Bush, 'Address Before a Joint Session of the Congress on the Persian Gulf Crisis and the Federal Budget Deficit', The American Presidency Project, 11 September 1990, https://www.presidency.ucsb.edu/documents/address-before-joint-session-the-congress-the-persian-gulf-crisis-and-the-federal-budget.

43 See Francis Fukuyama, *The End of History and the Last Man* (New York: Free Press, 1992).

44 Edward N. Luttwak, 'From Geo-politics to Geo-economics: Logic of Conflict, Grammar of Commerce', *National Interest*, no. 20, Summer 1990, pp. 17–23.

45 See, for example, Aaron L. Friedberg, 'Ripe for Rivalry: Prospects for Peace in a Multipolar Asia', *International Security*, vol. 18, no. 3, Winter 1993–94, pp. 5–33, especially p. 7. See also Desmond Ball, 'Arms and Affluence: Military Acquisitions in the Asia-Pacific Region', *International Security*, vol. 18, no. 3, Winter 1993–94, pp. 78–112.

46 For a useful summary of these arguments, see Bitzinger and Desker, 'Why East Asian War Is Unlikely', pp. 105–28.

47 See, for example, Robert S. Ross, 'The Geography of the Peace: East Asia in the Twenty-first Century', *International Security*, vol. 23, no. 4, Spring 1999, pp. 81–118. Ross argued that Asia's post-Cold War order would be bipolar, with China dominating its continental portions and the US its maritime regions. China and America would be strategic rivals, but geographical conditions meant that their rivalry would remain relatively peaceful and stable.

48 Charles Krauthammer, 'The Unipolar Moment', *Foreign Affairs*, vol. 70, no. 1, America and the World 1990, pp. 23–33, https://www.for-

eignaffairs.com/articles/1990-01-01/unipolar-moment.

49 See, for example, Walter Russell Mead, 'The Return of Geopolitics', *Foreign Affairs*, vol. 93, no. 3, May–June 2014, pp. 69–79, https://www.foreignaffairs.com/articles/china/2014-04-17/return-geopolitics.

50 Tanisha M. Fazal and Paul Poast, 'War Is Not Over', *Foreign Affairs*, vol. 98, no. 6, November–December 2019, pp. 74–83, especially p. 83, https://www.foreignaffairs.com/articles/2019-10-15/war-not-over.

51 Art, 'The Fungibility of Force', p. 3.

52 For further reading, see Brendan Taylor, *The Four Flashpoints: How Asia Goes to War* (Melbourne: La Trobe University Press, 2018).

53 ASEAN comprises Brunei, Cambodia, Indonesia, Laos, Malaysia, Myanmar, Philippines, Singapore, Thailand and Vietnam.

54 See, for example, Hillary Clinton, 'America's Pacific Century', *Foreign Policy*, 11 October 2011, https://foreignpolicy.com/2011/10/11/americas-pacific-century.

55 US Mission to ASEAN, 'Remarks by President Trump at APEC CEO Summit | Da Nang, Vietnam', 11 November 2017, https://asean.usmission.gov/remarks-president-trump-apec-ceo-summit-da-nang-vietnam.

56 US, Department of Defense, 'Indo-Pacific Strategy Report: Preparedness, Partnerships, and Promoting a Networked Region', p. 4; and US, Department of State, 'A Free and Open Indo-Pacific: Advancing a Shared Vision', 4 November 2019, p. 6, https://www.state.gov/wp-content/uploads/2019/11/Free-and-Open-Indo-Pacific-4Nov2019.pdf.

57 Sebastian Strangio, 'Is Biden Preparing to Tweak the Indo-Pacific Strategy?', *Diplomat*, 20 November 2020, https://thediplomat.com/2020/11/is-biden-preapring-to-tweak-the-indo-pacific-strategy.

58 Rory Medcalf, 'Indo-Pacific: What's in a Name?', *Interpreter*, 16 August 2012, https://archive.lowyinstitute.org/the-interpreter/indo-pacific-what-name.

59 See Rory Medcalf, 'Indo-Pacific Visions: Giving Solidarity a Chance', *Asia Policy*, vol. 14, no. 3, July 2019, pp. 79–95, especially p. 88.

60 Shri Narendra Modi, 'Keynote Address', 17th Asia Security Summit: The IISS Shangri-La Dialogue, 1 June 2018, https://www.iiss.org/events/shangri-la-dialogue/shangri-la-dialogue-2018.

61 Elouise Fowler, 'Quad Talks on Indo-Pacific Future Given Greater Status in New York', *Australian Financial Review*, 22 September 2019, https://www.afr.com/world/asia/quad-talks-on-indo-pacific-future-given-greater-status-in-new-york-20190922-p52tpq.

62 See, for example, Rory Medcalf, 'The Quad Has Seen Off Sceptics and It's Here to Stay', *Australian Financial Review*, 15 March 2021, https://www.afr.com/policy/foreign-affairs/the-quad-has-seen-off-the-sceptics-and-its-here-to-stay-20210314-p57amm.

63 China, Ministry of Foreign Affairs, 'Foreign Minister Wang Yi Meets the Press', 9 March 2018, https://www.fmprc.gov.cn/mfa_eng/zxxx_662805/t1540928.shtml.

64 Feng Zhang, 'China's Curious Nonchalance Towards the Indo-Pacific', *Survival: Global Politics and Strategy*, vol. 61, no. 3, June–July 2019, pp. 187–212.

65 Tom Mitchell, 'China's Xi Jinping Says He Is Opposed to Life-long Rule',

Financial Times, 16 April 2018, https://www.ft.com/content/2b449400-413a-11e8-803a-295c97e6fd0b.

66 The concept of a twenty-first-century Maritime Silk Road was introduced by Xi in a speech in 2013. See ASEAN–China Centre, 'Speech by Chinese President Xi Jinping to Indonesian Parliament', 2 October 2013, http://www.asean-china-center.org/english/2013-10/03/c_133062675.htm.

67 See IISS, *Asia-Pacific Regional Security Assessment 2018* (London: IISS, 2018), p. 27.

68 Peter Cai, 'Understanding China's Belt and Road Initiative', Lowy Institute, 22 March 2017, https://www.lowyinstitute.org/publications/understanding-belt-and-road-initiative.

69 Nadège Rolland, *China's Eurasian Century? Political and Strategic Implications of the Belt and Road Initiative* (Seattle, WA: National Bureau of Asian Research, 2017), p. 3.

70 See Daljit Singh, 'China's White Paper on Security Cooperation in the Asia-Pacific Region and Chinese Grand Strategy', ISEAS *Perspective*, no. 22, 7 April 2017, https://www.iseas.edu.sg/images/pdf/ISEAS_Perspective_2017_22.pdf.

71 Christopher K. Johnson, 'President Xi Jinping's "Belt and Road" Initiative', Center for Strategic and International Studies, March 2016, pp. 19–20, https://csis-website-prod.s3.amazonaws.com/s3fs-public/publication/160328_Johnson_PresidentXiJinping_Web.pdf.

72 See, for example, Denny Roy, 'Assertive China: Irredentism or Expansionism?', *Survival: Global Politics and Strategy*, vol. 61, no. 1, February–March 2019, pp. 51–74.

73 See, for example, Nadège Rolland, 'China's Vision for a New World Order', NBR Special Report, no. 83, January 2020, p. 51, https://www.nbr.org/wp-content/uploads/pdfs/publications/sr83_chinasvision_jan2020.pdf. Rolland contends that Beijing's ultimate objective is to exert influence over 'large portions of the "global South"'.

74 See Antony J. Blinken, 'Trump Is Ceding Global Leadership to China', *New York Times*, 8 November 2017, https://www.nytimes.com/2017/11/08/opinion/trump-china-xi-jinping.html; and Minxin Pei, 'China's Return to Strongman Rule', *Foreign Affairs*, 1 November 2017, https://www.foreignaffairs.com/articles/china/2017-11-01/chinas-return-strongman-rule.

75 Lee Hsien Loong, 'The Endangered Asian Century', *Foreign Affairs*, vol. 99, no. 4, July–August 2020, pp. 52–64, especially p. 52, https://www.foreignaffairs.com/articles/asia/2020-06-04/lee-hsien-loong-endangered-asian-century.

76 For an excellent summary of Indonesia's role in championing the ASEAN 'Outlook on the Indo-Pacific', see Dewi Fortuna Anwar, 'Indonesia and the ASEAN Outlook on the Indo-Pacific', *International Affairs*, vol. 96, no. 1, January 2020, pp. 111–29.

77 US, Department of State, 'A Free and Open Indo-Pacific: Advancing a Shared Vision', p. 6.

78 Yohei Muramatsu, 'Trump Skips ASEAN Summit Again, Ceding Influence to China', *Nikkei Asia*, 1 November 2019, https://asia.nikkei.com/Politics/International-relations/Trump-skips-ASEAN-Summit-again-ceding-influence-to-China.

79 Steve Holland and James Pomfret, 'Obama Cancels Asia Tour Over Shutdown; Raises Questions on U.S. Pivot', Reuters, 4 October 2013,

https://www.reuters.com/article/us-usa-fiscal-obama-cancel-idUS-BRE99302J20131004.

80 Ralph Cossa, 'Condoleezza Rice's Unfortunate Decision', *Japan Times*, 25 July 2005, https://www.japantimes.co.jp/opinion/2005/07/25/commnetary/condoleezza-rices-unfortunate-decision; and John Ruwitch, 'China Builds on Goodwill in SE Asia in U.S. Absence', Reuters, 29 July 2007, https://www.reuters.com/article/idINIndia-28707920070729.

81 William Choong, 'The Return of the Indo-Pacific Strategy: An Assessment', *Australian Journal of International Affairs*, vol. 73, no. 5, October 2019, pp. 415–30, especially p. 424.

82 Michael Mastanduno, 'Incomplete Hegemony: The United States and Security Order in Asia', in Muthiah Alagappa (ed.), *Asian Security Order: Instrumental and Normative Features* (Stanford, CA: Stanford University Press, 2003), pp. 141–70, especially p. 143.

83 Barry Buzan and Ole Wæver, *Regions and Powers: The Structure of International Security* (Cambridge: Cambridge University Press, 2003), pp. 47–8.

84 *Ibid.*, p. 96.

85 *Ibid.*, p. 94.

86 *Ibid.*, p. 60.

87 See, for example, Nick Bisley, 'Integrated Asia: Australia's Dangerous New Strategic Geography', *Centre of Gravity Series*, no. 31, May 2017, http://sdsc.bellschool.anu.edu.au/sites/default/files/publications/attachments/2017-05/cog_integrated_asia-may_2017_0.pdf.

88 For further reading, see Amitav Acharya, *Constructing a Security Community in Southeast Asia: ASEAN and the Problem of Regional Order* (London and New York: Routledge, 2001).

89 For further reading, see S.C.M. Paine, *The Japanese Empire: Grand Strategy from the Meiji Restoration to the Pacific War* (Cambridge: Cambridge University Press, 2017).

90 Buzan and Wæver, *Regions and Powers: The Structure of International Security*, p. 121.

91 Bilahari Kausikan, 'How the Coronavirus May Change the Geopolitics of Southeast Asia', *South China Morning Post*, 23 March 2020, https://www.scmp.com/week-asia/opinion/article/3076460/how-coronavirus-may-change-geopolitics-southeast-asia.

Chapter Two

1 For further reading, see Stephan Haggard and Marcus Noland, 'A Security and Peace Mechanism for Northeast Asia: The Economic Dimension', Peterson Institute for International Economics *Policy Briefs*, no. PB08–4, April 2008, https://www.piie.com/sites/default/files/publications/pb/pb08-4.pdf.

2 Eleanor Albert, 'China, South Korea, and Japan Make Nice in Chengdu', *Diplomat*, 28 December 2019, https://thediplomat.com/2019/12/china-south-korea-and-japan-make-nice-in-chengdu.

3 'Japan, China and South Korea to Delay Trilateral Summit to 2021', *Nikkei Asia*, 3 December 2020, https://asia.nikkei.com/Politics/International-relations/Japan-China-and-South-Korea-to-delay-trilateral-summit-to-2021.

4 Under the UN Convention on the

Law of the Sea, coastal states can claim EEZs out to 200 nautical miles in which they have sovereign rights over natural resources. The problems arise when such zones overlap with each other, which they frequently do, leading to competing claims.

5 'China Angered as Japan, Taiwan Sign Fishing Agreement', Reuters, 10 April 2013, https://www.reuters.com/article/us-china-japan-taiwan-idUS-BRE93909520130410.

6 Mallory Shelbourne, 'Davidson: China Could Try to Take Control of Taiwan in "Next Six Years"', USNI News, 9 March 2021, https://news.usni.org/2021/03/09/davidson-china-could-try-to-take-control-of-taiwan-in-next-six-years.

7 See Lev Nachman and Brian Hioe, 'No, Taiwan's President Isn't "Pro-independence"', Diplomat, 23 April 2020, https://thediplomat.com/2020/04/no-taiwans-president-isnt-pro-independence.

8 For further reading, see Brendan Taylor, Dangerous Decade: Taiwan's Security and Crisis Management, Adelphi 470–471 (Abingdon: Routledge for the IISS, 2019), pp. 43–59.

9 An ADIZ serves as a buffer between a country's airspace (which extends 12 nautical miles from its coast) and international airspace. While not formally recognised as sovereign airspace under international law, foreign aircraft customarily identify themselves and seek permission prior to entering a country's ADIZ. The US established an ADIZ over Taiwan in 1950 to guard against Chinese and Soviet intrusions. Many maps show this ADIZ extending over the entire strait and even over parts of the mainland, but in practice the median line in the strait has been the accepted boundary. For further reading, see Mercedes Trent, 'Over the Line: The Implications of China's ADIZ Intrusions in Northeast Asia', Federation of American Scientists, August 2020, https://fas.org/wp-content/uploads/2020/08/ADIZ-Report.pdf.

10 Ministry of National Defense of the Republic of China, '2006 National Defense Report: Republic of China', August 2006, p. 49; Nadia Chao, 'China Conducted Huge Drills in Strait', Taipei Times, 22 October 2004, http://www.taipeitimes.com/News/front/archives/2004/10/22/2003207884; and 'MND Confirms Chinese Jets Entered Local Airspace in June', China Post, 26 July 2011.

11 Derek Grossman et al., China's Long-range Bomber Flights: Drivers and Implications (Santa Monica, CA: RAND Corporation, 2018), pp. 20–5.

12 'Taiwan Says Military Under Pressure from China as Missions Mount', Asahi Shimbun, 6 October 2020, http://www.asahi.com/ajw/articles/13792699; and 'Taiwan Says Has Spent Almost $900 Million Scrambling Against China This Year', Reuters, 7 October 2020, https://www.reuters.com/article/us-taiwan-security-idUSKBN26S0K6.

13 Yimou Lee, David Lague and Ben Blanchard, 'China Launches "Gray-zone" Warfare to Subdue Taiwan', Reuters, 10 December 2020, https://www.reuters.com/investigates/special-report/hongkong-taiwan-military.

14 Gerry Shih, 'Taiwan Says Threat of Military Clash with China Is "On the Rise"', Washington Post, 22 July 2020, https://www.washingtonpost.com/world/asia_pacific/taiwan-says-threat-of-military-clash-with-china-is-on-the-rise/2020/07/22/6f6da4c8-cc0c-11ea-99b0-8426e26d203b_story.html.

15 'With the World Distracted, China Intimidates Taiwan', *The Economist*, 8 April 2020, https://www.economist.com/asia/2020/04/08/with-the-world-distracted-china-intimidates-taiwan.

16 John Dotson, 'Military Activity and Political Signalling in the Taiwan Strait in Early 2020', *China Brief*, vol. 20, no. 6, 1 April 2020, pp. 1–6.

17 Kelvin Chen, 'China Denies Existence of Median Line in Taiwan Strait', *Taiwan News*, 22 September 2020, https://www.taiwannews.com.tw/en/news/4014231.

18 Choe Sang-Hun, 'North Korea's Wrecking of Liaison Office a "Death Knell" for Ties with the South', *New York Times*, 16 June 2020, https://www.nytimes.com/2020/06/16/world/asia/north-korea-explosion-liaison-office.html.

19 'List of Border Incidents Involving North and South Korea', Wikipedia, last updated 9 May 2021, https://en.wikipedia.org/wiki/List_of_border_incidents_involving_North_and_South_Korea.

20 Jon M. Van Dyke, Mark J. Valencia and Jenny Miller Garmendia, 'The North/South Korea Boundary Dispute in the Yellow (West) Sea', *Marine Policy*, vol. 27, no. 2, March 2003, pp. 143–58; Jon Van Dyke, 'The Maritime Boundary Between North & South Korea in the Yellow (West) Sea', 38 North, 29 July 2010, https://www.38north.org/2010/07/the-maritime-boundary-between-north-south-korea-in-the-yellow-west-sea/; and International Crisis Group, 'North Korea: The Risks of War in the Yellow Sea', Asia Report no. 198, 23 December 2010, https://www.crisisgroup.org/asia/north-east-asia/korean-peninsula/north-korea-risks-war-yellow-sea.

21 For further reading, see Benjamin Schreer and Brendan Taylor, 'The Korean Crises and Sino-American Rivalry', *Survival: Global Politics and Strategy*, vol. 53, no. 1, February–March 2011, pp. 13–19.

22 Peter Baker and Choe Sang-Hun, 'Trump Threatens "Fire and Fury" Against North Korea if It Endangers U.S.', *New York Times*, 8 August 2017, https://www.nytimes.com/2017/08/08/world/asia/north-korea-un-sanctions-nuclear-missile-united-nations.html.

23 See Jesse Johnson, 'U.S. and North Korea Came Much Closer to War than Previously Thought, Book Claims', *Japan Times*, 21 September 2020, https://www.japantimes.co.jp/news/2020/09/21/asia-pacific/us-north-korea-war-bob-woodward-book.

24 Anna Fifield, 'U.S., South Korea Begin Air Combat Drills that Include Simulated Strikes on North Korea', *Washington Post*, 4 December 2017, https://www.washingtonpost.com/world/us-south-korea-begin-air-combat-drills-that-include-simulated-strikes-on-north-korea/2017/12/04/9f4b43e0-d8ca-11e7-8e5f-ccc94e22b133_story.html.

25 Richard Sokolsky, 'North and South Korea Take Important Steps to Demilitarize the Korean Peninsula', 38 North, 19 September 2018, https://www.38north.org/2018/09/rsokolsky091918.

26 See US Embassy and Consulate in Thailand, 'Joint Statement of President Trump and Chairman Kim Jong Un at the Singapore Summit', 12 June 2018, https://th.usembassy.gov/joint-statement-president-donald-j-trump-united-states-america-chairman-kim-jong-un-democratic-peoples-republic-korea-singapore-summit; and Johan Ahlander and Philip O'Connor, 'North Korea Breaks Off Nuclear

Talks with U.S. in Sweden', Reuters, 5 October 2019, https://www.reuters.com/article/us-northkorea-usa-sweden-idUSKCN1WK074.

[27] Bates Gill, 'China's North Korea Policy: Assessing Interests and Influences', United States Institute of Peace *Special Report*, no. 283, July 2011, p. 2, https://www.usip.org/sites/default/files/China's_North_Korea_Policy.pdf.

[28] Javier C. Hernández, 'When Xi Met Kim: How China and North Korea Depicted It', *New York Times*, 28 March 2018, https://www.nytimes.com/2018/03/28/world/asia/xi-jinping-kim-jong-un-meeting-.html.

[29] 'North Korea Summit: Putin Says Kim "Needs Guarantees"', BBC, 25 April 2019, https://www.bbc.com/news/world-asia-48047279.

[30] See Aidan Foster-Carter, 'North Korea–South Korea Relations: Pyongyang Shuns and Snarls; Seoul Seems in Denial', *Comparative Connections*, vol. 21, no. 2, September 2019, pp. 73–86, especially p. 76, http://cc.pacforum.org/wp-content/uploads/2019/09/09_1902_NKSK.pdf.

[31] Paul Farhi, 'Kim Jong Un Appears to Be Alive After All. So Why Did CNN and Other News Outlets Report He Was on His Deathbed?', *Washington Post*, 6 May 2020, https://www.washingtonpost.com/lifestyle/media/kim-jong-un-appears-to-be-alive-after-all-so-how-did-his-death-make-the-news/2020/05/05/e9cf7f0e-8d6c-11ea-a0bc-4e9ad4866d21_story.html.

[32] Desmond Ball, 'Intelligence Collection Operations and EEZs: The Implications of New Technology', *Marine Policy*, vol. 28, no. 1, January 2004, pp. 67–82, especially pp. 74–5.

[33] Toshu Noguchi, 'PRC Navy's Survey Operations Around Okinotori Island Increases by More Than Four-fold Over Last Year', *Sankei Shimbun*, 22 July 2004, cited in Richard Fisher, Jr, 'Growing Asymmetries in the China–Japan Naval Balance', 22 November 2005, http://www.strategycenter.net/research/pubID.83/pub_detail.asp.

[34] 'Mystery Sub Sparks Japan Alert', BBC, 10 November 2004, http://news.bbc.co.uk/2/hi/3998107.stm; and Nao Shimoyachi, 'Chinese Submarine Intrusion Considered An Act Of Provocation', *Japan Times*, 13 November 2004, https://www.japantimes.co.jp/news/2004/11/13/national/chinese-submarine-intrusion-considered-an-act-of-provocation.

[35] 'Unidentified Submarine Detected Between Shikoku and Kyushu', *Japan Times*, 15 September 2008, https://www.japantimes.co.jp/news/2008/09/15/national/unidentified-submarine-detected-between-shikoku-and-kyushu.

[36] Chris Buckley, 'China Cancels Japan Talks, Warns on Sea Dispute', Reuters, 11 September 2010, https://www.reuters.com/article/us-japan-china-idUSTRE68A0820100911.

[37] Martin Fackler, 'Japan Says China Aimed Military Radar at Ship', *New York Times*, 5 February 2013, https://www.nytimes.com/2013/02/06/world/asia/japan-china-islands-dispute.html; and 'Chinese Officials Admit to MSDF Radar Lock Allegations', *Japan Times*, 18 March 2013, https://www.japantimes.co.jp/news/2013/03/18/national/politics-diplomacvy/chinese-officials-admit-to-msdf-radar-lock-allegations.

[38] Shannon Tiezzi, 'A China–Japan Breakthrough: A Primer on Their 4 Point Consensus', *Diplomat*, 7 November 2014, https://thediplomat.com/2014/11/a-china-japan-

breakthrough-a-primer-on-their-4-point-consensus.

39 'Japan and China Launch Defense Communication Mechanism to Prevent Air and Sea Clashes', *Japan Times*, 8 June 2018, https://www.japantimes.co.jp/news/2018/06/08/national/politics-diplomacy/japan-china-launch-defense-communication-mechanism-prevent-air-sea-clashes.

40 Julian Ryall, 'Japan and China Hold First Joint Maritime Drills in Eight Years in Sign of Warming Ties', *South China Morning Post*, 22 October 2019, https://www.scmp.com/news/asia/east-asia/article/3034042/japan-and-china-hold-first-joint-maritime-drills-eight-years.

41 'Chinese Incursions Near Japan-held Islands Top 1,000 to Hit Record, Up 80% on Last Year', *Japan Times*, 6 December 2019, https://www.japantimes.co.jp/news/2019/12/06/national/politics-diplomacy/china-incursions-japan-held-islands-hit-record.

42 Mike Mochizuki and Jiaxiu Han, 'Is China Escalating Tensions with Japan in the East China Sea?', *Diplomat*, 16 September 2020, https://thediplomat.com/2020/09/is-china-escalating-tensions-with-japan-in-the-east-china-sea.

43 Steven Stashwick, 'Japan Sortieing More Jets During Heightened Senkaku Tensions', *Diplomat*, 21 July 2020, https://thediplomat.com/2020/07/japan-sortieing-more-jets-during-heightened-senkaku-tensions.

44 Japan, Ministry of Defense, 'Joint Staff Press Release: Statistics on Scrambles Through FY2019', 9 April 2020, https://www.mod.go.jp/js/Press/press2020/press_pdf/p20200409_02.pdf.

45 Japan, Ministry of Foreign Affairs, 'Japanese Territory', 1 March 2011, https://www.mofa.go.jp/region/europe/russia/territory/overview.html.

46 James D.J. Brown, 'Time for Japan to Reassess Its Russia Policy', *Japan Times*, 26 July 2019, https://www.japantimes.co.jp/opinion/2019/07/26/commentary/japan-commentary/time-japan-reassess-russia-policy.

47 Franz-Stefan Gady, 'Putin Offers Japan "Peace Treaty Without Any Pre-Conditions"', *Diplomat*, 14 September 2018, https://thediplomat.com/2018/09/putin-offers-japan-peace-treaty-without-any-pre-conditions.

48 Dmitri V. Streltsov, 'Will Japan and Russia Finally Settle Their Territorial Dispute?', *Diplomat*, 15 November 2018, https://thediplomat.com/2018/11/will-japan-and-russia-finally-settle-their-territorial-dispute.

49 See Michito Tsuruoka, 'Resetting Japan–Russia Relations', *Diplomat*, 7 October 2020, https://thediplomat.com/2020/10/resetting-japan-russia-relations.

50 'Russia Begins Military Drill on Disputed Islands Off Hokkaido', *Japan Times*, 12 March 2019, https://www.japantimes.co.jp/news/2019/03/12/national/politics-diplomacy/russia-begins-military-drill-disputed-islands-off-hokkaido.

51 Japan, Ministry of Defense, 'Defense of Japan 2019', p. 45, https://www.mod.go.jp/en/publ/w_paper/wp2019/pdf/DOJ2019_Full.pdf.

52 Japan Defense Agency, *Defense of Japan 1999* (Tokyo: Japan Defense Agency, 1999), p. 34.

53 Japan, Ministry of Defense, 'Joint Staff Press Release: Statistics on Scrambles Through FY2019'.

54 Jesse Johnson, 'Air Self-Defense Force Jets Scrambled as Russian Bombers and Fighters Skirt Japanese Coasts', *Japan Times*, 16 February 2019, https://www.japantimes.co.jp/news/2019/02/16/national/air-self-defense-force-jets-

scrambled-russian-bombers-fighters-skirt-japanese-coasts.

55 'Japan Scrambles Fighters After Russian Helicopter "Enters Airspace"', *Nikkei Asia*, 3 October 2020, https://asia.nikkei.com/Politics/International-relations/Japan-scrambles-fighters-after-Russian-helicopter-enters-airspace.

56 Japan, Ministry of Foreign Affairs, 'Japan–North Korea Relations: Abductions of Japanese Citizens by North Korea', 28 December 2018, https://www.mofa.go.jp/region/asia-paci/n_korea/abduction/index.html.

57 Tomohiro Osaki, 'Trump Pledges to Help Bring Home Japanese Citizens Abducted by North Korea', *Japan Times*, 27 May 2019, https://www.japantimes.co.jp/news/2019/05/27/national/politics-diplomacy/trump-pledges-help-bring-home-japanese-citizens-abducted-north-korea.

58 Jae-Soon Chang, 'North Korea Threatens "War" if Satellite Shot Down', NBC Washington, 9 March 2009, https://www.nbcwashington.com/local/natl-north-korea-threatens-war-if-satellite-shot-down/1867561.

59 Choe Sang-Hun and David E. Sanger, 'North Korea Fires Missile Over Japan', *New York Times*, 28 August 2017, https://www.nytimes.com/2017/08/28/world/asia/north-korea-missile.html.

60 Jesse Johnson, 'North Korean Missiles Again Flying Over Japan "Only a Matter of Time," Experts Say', *Japan Times*, 2 January 2020, https://www.japantimes.co.jp/news/2020/01/02/asia-pacific/politics-diplomacy-asia-pacific/north-korean-missiles-flying-japan-matter-time-experts-say.

61 Joseph Morgan and Mark Valencia (eds), *Atlas for Marine Policy in East Asian Seas* (Berkeley, CA: University of California Press, 1992), pp. 29–31.

62 See Dokdo Takeshima Liancourt Rocks – The Historical Facts of Korea's Dokdo Island, 'Japan's Takeshima X-Files II – Dokdo and Japan's Imperial Navy', https://www.dokdo-takeshima.com/japans-takeshima-x-files-ii.html.

63 'Seoul's Spat with Tokyo Boils Over', *Bangkok Post*, 15 July 2008, p. 4.

64 Ji-Young Lee and Mintaro Oba, 'Japan–Korea Relations: Hitting an All-time Low', *Comparative Connections*, vol. 29, no. 1, May 2019, pp. 105–14, especially p. 107.

65 Tomoyuki Tachikawa, 'Japan Hints at Ending Talks About Radar Lock-On Issue with S. Korea', Kyodo News, 1 June 2019, https://english.kyodonews.net/news/2019/06/870ce1b3783c-japanese-s-korean-defense-chiefs-meet-in-singapore-amid-strains.html.

66 Edward White, Kang Buseong and Henry Foy, 'S Korea Jets Fire Shots at Russian Military Aircraft Over Sea of Japan', *Financial Times*, 23 July 2019, https://www.ft.com/content/0c1e8550-acf4-11e9-8030-530adfa879c2.

67 'Japan Lodged Protest with South Korea, Russia After Jet Incident: Suga', Reuters, 23 July 2019, https://www.reuters.com/article/us-southkorea-russia-japan-govt/japan-lodged-protest-with-south-korea-russia-after-jet-incident-suga-idUSKCN1UI0R6.

68 Shin Kawashima, 'A Test of Japan–South Korea Relations', *Diplomat*, 6 December 2020, https://thediplomat.com/2020/12/a-test-of-japan-south-korea-relations.

69 For further reading, see Victor D. Cha, 'Complex Patchworks: U.S. Alliances as Part of Asia's Regional Architecture', *Asia Policy*, no. 11, January 2011, pp. 27–50, especially pp. 48–9.

70 Ju-min Park, 'Japan Official, Calling Taiwan "Red Line", Urges Biden to "Be Strong"', Reuters, 25 December 2020, https://www.reuters.com/article/us-japan-usa-taiwan-china-idUSKBN28Z0JR.

71 Shannon Tiezzi, 'Taiwan–Japan Fishing Dispute Heats Up', Diplomat, 3 May 2016, https://thediplomat.com/2016/05/taiwan-japan-fishing-dispute-heats-up.

72 Duncan DeAeth, 'Taiwan–Japan Revise Bilateral Fishery Agreement Around Diaoyu Islands', Taiwan News, 20 March 2018, https://www.taiwannews.com.tw/en/news/3385945; and 'Japan and Taiwan Sign Memorandum Of Understanding For Search And Rescue, But Fishing Dispute Remains Unresolved', Japan Times, 20 December 2017, https://www.japantimes.co.jp/news/2017/12/20/national/japan-taiwan-sign-search-rescue-memorandum-understanding-fishing-dispute-remains.

73 Wang Shu-fen and William Yen, 'Japan Scrambles Fighter Jets to Identify Taiwanese Aircraft: CAA', Focus Taiwan (CNA English News), 18 October 2017, https://focustaiwan.tw/society/201710180017.

74 Japan, Ministry of Defense, 'Joint Staff Press Release: Statistics on Scrambles Through FY2019', p. 3.

75 J. Berkshire Miller, 'China's Other Territorial Dispute: Baekdu Mountain', Diplomat, 23 December 2012, https://thediplomat.com/2012/12/baekdu-mountain-chinas-other-territorial-dispute.

76 'Kim Jong-Un: North Korean Leader Rides Up Mount Paektu', BBC News, 4 December 2019, https://www.bbc.com/news/world-asia-50655693.

77 Daniel Gomà Pinilla, 'Border Disputes Between China and North Korea', China Perspectives, no. 52, March–April 2004, pp. 64–70.

78 Joseph Bermudez and Victor Cha, 'New China–North Korea Tumen Road Bridge Nears Completion', CSIS Beyond Parallel, 22 July 2019, https://beyondparallel.csis.org/new-china-north-korea-tumen-road-bridge-nears-completion; and Andrew S. Erickson and Michael Monti, 'Trouble Ahead? Chinese–Korean Disputes May Intensify', National Interest, 20 February 2015, https://nationalinterest.org/feature/trouble-ahead-chinese-korean-disputes-may-intensify-12284.

79 'North Korea Is Lonelier Than Ever', The Economist, 22 October 2020, https://www.economist.com/asia/2020/10/24/north-korea-is-lonelier-than-ever.

80 Seokwoo Lee and Hee Eun Lee, 'South Korea', in Simon Chesterman, Hisashi Owada and Ben Saul (eds), The Oxford Handbook of International Law in Asia and the Pacific (Oxford: Oxford University Press, 2019), pp. 341–62, especially p. 358.

81 Lily Kuo, 'Will a Tiny, Submerged Rock Spark a New Crisis in the East China Sea?', Atlantic, 10 December 2013, https://www.theatlantic.com/china/archive/2013/12/will-a-tiny-submerged-rock-spark-a-new-crisis-in-the-east-china-sea/282155.

82 Terence Roehrig, 'South Korea–China Maritime Disputes: Toward a Solution', East Asia Forum, 27 November 2012, https://www.eastasiaforum.org/2012/11/27/south-korea-china-maritime-disputes-toward-a-solution.

83 Chang-Hoon Shin, 'South Korea's Inevitable Expansion of Its ADIZ', CSIS Asia Maritime Transparency Initiative, 8 December 2014, https://amti.csis.org/south-koreas-inevitable-expansion-of-its-adiz.

84 Ankit Panda, 'Chinese Fighter Violates South Korea's Air Defense Identification Zone', *Diplomat*, 28 February 2018, https://thediplomat.com/2018/02/chinese-fighter-violates-south-koreas-air-defense-identification-zone.

85 IISS, *The Military Balance 2021* (Abingdon: Routledge for the IISS, 2021), pp. 517–22. The Northeast Asia figure only includes the defence expenditures of China, Japan, South Korea and Taiwan, due to the absence of reliable data from North Korea.

86 For further reading, see Meia Nouwens and Lucie Béraud-Sudreau, 'Assessing Chinese Defence Spending: Proposals for New Methodologies', IISS, March 2020, https://www.iiss.org/blogs/research-paper/2020/03/assessing-chinese-defence-spending.

87 IISS, *The Military Balance 2021*, p. 249.

88 *Ibid.*, p. 23.

89 Desmond Ball, 'Arms Modernization in Asia: An Emerging Complex Arms Race', in Andrew T.H. Tan (ed.), *The Global Arms Trade: A Handbook* (London: Routledge, 2009), pp. 30–51.

90 Ball, 'Arms and Affluence: Military Acquisitions in the Asia-Pacific Region', pp. 78–112.

91 Darren Lake, 'South Korea Announces Record High Budget', *Jane's Defence Weekly*, 4 July 2001, p. 3; and Defence Intelligence Organisation, 'Defence Economic Trends in the Asia-Pacific 2007', p. 38, https://www.defence.gov.au/dio/documents/DET_07.pdf.

92 US, Defense Intelligence Agency, 'China Military Power: Modernizing a Force to Fight and Win', 16 January 2019, p. 20, https://www.dia.mil/Portals/27/Documents/News/Military%20Power%20Publications/China_Military_Power_FINAL_5MB_20190103.pdf.

93 Nick Childs and Tom Waldwyn, 'China's Naval Shipbuilding: Delivering on Its Ambition in a Big Way', IISS, *Military Balance* blog, 1 May 2018, https://www.iiss.org/blogs/military-balance/2018/05/china-naval-shipbuilding.

94 Robert Ross, 'The End of U.S. Naval Dominance in Asia', Lawfare, 18 November 2018, https://www.lawfareblog.com/end-us-naval-dominance-asia.

95 See US, Office of the Secretary of Defense, 'Military and Security Developments Involving the People's Republic of China 2020', p. 45, https://media.defense.gov/2020/Sep/01/2002488689/-1/-1/1/2020-dod-china-military-power-report-final.pdf. According to this report, China has an additional two SSBN hulls that are currently being fitted out. Reports earlier in the year in the Chinese media suggested that these Type-094 (*Jin*) SSBNs have already entered service. See, for example, Minnie Chan, 'Chinese Navy Puts Two New Nuclear Submarines into Service', *South China Morning Post*, 29 April 2020, https://www.scmp.com/print/news/china/military/article/3082195/chinese-navy-puts-two-new-nuclear-submarines-service.

96 US, Office of the Secretary of Defense, 'Military and Security Developments Involving the People's Republic of China 2019', p. 36, https://media.defense.gov/2019/May/02/2002127082/-1/-1/1/2019_china_military_power_report.pdf; and IISS, *The Military Balance 2020* (Abingdon: Routledge for the IISS, 2020), p. 235.

97 US, Defense Intelligence Agency, 'China Military Power: Modernizing a Force to Fight and Win', p. 70; and US Department of Defense, 'Military and

Security Developments Involving the People's Republic of China 2019', p. 36.

98 See IISS, Military Balance+ database, https://milbalplus.iiss.org, accessed July 2021; and US Defense Intelligence Agency, 'China Military Power: Modernizing a Force to Fight and Win', p. 70.

99 IISS, *The Military Balance 2020*, p. 235.

100 IISS, Military Balance+ database, https://milbalplus.iiss.org, accessed July 2021.

101 Rajeswari Pillai Rajagopalan, 'China's Second Aircraft Carrier: A Sign of PLA Naval Muscle?', *Diplomat*, 26 December 2019, https://thediplomat.com/2019/12/chinas-second-aircraft-carrier-a-sign-of-pla-naval-muscle; and US, Office of the Secretary of Defense, 'Military and Security Developments Involving the People's Republic of China 2019', p. 37.

102 Minnie Chan, 'Chinese Navy Set to Build Fourth Aircraft Carrier, but Plans for a More Advanced Ship Are Put On Hold', *South China Morning Post*, 28 November 2019, https://www.scmp.com/news/china/military/article/3039653/chinese-navy-set-build-fourth-aircraft-carrier-plans-more.

103 Rear Admiral (Retd) Michael A. McDevitt, 'China's Navy Will Be the World's Largest in 2035', US Naval Institute, February 2020, https://www.usni.org/magazines/proceedings/2020/february/chinas-navy-will-be-worlds-largest-2035.

104 US, Office of the Secretary of Defense, 'Military and Security Developments Involving the People's Republic of China 2019', p. 36.

105 See, for example, China Power Team, 'Does China Have an Effective Sea-based Nuclear Deterrent?', CSIS ChinaPower, https://chinapower.csis.org/ssbn; and Bill Gertz, 'China Tests Submarine-launched JL-3 Missile

Capable of Hitting U.S. with Nuke', *Washington Times*, 24 December 2019, https://www.washingtontimes.com/news/2019/dec/24/china-tests-submarine-launched-jl-3-missile-capabl.

106 Michael Zennie, 'President Trump Visited Japan's Biggest Warship Since World War II. Here's What to Know About the JS Kaga', *Time*, 28 May 2019, https://time.com/5597046/japanese-aircraft-carrier-kaga-izumo.

107 Gabriel Dominguez, 'Japan Launches Second Soryu-class Submarine Equipped with Lithium-ion Batteries', Janes, 6 November 2019, https://www.janes.com/defence-news/news-detail/japan-launches-second-soryu-class-submarine-equipped-with-lithium-ion-batteries. These are the first diesel-electric attack submarines in the world to use such batteries.

108 Steven Stashwick, 'Japan Launches New Submarine Class', *Diplomat*, 15 October 2020, https://thediplomat.com/2020/10/japan-launches-new-submarine-class.

109 For further reading, see Vann H. Van Diepen, 'Cutting Through the Hype About the North Korean Ballistic Missile Submarine Threat', 38 North, 6 September 2019, https://www.38north.org/2019/09/vvandiepen090619.

110 Oh Seok-Min, 'S. Korea to Launch New 3,000-ton Submarine', Yonhap News Agency, 10 November 2020, https://en.yna.co.kr/view/AEN20201110001300325.

111 Ridzwan Rahmat, 'South Korea's First KSS-3 Submarine Begins Sea Trials', Janes, 17 June 2019, https://www.janes.com/defence-news/news-detail/south-koreas-first-kss-3-submarine-begins-sea-trials; and Matteo Scarano, 'DSME Awarded Contract to Design, Build Upgraded KSS-III-class

Submarine', Janes, 11 October 2019, https://www.janes.com/defence-news/news-detail/dsme-awarded-contract-to-design-build-upgraded-kss-iii-class-submarine.

[112] Lucie Béraud-Sudreau and Joseph Dempsey, 'Indigenous Submarines: Not Quite Made in Taiwan?', IISS, *Military Balance* blog, 20 August 2018, https://www.iiss.org/blogs/military-balance/2018/08/indigenous-submarines-taiwan.

[113] Nick Aspinwall, 'Taiwan Starts Production of First Domestically Made Submarines', *Diplomat*, 28 November 2020, https://thediplomat.com/2020/11/taiwan-starts-production-of-first-domestically-made-submarines.

[114] Lawrence Chung, 'US–Taiwan Relations: Biden Administration Gives Green Light to Exports of Key Submarine Technology', *South China Morning Post*, 16 March 2021, https://www.scmp.com/news/china/military/article/3125640/us-taiwan-relations-biden-administration-gives-green-light.

[115] For further reading, see Mark Fitzpatrick, *Asia's Latent Nuclear Powers: Japan, South Korea and Taiwan*, Adelphi 455 (London: Routledge for the IISS, 2015).

[116] Hans M. Kristensen and Matt Korda, 'Russian Nuclear Forces, 2020', *Bulletin of the Atomic Scientists*, vol. 76, no. 2, February 2020, pp. 102–17; and Hans M. Kristensen and Matt Korda, 'United States Nuclear Forces, 2020', *Bulletin of the Atomic Scientists*, vol. 76, no. 1, January 2020, pp. 46–60.

[117] Hans M. Kristensen and Matt Korda, 'Chinese Nuclear Forces, 2020', *Bulletin of the Atomic Scientists*, vol. 76, no. 6, December 2020, pp. 443–57.

[118] IISS, *North Korean Security Challenges: A Net Assessment* (London: IISS, 2011), pp. 117–18.

[119] See Ankit Panda and Vipin Narang, 'Welcome to the H-Bomb Club, North Korea', *Diplomat*, 5 September 2017, https://thediplomat.com/2017/09/welcome-to-the-h-bomb-club-north-korea.

[120] Hans M. Kristensen and Robert S. Norris, 'North Korean Nuclear Capabilities, 2018', *Bulletin of the Atomic Scientists*, vol. 74, no. 1, 2018, p. 48.

[121] Minnie Chan, 'Chinese Military Beefs Up Coastal Forces As It Prepares For Possible Invasion Of Taiwan', *South China Morning Post*, 18 October 2020, https://www.scmp.com/news/china/diplomacy/article/3105953/chinese-military-beefs-coastal-forces-it-prepares-possible.

[122] Ankit Panda, 'Is China's DF-17 Hypersonic Missile A Serious Threat to the United States?', *South China Morning Post*, 5 October 2019, https://www.scmp.com/news/china/military/article/3031404/chinas-df-17-hypersonic-missile-serious-threat-united-states.

[123] Kristensen and Norris, 'North Korean Nuclear Capabilities, 2018', p. 48.

[124] See Michael Elleman, 'Does Size Matter? North Korea's Newest ICBM', 38 North, 21 October 2020, https://www.38north.org/2020/10/melleman102120.

[125] Ankit Panda, 'What Was Behind North Korea's Busy March 2020 Missile Launches?', *Diplomat*, 8 April 2020, https://thediplomat.com/2020/04/what-was-behind-north-koreas-busy-march-2020-missile-launches.

[126] Michael Elleman, 'North Korea's New Short-range Missiles: A Technical Evaluation', 38 North, 9 October 2019, https://www.38north.org/2019/10/melleman100919.

[127] Richard D. Fisher, Jr, 'Taiwan Reviews Its Missiles Programmes', *Jane's*

Intelligence Review, 27 March 2018.

[128] Ian Easton, *The Chinese Invasion Threat: Taiwan's Defense and American Strategy in* Asia (Arlington, VA: The Project 2049 Institute, 2017), p. 222.

[129] 'Harpoon', Missile Threat, Center for Strategic and International Studies, https://missilethreat.csis.org/missile/harpoon.

[130] 'Missiles of South Korea', Missile Threat, Center for Strategic and International Studies, https://missilethreat.csis.org/country/south-korea.

[131] Gabriel Dominguez, 'HHI To Build First Of Second Batch Of KDX-III Destroyers For RoKN', *Jane's Defence Weekly*, 11 October 2019, https://www.janes.com/article/91857/hhi-to--build-first-of-second-batch-of-kdx-iii-destroyers-for-rokn.

[132] IISS, *The Military Balance 2020*, p. 246.

[133] Brad Glosserman, 'Seoul Draws Wrong Thaad Lessons', *Japan Times*, 27 January 2020, https://www.japantimes.co.jp/opinion/2020/01/27/commentary/japan-commentary/seoul-draws-wrong-thaad-lessons.

[134] Japan, Ministry of Defense, 'Defense of Japan 2019', p. 281.

[135] *Ibid.*

[136] See, for example, Jeffrey W. Hornung, 'Is Japan's Interest In Strike Capabilities A Good Idea?', War on the Rocks, 17 July 2020, https://warontherocks.com/2020/07/is-japans-interest-in-strike-capabilities-a-good-idea/.

[137] Junnosuke Kobara, 'Japan's Plan For 2 Superdestroyers To Cost More Than Aegis Ashore', *Nikkei Asia*, 25 November 2020, https://asia.nikkei.com/Politics/Japan-s-plan-for-2-superdestroyers-to-cost-more-than-Aegis-Ashore.

[138] IISS, 'Ballistic Missile Defence in East Asia', *Asia-Pacific Regional Security Assessment 2018* (London: IISS, 2018), p. 94.

[139] US, Office of the Secretary of Defense, 'Military and Security Developments Involving the People's Republic of China 2020', pp. 52, 73.

[140] *Ibid.*, p. 73.

[141] *Ibid.*

[142] Franz-Stefan Gady, 'Russia Completes Delivery of Second S-400 Regiment to China', *Diplomat*, 3 February 2020, https://thediplomat.com/2020/02/russia-completes-delivery-of-second-s-400-regiment-to-china.

[143] Paul Dibb, 'How the Geopolitical Partnership between China and Russia Threatens the West', *Special Report*, Australian Strategic Policy Institute, November 2019, p. 24.

[144] See Nigel Inkster, 'Measuring Military Cyber Power', *Survival: Global Politics and Strategy*, vol. 59, no. 4, August–September 2017, p. 28; and Marcus Willett, 'Assessing Cyber Power', *Survival: Global Politics and Strategy*, vol. 61, no. 1, February–March 2019, p. 87.

[145] Inkster, 'Measuring Military Cyber Power', p. 32; and Willett, 'Assessing Cyber Power', pp. 85–6.

[146] Desmond Ball, 'China's Cyber Warfare Capabilities', *Security Challenges*, vol. 7, no. 2, Winter 2011, p. 81.

[147] IISS, Military Balance+ database, https://milbalplus.iiss.org, accessed July 2021.

[148] IISS, 'China's Cyber Power in a New Era', *Asia-Pacific Regional Security Assessment 2019* (London: IISS, 2019), p. 82; and Greg Austin, 'The Strategic Implications of China's Weak Cyber Defences', *Survival: Global Politics and Strategy*, vol. 62, no. 5, October–November 2020, pp. 119–38.

[149] 'China Is Seeking To Become A "Cyber Superpower"', *The Economist*, 20 March 2018, https://

www.economist.com/graphic-detail/2018/03/20/china-is-seeking-to-become-a-cyber-superpower.

[150] Stephanie Kleine-Ahlbrandt, 'North Korea's Illicit Cyber Operations: What Can Be Done?', 38 North, February 2020, https://www.38north.org/2020/02/skleineahlbrandt022820.

[151] IISS, Military Balance+ database, https://milbalplus.iiss.org, accessed July 2021.

[152] Dan Strumpf, 'North Korean Cyber-criminals Implicated in Taiwan Bank Theft', Wall Street Journal, 17 October 2017, https://www.wsj.com/articles/north-korea-link-suspected-in-taiwan-bank-cyberheist-1508246101.

[153] Nick Kostov, Jenny Gross and Stu Woo, 'Cyberattack Is Likely to Keep Spreading', Wall Street Journal, 15 May 2017, https://www.wsj.com./articles/list-of-cyberattack-victims-grows-to-more-than-200-000-1494764594.

[154] 'North Korean Hackers Said Possibly Behind Massive Coincheck Heist', Japan Times, 6 February 2018, https://www.japantimes.co.jp/news/2018/02/06/business/tech/north-korean-hackers-said-possibly-behind-massive-coincheck-heist.

[155] Japan, Ministry of Defense, 'National Defense Program Guidelines for FY2019 and Beyond', 18 December 2018, https://warp.da.ndl.go.jp/info:ndljp/pid/11591426/www.mod.go.jp/j/approach/agenda/guideline/2019/pdf/20181218_e.pdf.

[156] See Franz-Stefan Gady and Yuka Koshino, 'Japan And Cyber Capabilities: How Much Is Enough?',

IISS, Military Balance blog, 28 August 2020, https://www.iiss.org/blogs/military-balance/2020/08/japan-cyber-capabilities.

[157] Ibid.

[158] See Japan, Ministry of Foreign Affairs, 'Joint Statement of the Security Consultative Committee', 19 April 2019, https://www.mofa.go.jp/files/000470738.pdf.

[159] See Japan–US Security Consultative Committee, 'The Guidelines for U.S.–Japan Defense Cooperation', 27 April 2015, https://archive.defense.gov/pubs/20150427_--_GUIDELINES_FOR_US-JAPAN_DEFENSE_COOPERATION.pdf.

[160] Katherin Hille, 'Us And Taiwan Host Security Exercise To Boost Cyber Defence', Financial Times, 4 November 2019, https://www.ft.com/content/7d6c78cc-fec8-11e9-b7bc-f3fa4e77dd47.

[161] Philip Sherwell, 'China Uses Taiwan For AI Target Practice To Influence Elections', Australian, 5 January 2020, https://www.theaustralian.com.au/world/the-times/china-uses-taiwan-for-ai-target-practice-to-influence-elections/news-story/57499d2650d4d359a3857688d416d1e5.

[162] For further reading, see US, Office of the Secretary of Defense, 'Military and Security Developments Involving the People's Republic of China 2019', p. 88.

[163] 'Us And Taiwan Hold First Joint Cyber-War Exercise', BBC News, 4 November 2019, https://www.bbc.com/news/technology-50289974.

Chapter Three

1 For further reading, see David Shambaugh, *Where Great Powers Meet* (New York: Oxford University Press, 2021).

2 See, for example, 'Us "Neglect" Drives Asean Towards China In Superpower Economic Rivalry, Analysts Say', *South China Morning Post*, 17 February 2021, https://www.scmp.com/economy/china-economy/article/3121908/us-neglect-drives-asean-towards-china-superpower-economic.

3 For further reading, see Cheng Guan Ang, *Lew Kuan Yew's Strategic Thought* (London and New York: Routledge, 2013).

4 Lee Hsien Loong, 'Keynote Address', 18th Asia Security Summit: The IISS Shangri-La Dialogue, 31 May 2019, https://www.iiss.org/-/media/files/shangri-la-dialogue/2019/speeches/keynote-address---lee-hsien-loong-prime-minister-of-singapore-full-transcript.pdf.

5 Singapore, Ministry of Defence, 'Fact Sheet: Enhanced Agreement on Defence Exchanges and Security Cooperation (ADESC)', 20 October 2019, https://www.mindef.gov.sg/web/portal/mindef/news-and-events/latest-releases/article-detail/2019/October/20oct19_fs.

6 Lindsay Murdoch, 'Philippines Divided Over US Return to Subic Bay', *Sydney Morning Herald*, 20 November 2012, https://www.smh.com.au/world/philippines-divided-over-us-return-to-subic-bay-20121119-29m4m.html.

7 Seth Robson, 'Facility for US Forces Opens on Philippines' Main Island; Another Slated for Palawan', *Stars and Stripes*, 31 January 2019, https://www.stripes.com/news/pacific/facility-for-us-forces-opens-on-philippines-main-island-another-slated-for-palawan-1.566695.

8 See Zack Cooper and Jake Douglas, 'Successful Signaling at Scarborough Shoal?', War on the Rocks, 2 May 2016, https://warontherocks.com/2016/05/successful-signaling-at-scarborough-shoal.

9 Prashanth Parameswaran, 'Duterte Says Philippines Will Accept China Arms Deal', *Diplomat*, 13 December 2016, https://thediplomat.com/2016/12/duterte-says-philippines-will-accept-china-arms-deal.

10 An Baijie, 'China, the Philippines Sign 29 Agreements during Xi's Visit', *China Daily*, http://www.chinadaily.com.cn/a/201811/20/WS5bf404e8a-310eff303289ecc.html.

11 Cliff Venzon, '"A Little Accident" – Duterte Plays Down Sinking of Fishing Boat', *Nikkei Asia*, 18 June 2019, https://asia.nikkei.com/Politics/International-relations/A-little-accident-Duterte-plays-down-China-sinking-of-fishing-boat.

12 Richard Heydarian, 'How Washington's Ambiguity in South China Sea Puts the Philippine–US Alliance at a Crossroads', *South China Morning Post*, 31 January 2019, https://www.scmp.com/news/china/diplomacy/article/2184390/how-washingtons-ambiguity-south-china-sea-puts-philippine-us.

13 Ankit Panda, 'In Philippines, Pompeo Offers Major Alliance Assurance on South China Sea', *Diplomat*, 4 March 2019, https://thediplomat.com/2019/03/in-philippines-pompeo-offers-major-alliance-assurance-on-south-china-sea.

14 Eimor Santos, 'Philippines Formally Ends Visiting Force Agree-

ment with US', CNN Philippines, 11 February 2020, https://cnnphil-ippines.com/news/2020/2/11/Phil-ippines-ends-VFA-United-States.html?fbclid=IwAR2M_WNSz3lHD-7GOx5a_yGBrvGTMwEdyeqCcbk-bLdLKigDqVDlMdbCWSEOc.

15 'China, Thailand to Establish Compre-hensive Strategic Cooperative Partner-ship', Xinhua, 19 April 2012, https://www.china.org.cn/world/2012-04/19/content_25188715.htm.

16 On Thailand's traditionally flexible foreign policy and challenges to this approach, see Pongphisoot Busbarat, '"Bamboo Swirling in the Wind": Thailand's Foreign Policy Imbal-ance between China and the United States', *Contemporary Southeast Asia*, vol. 38, no. 2, August 2016, pp. 233–57; and Gregory Vincent Raymond, *Thai Military Power: A Culture of Strategic Accommodation* (Copenhagen: NIAS Press, 2018).

17 'Joint Press Statement Special ASEAN Foreign Ministers Meeting to Issue the Declaration of Zone of Peace, Freedom and Neutrality', Kuala Lumpur, 25–26 November 1971, https://asean.org/?static_post=joint-press-statement-special-asean-foreign-ministers-meet-ing-to-issue-the-declaration-of-zone-of-peace-freedom-and-neutrality-kuala-lumpur-25-26-november-1971.

18 US, Department of State, 'United States–Indonesia Comprehen-sive Partnership', 8 October 2013, https://2009-2017.state.gov/r/pa/prs/ps/2013/10/215196.htm.

19 See, for example, 'Statement by H.E. Dr. R.M. Marty M. Natalegawa, Min-ister for Foreign Affairs, Republic of Indonesia, at the General Debate of the 66th Session of the United Nations General Assembly', 26 September 2011, https://gadebate.un.org/sites/default/files/gastatements/66/ID_en.pdf.

20 Evan Laksmana, 'An Indo-Pacific Construct with "Indonesian Charac-teristics"', *Strategist*, 6 February 2018, https://www.aspistrategist.org.au/indo-pacific-construct-indonesian-characteristics.

21 Dewi Fortuna Anwar, 'Indonesia and the ASEAN Outlook on the Indo-Pacific', *International Affairs*, vol. 96, no. 1, 2020, pp. 111–29.

22 See, for example, Margareth S. Ari-tonang and Novan Iman Santosa, 'China, RI Begin Missile Talks', *Jakarta Post*, 27 July 2012, https://www.the-jakartapost.com/news/2012/07/27/china-ri-begin-missile-talks.html.

23 Aaron Connelly, 'Indonesia and the South China Sea under Jokowi', in IISS, *Asia-Pacific Regional Security Assessment 2020* (London: IISS, 2020), pp. 103–4.

24 *Ibid.*, pp. 110–12.

25 Prashanth Parameswaran, 'Is New Malaysia's China–US Balance Chang-ing Under Mahathir?', *Diplomat*, 14 March 2019, https://thediplomat.com/2019/03/is-new-malaysias-china-us-balance-changing-under-mahathir/.

26 'Boosting Malaysia–China Investments and Trade', *Star*, 1 January 2021, https://www.thestar.com.my/business/busi-ness-news/2021/01/01/boosting-malay-sia-china-investments-and-trade.

27 James Crabtree and Blake Berger, 'Malaysia GE a Wake-up Call on China Projects', *Straits Times*, 14 May 2018, https://www.straitstimes.com/opinion/malaysia-ge-a-wake-up-call-on-china-projects.

28 Joseph Sipalan, 'China, Malaysia Restart Massive "Belt and Road" Project after Hiccups', Reuters, 25 July 2019, https://in.reuters.com/article/us-

china-silkroad-malaysia/china-malay-sia-restart-massive-belt-and-road-project-after-hiccups-idINKCN1UK0DG.

29 'Malaysian Deputy PM Says Must Defend Sovereignty in South China Sea Dispute', Reuters, 14 November 2015, https://www.reuters.com/article/us-southchinasea-asean/malaysian-deputy-pm-says-must-defend-sovereignty-in-south-china-sea-dispute-idUSKCN0T30LU20151114.

30 'Malaysia Pushes Joint Development to Solve Asia Sea Disputes', *Bangkok Post*, 4 June 2013, https://www.bangkokpost.com/thailand/general/353412/malaysia-pushes-joint-development-to-solve-asia-sea-disputes.

31 Sharon Chen, 'Malaysia Splits with Asean Claimants on China Sea Threat', Bloomberg, 29 August 2013, https://www.bloomberg.com/news/articles/2013-08-28/malaysia-splits-with-other-asean-claimants-over-china-sea-threat.

32 David Han, 'Why Malaysia's South China Sea Policy Seems Confused', *Straits Times*, 5 May 2016, https://www.straitstimes.com/opinion/why-malaysias-south-china-sea-policy-seems-confused.

33 Cheng-Chwee Kuik and Chin Tong Liew, 'What Malaysia's "Mahathir Doctrine" Means for China–US Rivalry', *South China Morning Post*, 20 August 2018, https://www.scmp.com/week-asia/geopolitics/article/2160552/what-malaysias-mahathir-doctrine-means-china-us-rivalry.

34 For further reading, see Euan Graham, 'U.S. Naval Standoff with China Fails to Reassure Regional Allies', *Foreign Policy*, 4 May 2020, https://foreignpolicy.com/2020/05/04/malaysia-south-china-sea-us-navy-drillship-standoff.

35 Johan Saravanamuttu, 'Malaysia–China Relations in the Time of COVID-19', *East Asia Forum*, 1 April 2020, https://www.eastasiaforum.org/2020/04/01/malaysia-china-relations-in-the-time-of-covid-19/.

36 UK Government, 'Press Release: PM Meeting with His Majesty the Sultan of Brunei', 4 February 2020, https://www.gov.uk/government/news/pm-meeting-with-his-majesty-the-sultan-of-brunei-4-february-2020.

37 Stephen Druce and Abdul Hai Julay, 'The Road to Brunei's Economic Diversification: Contemporary Brunei–China Relations', in Alvin Cheng-Hin Lim and Frank Cibulka (eds), *China and Southeast Asia in the Xi Jinping Era* (Lanham, MD: Lexington Books, 2019), pp. 139–52.

38 Ralph Jennings, 'If Brunei Takes China's Energy Deal, Neighbors May Follow', Voice of America, 7 December 2018, https://www.voanews.com/east-asia-pacific/if-brunei-takes-chinas-energy-deal-neighbors-may-follow.

39 China, Ministry of Foreign Affairs, 'Wang Yi Talks about China's Four-point Consensus on South China Sea Issue with Brunei, Cambodia, Laos', 23 April 2016, https://www.fmprc.gov.cn/mfa_eng/zxxx_662805/t1358478.shtml.

40 Druce and Hai, 'The Road to Brunei's Economic Diversification', p. 147.

41 For further reading, see Michael Green et al., *Countering Coercion in Maritime Asia: The Theory and Practice of Gray Zone Deterrence* (Boulder, New York and London: Rowman & Littlefield for the Center for Strategic and International Studies, 2017), pp. 202–23.

42 Khanh Vu, 'Vietnam Protests Beijing's Sinking of South China Sea Boat', Reuters, 4 April 2020, https://www.reuters.com/article/us-vietnam-china-southchinasea-idUSKBN21M072.

43 'Viet Nam, China Trade Ties Continue to Develop', *Viet Nam News*, 25 April 2019, https://vietnamnews.vn/economy/519131/viet-nam-china-trade-ties-continue-to-develop.html.

44 'Vietnam Vows to Boost Political Ties with China in Visit', Bloomberg, 15 October 2013, https://www.bloomberg.com/news/articles/2013-10-14/vietnam-seeks-to-boost-political-trust-with-china-during-li-trip.

45 Xuan Quynh Nguyen, 'Vietnam, China Foreign Ministers Seek to Control South China Sea Tensions', Bloomberg, 22 July 2020, https://www.bloomberg.com/news/articles/2020-07-22/vietnam-china-foreign-ministers-seek-to-control-sea-tensions.

46 US, Department of Defense, and Vietnam, Ministry of National Defense, 'U.S.–Viet Nam Joint Vision Statement on Defense Relations', 1 June 2015, https://web.archive.org/web/*/https://photos.state.gov/libraries/vietnam/8621/pdf-forms/usvn_defense_relations_jvs2015.pdf.

47 Ian Storey, 'China's Tightening Relationship with Cambodia', *China Brief*, vol. 6, no. 9, 2006, https://jamestown.org/program/chinas-tightening-relationship-with-cambodia.

48 Chansambath Bong, 'Cambodia's Disastrous Dependence on China: A History Lesson', *Diplomat*, 4 December 2019, https://thediplomat.com/2019/12/cambodias-disastrous-dependence-on-china-a-history-lesson.

49 Anna Fifield, 'Asia's Tourist Spots Brace for Leaner Times as Coronavirus Keeps Chinese Visitors at Home', *Washington Post*, 31 January 2020, https://www.washingtonpost.com/world/asia_pacific/asias-tourist-spots-brace-for-leaner-times-as-coronavirus-keeps-chinese-visitors-at-home/2020/01/31/e31fc550-42bd-11ea-99c7-1dfd4241a2fe_story.html.

50 Jeremy Page, Gordon Lubold and Rob Taylor, 'Deal for Naval Outpost in Cambodia Furthers China's Quest for Military Network', *Wall Street Journal*, 22 July 2019, https://www.wsj.com/articles/secret-deal-for-chinese-naval-outpost-in-cambodia-raises-u-s-fears-of-beijings-ambitions-11563732482.

51 George Styllis, 'Cambodia Awaits Payday as Hun Sen Cozies up to China', Nikkei Asia, 17 April 2020, https://asia.nikkei.com/Politics/International-relations/Cambodia-awaits-payday-as-Hun-Sen-cozies-up-to-China.

52 Eleanor Albert, 'China Digs Deep In Landlocked Laos', *Diplomat*, 24 April 2019, https://thediplomat.com/2019/04/china-digs-deep-in-landlocked-laos.

53 Edgar Pang, '"Same-same but Different": Laos and Cambodia's Political Embrace of China', *Perspective*, ISEAS Yusof Ishak Institute, 5 September 2017, https://www.iseas.edu.sg/images/pdf/ISEAS_Perspective_2017_66.pdf.

54 Bertil Lintner, 'Myanmar Morphs to US–China Battlefield', *Asia Times Online*, 2 May 2013, http://www.atimes.com/atimes/Southeast_Asia/SEA-01-020513.html.

55 Tin Maung Maung Than, 'Myanmar and China: A Special Relationship?', in Institute of Southeast Asian Studies, *Southeast Asian Affairs 2003* (Singapore: Institute of Southeast Asian Studies, 2003), pp. 189–210.

56 Thomas Fuller, 'Myanmar Backs Down, Suspends Dam Project', *New York Times*, 30 September 2011, https://www.nytimes.com/2011/10/01/world/asia/myanmar-suspends-construction-of-controversial-dam.html.

57 'US Rebalance: Potential and Limits in Southeast Asia', *IISS Strategic*

Comments, vol. 18, no. 10, 3 January 2013, https://www.tandfonline.com/doi/abs/10.1080/13567888.2012.761849.

58 Dai Yonghong and Zhang Guoxuan, 'No Sign of a Sea Change for Myanmar's Foreign Policy', East Asia Forum, 23 December 2016, https://www.eastasiaforum.org/2016/12/23/no-sign-of-a-sea-change-for-myanmars-foreign-policy.

59 Jane Perlez and Wai Moe, 'China Helps Aung San Suu Kyi with Peace Talks in Myanmar', *New York Times*, 20 August 2016, https://www.nytimes.com/2016/08/21/world/asia/aung-san-suu-kyi-myanmar-china.html.

60 Ruosiu Zhang, 'Chinese Investment in Myanmar: Beyond Myitsone Dam', *Diplomat*, 22 July 2020, https://thediplomat.com/2020/07/chinese-investment-in-myanmar-beyond-myitsone-dam.

61 Camille Diola, 'Japan PM: 10 Patrol Ships for Phl Coast Guard Soon', *Philippine Star*, 10 October 2013, http://www.philstar.com/headlines/2013/10/10/1243651/japan-pm-10-patrol-ships-phl-coast-guard-soon.

62 'Hand in Hand, Facing Regional and Global Challenges', Joint Statement of the ASEAN–Japan Commemorative Summit, 14 December 2013, https://asean.org/hand-in-hand-facing-regional-and-global-challenges.

63 Mike Yeo, 'Japan Secures First-ever Major Defense Export with Philippine Radar Order', *Defense News*, 28 August 2020, https://www.defensenews.com/global/asia-pacific/2020/08/28/japan-secures-first-ever-defense-export-with-philippine-radar-order.

64 'Japan, Vietnam Reach Broad Agreement on Transfer of Defence Gear', Channel News Asia, 19 October 2020, https://www.channelnewsasia.com/news/asia/japan-vietnam-relations-defence-export-suga-13312316.

65 See Tim Huxley, 'India's Defence and Strategic Relations with Southeast Asia', in N.S. Sisodia and Sreeradha Datta (eds), *Changing Security Dynamics in Southeast Asia* (New Delhi: Magnum Books, 2008), pp. 347–54.

66 'Sushma Swaraj Tells Indian Envoys to Act East and Not Just Look East', *Economic Times*, 26 August 2014, https://economictimes.indiatimes.com/news/politics-and-nation/sushma-swaraj-tells-indian-envoys-to-act-east-and-not-just-look-east/articleshow/40907671.cms?from=mdr.

67 Sanjeev Miglani and Greg Torode, 'India to Build Satellite Tracking Station in Vietnam that Offers Eye on China', Reuters, 25 January 2016, https://www.reuters.com/article/india-vietnam-satellite-china-idINKCN0V309W.

68 Rahul Bedi, 'Four Years after Modi's "Act East" Promise, India No Closer to Selling BrahMos to Vietnam', *Wire*, 2 July 2020, https://thewire.in/security/india-vietnam-brahmos-missile.

69 For further reading on the history of Australia's Southeast Asian defence engagement, see Desmond Ball and Pauline Kerr, *Presumptive Engagement: Australia's Asia-Pacific Security Policy in the 1990s* (St Leonards, NSW: Allen & Unwin, 1996).

70 Australian Government, '2017 Foreign Policy White Paper', 2017, p. 1, https://www.dfat.gov.au/sites/default/files/2017-foreign-policy-white-paper.pdf.

71 Richard Maude, 'Australia Gets More Diplomatic Firepower in Southeast Asia', Asia Society Policy Institute, 16 November 2020, https://asiasociety.org/australia/australia-gets-more-diplomatic-firepower-southeast-asia.

72 Australia, Department of Defence, 'Defending Australia and Its Interests', 1 July 2020, https://www.minister.defence.gov.au/minister/lreynolds/media-releases/defending-australia-and-its-interests.

73 Lee Hsien Loong, 'Keynote Address'.

74 See Tim Huxley, *Defending the Lion City: The Armed Forces of Singapore* (Sydney, NSW: Allen & Unwin, 2000).

75 Huong Le Thu, 'Vietnam Draws Lines in the Sea', *Foreign Policy*, 6 December 2019, https://foreignpolicy.com/2019/12/06/vietnam-south-china-sea-united-states-draws-lines-in-the-sea; and Prashanth Parameswaran, 'Vietnam's New Defense White Paper in the Spotlight', *Diplomat*, 26 November 2019, https://thediplomat.com/2019/11/vietnams-new-defense-white-paper-in-the-spotlight.

76 See Benjamin Schreer, *Moving Beyond Ambitions? Indonesia's Military Modernisation* (Canberra: Australian Strategic Policy Institute, 2013).

77 'Indonesian Politicians Are Giving the Armed Forces a Big Role in Government', *The Economist*, 31 October 2019, https://www.economist.com/asia/2019/10/31/indonesian-politicians-are-giving-the-armed-forces-a-big-role-in-government.

78 Adrian David, 'Defence White Paper Will Protect Msia's Secrets, Sovereignty', *New Straits Times*, 2 December 2019, https://www.nst.com.my/news/exclusive/2019/12/543917/defence-white-paper-will-protect-msias-secrets-sovereignty.

79 Mike Yeo, 'Malaysia Points to Top Concerns in First-ever Defense White Paper', *Defense News*, 3 December 2019, https://www.defensenews.com/global/asia-pacific/2019/12/03/malaysia-points-to-top-concerns-in-first-ever-defense-whitepaper.

80 Renato Cruz De Castro, 'The Next Phase of Philippine Military Modernization: Looking to External Defense', Asian Maritime Transparency Initiative, 12 July 2018, https://amti.csis.org/the-next-phase-of-philippine-military-modernization-looking-to-external-defense.

81 IISS, *The Military Balance 2021* (Abingdon: Routledge for the IISS, 2021), pp. 223, 246.

82 IISS, *The Military Balance 2019* (Abingdon: Routledge for the IISS, 2019), pp. 242–6.

83 Thailand, Department of Mineral Resources, 'Status of Coastal Geoenvironment in Thailand', 2015, http://www.dmr.go.th/main.php?filename=Coastal2015___EN.

84 'The 10th Central Committee of the Lao People's Revolutionary Party', Lao News Agency, http://kpl.gov.la/En/Page/Politic/partyx.aspx.

85 'Members of the Lao Government', Lao News Agency, http://kpl.gov.la/En/Page/Politic/governmentVIII.aspx.

86 See the website of the ASEAN Defence Ministers' Meeting: https://admm.asean.org/.

87 Source for all defence-economics data: IISS, Military Balance+ database, https://milbalplus.iiss.org, accessed July 2021.

88 Joseph Sipalan, 'Malaysia Hopes to Pay for Military Equipment with Palm Oil', Reuters, 26 August 2019, https://www.reuters.com/article/us-malaysia-defence-idUSKCN1VG12Q.

89 Ridzwan Rahmat, 'South Korean Officials Arrive in Jakarta to Renegotiate KFX/IFX Fighter Aircraft Programme', Janes, 10 June 2020, https://www.janes.com/defence-news/news-detail/south-korean-officials-arrive-in-jakarta-to-renegotiate-kfxifx-

fighter-aircraft-programme.

90 Source for all data on arms orders and deliveries, unless otherwise stated: IISS, Military Balance+ database, https://milbalplus.iiss.org, accessed July 2021.

91 Singapore, Ministry of Defence, Committee of Supply Debate, 'Building the Next Generation SAF', https://www.mindef.gov.sg/web/portal/mindef/news-and-events/latest-releases/article-detail/2019/cos2019.

92 Lim Min Zhang, 'Customisation of Type 218SG Submarine Includes Use of Materials Suited to Saltier Singapore Waters', Straits Times, 18 February 2019, https://www.straitstimes.com/singapore/customisation-of-type-218sg-submarine-includes-use-of-materials-suited-to-saltier.

93 Xavier Vavasseur, 'Singapore MINDEF Outlines Future Procurement Plans', Naval News, 7 March 2019, https://www.navalnews.com/naval-news/2019/03/singapore-mindef-outlines-future-procurement-plans/.

94 Singapore, Ministry of Defence, 'Fact Sheet: Hunter Armoured Fighting Vehicle', 11 June 2019, https://www.mindef.gov.sg/web/portal/mindef/news-and-events/latest-releases/article-detail/2019/june/11jun19_fs.

95 NEC, 'NEC to Provide Vietnam with "LOTUSat-1" Earth Observation Satellite System', 23 April 2020, https://www.nec.com/en/press/202004/global_20200423_02.html.

96 US, Department of Defense, 'Contracts for May 31, 2019', https://www.defense.gov/Newsroom/Contracts/Contract/Article/1863144.

97 Thales, 'Len Industries and Thales to Modernise Indonesia's Naval Capabilities', 10 March 2020, https://www.thalesgroup.com/en/netherlands/press_release/len-industri-and-thales-modernise-indonesias-naval-capabilities.

98 Prashanth Parameswaran, 'Indonesia's Naval Modernization in Focus with New Fast Attack Craft Order', Diplomat, 9 January 2019, https://thediplomat.com/2019/01/indonesias-naval-modernization-in-focus-with-new-fast-attack-craft-order.

99 'Indonesia Set to Renegotiate KFX Jet Fighter Project Funding with South Korea', Jakarta Post, 8 September 2020, https://www.thejakartapost.com/news/2020/09/08/indonesia-set-to-renegotiate-kfx-jet-fighter-project-funding-with-south-korea.html.

100 Koya Jibiki and Shotaro Tani, 'Indonesia's Prabowo Trots Globe to Cut Fighter Jet Deal', Nikkei Asia, 11 November 2020, https://asia.nikkei.com/Business/Aerospace-Defense/Indonesia-s-Prabowo-trots-globe-to-cut-fighter-jet-deal.

101 Mike Yeo, 'Plagued by Defence Budget Curbs – the Royal Malaysian Air Force in Crisis', Channel News Asia, 2 April 2019, https://www.channelnewsasia.com/news/commentary/rmaf-defence-budget-curbs-royal-malaysian-air-force-fighter-jets-11400902.

102 Martin Carvalho, Rhimy Rahim and Hanis Zainal, 'Mat Sabu: No Plans to Acquire New Fighter Jets', Star, 21 November 2019, https://www.thestar.com.my/news/nation/2019/11/21/mat-sabu-no-plans-to-acquire-new-fighter-jets.

103 Ridzwan Rahmat, 'Hindered Ambitions: Delays Thwart Malaysia's Naval Transformation Plans', Janes Navy International, 25 November 2019.

104 Priam Nepomuceno, 'PAF New Jet Fighters Lauded for Role in Marawi Victory', Philippines News Agency, 25 May 2018, https://www.pna.gov.ph/articles/1036455.

105 'BrahMos Program in Progress, Funds Yet to Be Available: DND', Philippine News Agency, 24 November 2020, https://www.pna.gov.ph/articles/1122736.

106 Priam Nepomuceno, 'Missile Frigate BRP Jose Rizal to Conduct Sea Trials', Philippines News Agency, 22 November 2019, https://www.pna.gov.ph/articles/1086765.

107 Saab Thailand, 'Saab in Thailand', https://saab.com/region/thailand/about-saab/saab-in-thailand; and Craig Hoyle, 'How Gripen Became the Prize Thai Fighter', FlightGlobal, 7 January 2019, https://www.flightglobal.com/news/articles/analysis-how-gripen-became-prize-thai-fighter-454776.

108 Masayuki Yuda, 'Thailand Shelves Chinese Submarine Deal after Public Backlash', Nikkei Asia, 31 August 2020, https://asia.nikkei.com/Politics/Turbulent-Thailand/Thailand-shelves-Chinese-submarine-deal-after-public-backlash.

109 Greg Waldron, 'Myanmar Signs Order for Six Su-30s', FlightGlobal, 23 January 2018, https://www.flightglobal.com/myanmar-signs-order-for-six-su-30s/126797.article#.

110 Mohammad Rubaiyat Rahman, 'What Myanmar's New Amphibious Ship Says About Its Naval Ambitions', Diplomat, 9 November 2019, https://thediplomat.com/2019/11/what-myanmars-new-amphibious-ship-says-about-its-naval-ambitions; and Anthony Davis, 'Myanmar Air Force Commissions 10 New Aircraft to Boost Counter-insurgency Capabilities', Janes, 10 June 2020, https://www.janes.com/defence-news/news-detail/myanmar-air-force-commissions-10-new-aircraft-to-boost-counter-insurgency-capabilities.

111 Marwaan Macan-Markar, 'Myanmar Embraces Russian Arms to Offset China's Influence', Nikkei Asia, 9 February 2021, https://asia.nikkei.com/Spotlight/Myanmar-Coup/Myanmar-embraces-Russian-arms-to-offset-China-s-influence.

112 A typical example involved the Philippine Air Force flying combat aircraft over the 'swarming and threatening presence' of more than 200 boats allegedly crewed by Chinese maritime-militia personnel at Whitsun Reef, inside the Philippines' EEZ, in March 2021. See 'Philippine Fighter Jets Sent to Fly Over Chinese Boats in S. China Sea', Straits Times, 29 March 2021, https://www.straitstimes.com/asia/philippine-fighter-jets-sent-to-fly-over-chinese-boats-in-s-china-sea.

113 See Tim Huxley, 'Why Asia's "Arms Race" Is Not Quite What It Seems', World Economic Forum, 12 September 2018, https://www.weforum.org/agenda/2018/09/asias-arms-race-and-why-it-doesnt-matter.

Chapter Four

1   For further reading on the contested concept of 'hybrid warfare', see Lawrence Freedman, *The Future of War: A History* (New York: PublicAffairs, 2017), pp. 222–9.

2   Panikkar's address to the Indian School of International Studies, New Delhi, 13 February 1961, reproduced in Sardar K.M. Panikkar, 'International Studies', *International Studies*, vol. 22, no. 3, July 1985, p. 193. See also K.M. Panikkar, *Geographical Factors in Indian History* (Bombay: Bharatiya Vidya Bhavan, 1955).

3   For further reading on the concept of the 'Great Game', see Seymour Becker, 'The "Great Game": The History of an Evocative Phrase', *Asian Affairs*, vol. 43, no. 1, 2012, pp. 61–80; Malcolm Yapp, 'The Legend of the Great Game', Elie Kedouri Memorial Lecture, British Academy, London, 16 May 2000; and Peter John Brobst, *Future of the Great Game: Sir Olaf Caroe, India's Independence and the Defence of Asia* (Akron, OH: University of Akron Press, 2005).

4   See John K. Cooley, *Unholy Wars: Afghanistan, America and International Terrorism* (London: Pluto Press, 2000); and John Prados, 'Notes on the CIA's Secret War in Afghanistan', *Journal of American History*, vol. 89, no. 2, 2002, pp. 466–71.

5   Samina Ahmed, 'Pakistan's Nuclear Weapons Program: Turning Points and Choices', *International Security*, vol. 23, no. 4, Spring 1999, pp. 178–204. See also Dennis Kux, *Disenchanted Allies: The United States and Pakistan, 1947–2000* (Washington DC: Johns Hopkins University Press, 2001).

6   See Rajiv Chandrasekharan, *Little America: The War Within the War for Afghanistan* (New York: Alfred A. Knopf, 2012); Christopher Kolenda, 'Slow Failure: Understanding America's Quagmire in Afghanistan', *Journal of Strategic Studies*, vol. 42, no. 7, 2019, pp. 992–1014; and Carter Malkasian, 'How the Good War Went Bad: America's Slow Motion Failure in Afghanistan', *Foreign Affairs*, vol. 99, no. 2, March/April 2020, pp. 77–91.

7   Mark Landler, 'The Afghan War and the Evolution of Obama', *New York Times*, 1 January 2017, https://www.nytimes.com/2017/01/01/world/asia/obama-afghanistan-war.html.

8   US, Department of State, 'Agreement for Bringing Peace to Afghanistan between the Islamic Emirate of Afghanistan which is not Recognized by the United States as a State and is Known as the Taliban and the United States of America', 29 February 2020, https://www.state.gov/wp-content/uploads/2020/02/Agreement-For-Bringing-Peace-to-Afghanistan-02.29.20.pdf.

9   'Donald Trump Risks Handing Afghanistan to the Taliban', *The Economist*, 21 November 2020, https://www.economist.com/leaders/2020/11/19/donald-trump-risks-handing-afghanistan-to-the-taliban.

10 See, for example, Zachary Constantino, 'The India–Pakistan Rivalry in Afghanistan', United States Institute of Peace *Special Report*, 29 January 2020, https://www.usip.org/publications/2020/01/india-pakistan-rivalry-afghanistan.

11 For a discussion of the complex relationship between Pakistan and the Taliban, see Tricia Bacon, 'Slipping the

Leash: Pakistan's Relationship with the Afghan Taliban', *Survival: Global Politics and Strategy*, vol. 60, no. 5, October–November 2018, pp. 159–80.

12 See Satinder Lambah, *The Durand Line* (New Delhi: Aspen Institute, 2011).

13 India, Ministry of External Affairs, 'Text of Agreement on Strategic Partnership between Republic of India and the Islamic Republic of Afghanistan', 4 October 2011, https://mea.gov.in/bilateral-documents.htm?dtl/5383/Text+of+Agreement+on+Strategic+Partnership+between+the+Republic+of+India+and+the+Islamic+Republic+of+Afghanistan.

14 Gurmeet Kanwal, 'If Invited, India Must Send Troops to Kabul', *Tribune* (India), 11 February 2020, https://www.tribuneindia.com/news/comment/if-invited-india-must-send-troops-to-kabul-39015; Prakash Katoch, 'Sending Troops to Afghanistan Would Be Ludicrous', *Indian Defence Review*, 15 February 2020, http://www.indiandefencereview.com/news/sending-troops-to-afghanistan-would-be-ludicrous/; and Avinash Paliwal, 'India Must Support Its Allies in Kabul', *Hindustan Times*, 24 February 2020, https://www.hindustantimes.com/analysis/india-must-support-its-allies-in-kabul/story-obw9seh5gQu7dq9hAvnJqJ.html.

15 'Modi Questions Pak. on Rights Abuses in Balochistan', *Hindu*, 15 August 2016, https://www.thehindu.com/news/national/Modi-questions-Pak.-on-rights-abuses-in-Balochistan-PoK/article14571403.ece; and Ashan Butt, 'What the Kulbhushan Jadhav Saga Reveals About India and Pakistan's Balochistan Problems', *Diplomat*, 11 January 2018, https://thediplomat.com/2018/01/what-the-kulbhushan-jadhav-saga-reveals-about-india-and-pakistans-balochistan-problems.

16 For a review of the crises during the period 1987–2002, see P.R. Chari, Pervaiz Iqbal Cheema and Stephen P. Cohen, *Four Crises and a Peace Process: American Engagement in South Asia* (Washington DC: Brookings Institution Press, 2007). For a later study that includes the 2008 tensions, see Michael Krepon and Nate Cohn (eds), *Crises in South Asia: Trends and Consequences* (Washington DC: Stimson Center, 2011); and Sameer Lalwani et al., 'From Kargil to Balakot: Southern Asian Crisis Dynamics and Future Trajectories', Stimson Center, 2020.

17 For the history and complexities of the Jammu and Kashmir dispute, see Alastair Lamb, *Kashmir: A Disputed Legacy, 1846–1990* (Karachi: Oxford University Press, 1991); and Victoria Schofield, *Kashmir in Conflict: India, Pakistan and the Unending War* (London: I.B. Tauris, 2010).

18 For a comprehensive assessment, see P.R. Chari and Pervaiz Iqbal Cheema, *The Shimla Agreement, 1972: Its Wasted Promise* (New Delhi: Manohar, 2001).

19 See T.V. Paul, 'Chinese Pakistani Nuclear Missile Ties and Balance of Power Politics', *Nonproliferation Review*, vol. 10, no. 2, 2003, pp. 1–9; and Shirley A. Kan, *China and Proliferation of Weapons of Mass Destruction and Missiles* (Washington DC: Congressional Research Service, 2009).

20 See Ashley J. Tellis, C. Christine Fair and Jamison Jo Medby, *Limited Conflicts under the Nuclear Umbrella: Indian and Pakistani Lessons from the Kargil Crisis* (Santa Monica, CA: Rand, 2001); and Peter Lavoy (ed.), *Asymmetric Warfare in South Asia: The Causes and Consequences of the Kargil Conflict* (Cambridge: Cambridge University Press, 2009).

21 See Chari, Cheema and Cohen, *Four Crises and a Peace Process*.

22 For insights into the debate in New Delhi following the November 2008 Mumbai terror attacks, see Pranab Samanta, 'How India Debated a War with Pakistan That November', *Indian Express*, 26 November 2010, p. 1.

23 'India's Surgical Strikes Across the LoC: Full Statement by DGMO Lt Gen Ranbir Singh', *Hindustan Times*, 29 September 2016, https://www.hindustantimes.com/india-news/india-s-surgical-strikes-across-loc-full-statement-by-dgmo-lt-gen-ranbir-singh/story-Q5yrpogjvxKPGazDzAnVsM.html.

24 For an insightful discussion, see Ashley Tellis, 'Smoldering Volcano: Pakistan and Terrorism after Balakot', Carnegie Endowment for International Peace, 14 March 2019, https://carnegieendowment.org/2019/03/14/smoldering-volcano-pakistan-and-terrorism-after-balakot-pub-78593.

25 See, for example, Arzan Tarapore, 'Balakot, Deterrence and Risk: How This India–Pakistan Crisis Will Shape the Next', War on the Rocks, 11 March 2019, https://warontherocks.com/2019/03/balakot-deterrence-and-risk; and Patrick C. Bratton, 'The Not So Gray Zone in South Asia', *Comparative Strategy*, vol. 39, no. 1, 2020, pp. 41–61.

26 Tellis, 'Smoldering Volcano: Pakistan and Terrorism after Balakot'.

27 World Bank, GDP by country 2019, https://databank.worldbank.org/data/download/GDP.pdf.

28 For a comparison in terms of nominal GDP, see the World Bank data, https://data.worldbank.org/indicator/NY.GDP.MKTP.CD?end=2019&most_recent_year_desc=true&start=1960.

29 *Ibid.*

30 See, for example, Abhijnan Rej, 'Government Misspend on Defence Will Widen Gap between Intent and Capability', Firstpost, 25 March 2019, https://www.firstpost.com/india/government-misspend-on-defence-will-widen-gap-between-intent-and-capability-6321261.html.

31 Ashley Tellis, 'The Merits of Dehyphenation: Explaining U.S. Success in Engaging India and Pakistan', *Washington Quarterly*, vol. 31, no. 4, 2008, pp. 21–42.

32 US, Department of Defense, and India, Ministry of Defence, 'New Framework for the U.S–India Defense Relationship', 28 June 2005, http://library.rumsfeld.com/doclib/sp/3211/2005-06-28%20New%20Framework%20for%20the%20US-India%20Defense%20Relationship.pdf. See also White House, 'Joint Statement Between President George W. Bush and Prime Minister Manmohan Singh', 18 July 2005, http://georgewbush-whitehouse.archives.gov/news/releases/2005/07/20050718-6.html.

33 Christopher Colley and Sumit Ganguly, 'The Obama Administration and India', in Oliver Turner and Inderjeet Parmar (eds), *The United States and the Indo-Pacific: Obama's Legacy and the Trump Transition* (Manchester: Manchester University Press, 2020), pp. 44–62.

34 'US Tilt Towards India Creates an Imbalance in South Asia: Pakistan Envoy', *Economic Times*, 8 April 2018, https://economictimes.indiatimes.com/news/defence/us-tilt-towards-india-creates-an-imbalance-in-south-asia-pakistan-envoy/articleshow/63667318.cms?from=mdr.

35 Sitara Noor, 'Pulwama/Balakot and the Evolving Role of Third Parties

in India–Pakistan Crises', Visiting Fellow *Policy Memo*, Stimson Center, 25 March 2020, https://www.stimson.org/2020/pulwama-balakot-and-the-evolving-role-of-third-parties-in-india-pakistan-crises.

36 Nidhi Razdan, 'How the US, UAE and Saudi Arabia Put Pressure on Pakistan', NDTV.com, 1 March 2019, https://www.ndtv.com/india-news/abhinandan-varthaman-release-how-the-us-uae-and-saudi-arabia-put-pressure-on-pakistan-2000874.

37 Michael Kugelman, 'An Obscure Organisation with Outsize Importance', Asia Dispatches, Wilson Center, 25 June 2019, https://www.wilsoncenter.org/blog-post/obscure-organization-outsize-importance.

38 Laya Maheshwari, 'How the Indian Government Changed the Legal Status of Jammu and Kashmir', Lawfare, 12 August 2019, https://www.lawfareblog.com/how-indian-government-changed-legal-status-jammu-and-kashmir.

39 Dipanjan Roy Chaudhuri, 'P4 Foils China's Attempt to Discuss Kashmir at UNSC', *Economic Times*, 19 December 2019, https://economictimes.indiatimes.com/news/defence/p4-foils-chinas-attempt-to-discuss-kashmir-at-unsc/articleshow/72861820.cms.

40 C. Raja Mohan, 'Terms of Engagement', *Indian Express*, 13 June 2019, https://indianexpress.com/article/opinion/columns/india-pakistan-relations-imran-khan-pm-modi-talks-5777730.

41 Ashley Tellis, 'Pakistan.Will.Not.Change', Carnegie Endowment for International Peace, 25 February 2019, https://carnegieendowment.org/2019/02/25/pakistan.will.not.change-pub-78440; and Paul Stani-

land, 'India's New Security Order', War on the Rocks, 17 December 2019, https://warontherocks.com/2019/12/indias-new-security-order.

42 For a comprehensive review of the bilateral relationship, see Kanti Bajpai, Selina Ho and Manjari Chatterjee Miller (eds), *Routledge Handbook of China–India Relations* (New York: Routledge, 2020).

43 For an analysis of the India–China military confidence-building measures in the 1990s, see Waheguru Pal, Singh Sidhu and Jing-dong Yuan, *China and India: Cooperation or Conflict?* (New Delhi: India Research Press, 2003), pp. 113–40; and Jeff Smith, *Cold Peace: China–India Rivalry in the Twenty-first Century* (Lanham, MD: Lexington Books, 2015).

44 Brahma Chellaney, 'Vajpayee Kowtows to China', *Japan Times*, 8 July 2003, https://www.japantimes.co.jp/opinion/2003/07/08/commentary/vajpayee-kowtows-to-china.

45 John W. Garver, 'China's Kashmir Policies', *India Review*, vol. 3, no. 1, 2004, pp. 1–24.

46 India, Ministry of External Affairs, 'Country Brief on China', September 2019, http://mea.gov.in/Portal/ForeignRelation/china_brief_sep_2019.pdf.

47 India, Ministry of External Affairs, 'Agreement between the Government of the Republic of India and the Government of the People's Republic of China on the Political Parameters and Guiding Principles for the Settlement of the India–China Boundary Question', 11 April 2005, https://www.mea.gov.in/bilateral-documents.htm?dtl/6534/Agreement+between+the+Government+of+the+Republic+of+India+and+the+Government+of+the+Peoples+

Republic+of+China+on+the+Political+ Parameters+and+Guiding+Principles +f o r + t h e + S e t t l e m e n t + o f + t h e + IndiaChina+Boundary+Question. See also Mihir Bhonsale, 'Breaking the Border Juggernaut: India–China at 70', Diplomatist, 4 March 2020, http://diplomatist.com/2020/03/04/ breaking-the-border-juggernaut-india-china-at-70.

48 For a recent discussion of the multiple issues involved, see Phunchok Stobdan, *The Great Game in the Buddhist Himalayas: India and China's Quest for Strategic Dominance* (Delhi: Penguin, 2019).

49 Rajeshwari Rajagopalan and Pulkit Mohan, 'PLA Joint Exercises in Tibet: Implications for India', *ORF Occasional Paper*, no. 238, Observer Research Foundation, February 2020, https://www.orfonline.org/ research/pla-joint-exercises-in-tibet-implications-for-india-61735.

50 Gurmeet Kanwal, 'China's New War Concepts for 21st Century Battlefields', *IPCS Issue Brief*, no. 48, July 2007, http://www.ipcs.org/issue_briefs/ issue_brief_pdf/1577903632IPCS-IssueBrief-No48.pdf.

51 For further reading on the 'Active Defence' doctrine, see M. Taylor Fravel, *Active Defense: China's Military Strategy Since 1949* (Princeton, NJ: Princeton University Press, 2019). See also Kevin McCauley, 'Himalayan Impasse: How China Would Fight an Indian Border Conflict', *China Brief*, vol. 17, no. 12, 20 September 2017, https://jamestown.org/program/him-alayan-impasse-how-china-would-fight-an-indian-border-conflict.

52 Arun Sahgal, 'China's Military Modernization: Responses from India', in Ashley J. Tellis and Travis Tanner

(eds), *Strategic Asia 2012–13: China's Military Challenge* (Seattle, WA: National Bureau of Asian Research, 2012), p. 294. See also Yogesh Joshi and Anit Mukherjee, 'From Denial to Punishment: The Security Dilemma and Changes in India's Military Strategy Towards China', *Asian Security*, vol. 15, no. 1, 2019, pp. 25–43.

53 For a detailed review of the incursions, see Mihir Bhonsale, 'Understanding Sino-Indian Border Issues: An Analysis of Incidents Reported in the Indian Media', *ORF Occasional Paper*, no. 143, Observer Research Foundation, February 2018, https://www.orfonline.org/ wp-content/uploads/2018/02/ORF_ Occasional_Paper_143_India-China.pdf.

54 See Deldan Kunzes Angmo Nyachu, 'The Depsang Standoff at the India–China Border along the LAC', *Himalayan and Central Asian Studies*, vol. 17, no. 3 and 4, July–December 2013, pp. 171–83.

55 Interview with a senior Indian official, September–October 2014.

56 See Joel Wuthnow, Satu Limaye and Nilanthi Samaranayake, 'Doklam One Year Later: China's Long Game in the Himalayas', War on the Rocks, 7 June 2018, https://warontherocks. com/2018/06/doklam-one-year-later-chinas-long-game-in-the-himalayas.

57 Interview with a senior Indian official engaged with the China relationship, December 2019.

58 Steven Lee Myers, 'Beijing Takes Its South China Sea Strategy to the Himalayas', *New York Times*, 27 November 2020, https://www.nytimes. com/2020/11/27/world/asia/china-bhutan-india-border.html.

59 Amy Kazmin and Christian Shepherd, 'Himalayan Border Tension Is "Accident Waiting to Happen"', *Financial*

Times, 7 September 2020, p. 4.

60 Steven Lee Myers and Sameer Yasir, 'India and China Dial Back Tensions at Himalayan Border', *New York Times*, 12 September 2020, p. 12.

61 M. Taylor Fravel, 'China and India Are Pulling Back from the Brink. They've Created a Buffer Zone and Started Talks', *Washington Post*, 3 March 2021, https://www.washingtonpost.com/politics/2021/03/03/china-india-are-pulling-back-brink-theyve-created-buffer-zone-started-talks.

62 Naeem Salik, 'Pakistan's Nuclear Force Structure in 2025', *Regional Insight,* Carnegie Endowment for International Peace, 30 June 2016, https://carnegieendowment.org/2016/06/30/pakistan-s-nuclear-force-structure-in-2025-pub-63912; and Sadia Tasleem and Toby Dalton, 'Nuclear Emulation: Pakistan's Nuclear Trajectory', *Washington Quarterly*, vol. 41, no. 4, Winter 2018, pp. 135–55.

63 Arms Control Association, 'Nuclear Weapons: Who Has What at a Glance', August 2020, https://www.armscontrol.org/factsheets/Nuclearweaponswhohaswhat.

64 India, Ministry of External Affairs, 'Suo-Motu Statement by Prime Minister Dr. Manmohan Singh on Discussions on Civil Nuclear Energy Cooperation with the US: Implementation of India's Separation Plan', 7 March 2006, https://www.mea.gov.in/Speeches-Statements.htm?dtl/2167/SuoMotu+Statement+by+Prime+Minister+Dr+Manmohan+Singh+on+Discussions+on+Civil+Nuclear+Energy+Cooperation+with+the+US+Implementation+of+Indias+Separation+Plan.

65 Christopher Clary and Vipin Narang, 'India's Counterforce Temptations: Strategic Dilemmas, Doctrine and

Capabilities', *International Security*, vol. 43, no. 3, Winter 2018/19, pp. 7–52. Some Indian analysts, however, question the assessment that New Delhi is drifting towards a counterforce doctrine. See Rajesh Rajagopalan, 'India and Counterforce: A Question of Evidence', *ORF Occasional Paper*, no. 247, Observer Research Foundation, May 2020, https://www.orfonline.org/research/india-and-counterforce-a-question-of-evidence-66126.

66 For an assessment, see Walter C. Ladwig III, 'A Cold Start for Hot Wars? The Indian Army's New Limited War Doctrine', *International Security*, vol. 32, no. 3, Winter 2007/08, pp. 158–90. For an Indian view, see Ali Ahmed, 'Towards a Proactive Military Strategy: "Cold Start and Stop"', *Strategic Analysis*, vol. 35, no. 3, 2011, pp. 401–16.

67 For a Pakistani assessment, see Masood Ur Rehman Khattak, 'Indian Military's Cold Start Doctrine: Capabilities, Limitations and Possible Response from Pakistan', South Asian Strategic Stability Institute research paper 31, March 2011.

68 See Shashank Joshi, 'India's Military Instrument: A Doctrine Stillborn', *Journal of Strategic Studies*, vol. 36, no. 4, 2013, pp. 512–40.

69 See Ashley J. Tellis, 'The Evolution of U.S.–Indian Ties: Missile Defense in an Emerging Strategic Relationship', *International Security*, vol. 30, no. 4, Spring 2006, p. 125.

70 Rajat Pandit, 'Missile Shield Over Delhi: India May Buy NASAMS-II Air Defence System From US', *Times of India*, 11 February 2020, https://timesofindia.indiatimes.com/india/missile-shield-over-delhi-india-may-buy-nasams-ii-air-defence-system-

from-us/articleshow/74071029.cms; and Franz-Stefan Gady, 'Report: India's Homemade Anti-ballistic Missile Shield Ready', *Diplomat*, 8 January 2020, https://thediplomat.com/2020/01/report-indias-homemade-anti-ballistic-missile-shield-ready.

71 Zachary Keck, 'Pakistan Has Just Tested the Ultimate Nuclear Missile', *National Interest*, 9 March 2018, https://nationalinterest.org/blog/the-buzz/pakistan-has-just-tested-the-ultimate-nuclear-missile-24834; and Haris Bilal Malik, 'Assessing India's Enhanced Air-defence Shield with Reference to Pakistan's MIRV Capabilities', *Modern Diplomacy*, 18 February 2020, https://moderndiplomacy.eu/2020/02/18/assessing-indias-enhanced-air-defence-shield-with-reference-to-pakistans-mirv-capabilities.

72 Kenneth N. Luongo, 'Loose Nukes in New Neighborhoods: The Next Generation of Proliferation Prevention', *Arms Control Association*, May 2009, https://www.armscontrol.org/act/2009-05/features/loose-nukes-new-neighborhoods-next-generation-proliferation-prevention. See also Paul K. Kerr and Mary Beth Nikitin, 'Pakistan's Nuclear Weapons', CRS Report for Congress, 1 August 2016, http://www.fas.org/sgp/crs/nuke/RL34248.pdf; Pervez Hoodbhoy and Zia Mian, 'Securing Pakistan's Nuclear Arsenal: The Threat from Within', in Brech Volders and Tom Sauer (eds), *Nuclear Terrorism: Countering the Threat* (New York: Routledge, 2016), pp. 182–94; and Rizwan Naseer and Musrat Ameen, 'Nuclear Terrorism: Hype, Risk and Reality – A Case of Pakistan', *South Asian Studies*, vol. 34, no. 2, 2019, pp. 383–99.

73 David Sanger and William Broad, 'US Secretly Aids Pakistan in Guarding Nuclear Arms', *New York Times*, 18 November 2007, https://www.nytimes.com/2007/11/18/washington/18nuke.html; Jeffrey Goldberg and Marc Abinder, 'The Pentagon's Secret Plans to Secure Pakistan's Nuclear Arsenal', *National Journal*, 9 November 2011, https://www.nti.org/gsn/article/the-pentagons-secret-plans-to-secure-pakistans-nuclear-arsenal; Shajjad Shaukat, 'Conspiracy to "Denuclearise" Pakistan', *News*, August 2012, https://web.archive.org/web/20160316202306/http://www.newscenterpk.com/conspiracy-to-denuclearise-pakistan; and Brig Asif Haroon Raja, 'The US Veiled Designs Against Pakistan No More Secret', *Opinion Maker*, 10 July 2012, https://web.archive.org/web/20130211150624/http://www.opinion-maker.org/2012/07/us-attacking-pakistan.

74 For Pakistan's perception, see Cyril Almeida, 'Pakistan the "Most Bullied" U.S. Ally', *Dawn*, 29 November 2010, http://dawn.com/2010/11/30/pakistan-the-most-bullied-us-ally.

75 For WikiLeaks reports on denuclearising Pakistan, see Declan Walsh and Julian Borger, 'US Embassy Cables: U.S. and Pakistan Deny Revelations of Mutual Mistrust', *Guardian*, 1 December 2010, http://www.guardian.co.uk/world/2010/dec/01/wikileaks-pakistan-us-suspicion-mistrust.

76 See, for example, 'Joint Statement by President Obama and Prime Minister Nawaz Sharif', 23 October 2013, https://obamawhitehouse.archives.gov/the-press-office/2013/10/23/joint-statement-president-obama-and-prime-minister-nawaz-sharif.

77 Toby Dalton and Jaclyn Tandler,

'Understanding the Arms "Race" in South Asia', Carnegie Endowment for International Peace, September 2012, p. 1.

[78] W.P.S. Sidhu, 'Evolution of India's Nuclear Doctrine', *Occasional Paper*, no. 9, Centre for Policy Research, April 2004, p. 8.

[79] Rikhi Jaipal, 'The Indian Nuclear Explosion', *International Security*, vol. 1, no. 4, Spring 1977, pp. 44–51.

[80] K. Subrahmanyam, who was involved in nuclear planning, asserts that Rajiv Gandhi ordered the weaponisation of the programme in 1988. Author's interview in 1998.

[81] Andrew Kennedy, 'India's Nuclear Odyssey: Implicit Umbrellas, Diplomatic Disappointments, and the Bomb', *International Security*, vol. 36, no. 2, Fall 2011, p. 143.

[82] See Jonathan McLaughlin, 'India's Expanding Missile Force', Wisconsin Project on Nuclear Arms Control, 20 October 2020, https://www.wisconsinproject.org/indias-expanding-missile-force. For a critical questioning of the need for the ICBM and the SLBM, see Frank O'Donnell and Alexander Bollfrass, 'India Is Building Nuclear Submarines and ICBMs. That's a $14bn Mistake', *Bulletin of the Atomic Scientists*, 26 February 2020, https://thebulletin.org/2020/02/india-is-building-nuclear-submarines-and-icbms-thats-a-14-billion-mistake.

[83] See 'Satellite Imagery Reveals Presence of Chinese Nuclear Submarine in Karachi', *Economic Times*, 12 July 2018, https://economictimes.indiatimes.com/news/defence/chinese-nuclear-submarine-spotted-at-karachi-revealed-in-satellite-imagery/articleshow/56375723.cms.

[84] Vishnu Som, 'Pakistan Likely to Acquire Chinese Nuclear Attack Submarines', NDTV.com, 10 January 2017, https://www.ndtv.com/world-news/pakistan-likely-to-acquire-chinese-nuclear-attack-submarines-ndtv-exclusive-1647370.

[85] See Robert Einhorn and W.P.S. Sidhu, 'The Strategic Chain: Linking Pakistan, India, China, and the United States', Arms Control and Non-Proliferation Series Paper no. 14, Brookings Institution, March 2017, p. 14.

[86] Condoleezza Rice, 'Promoting the National Interest', *Foreign Affairs*, vol. 79, no. 1, January/February 2000, pp. 45–62.

[87] See Mohammed Ayoob, 'India, Pakistan and Super-power Rivalry', *World Today*, vol. 38, no. 5, May 1982, pp. 194–202; and C. Raja Mohan, 'India and the Balance of Power', *Foreign Affairs*, vol. 85, no. 4, July/August 2006, pp. 17–32.

[88] John W. Garver, 'The Future of the Sino-Pakistani Entente Cordiale', in Michael R. Chambers (ed.), *South Asia in 2020: Future Strategic Balances and Alliances* (Carlisle, PA: Strategic Studies Institute, US Army War College, November 2002), p. 385.

[89] See Evan A. Feigenbaum, 'India's Rise, America's Interest', *Foreign Affairs*, vol. 89, no. 2, March/April 2010, pp. 76–91. See also 'India's Rise and the Promise of U.S.–Indian Partnership', speech delivered by Under Secretary of State William J. Burns, Council on Foreign Relations, Washington DC, 1 June 2010, https://2009-2017.state.gov/p/us/rm/2010/136718.htm.

[90] Ashton Carter and Manohar Parrikar, 'Framework for the U.S.–India Defense Relationship', available at Manohar Parrikar Institute for Defence Studies and Analyses, 28

June 2005, https://idsa.in/resources/documents/Ind-US-Def-Rel-28.06.05.

91 Zach Montague, 'U.S.–India Defense Ties Grow Closer as Shared Concerns in Asia Loom', *New York Times*, 20 November 2019, https://www.nytimes.com/2019/11/20/world/asia/india-military-exercises-trump.html.

92 US, Department of State, 'US Security Cooperation with India: A Fact Sheet', 4 June 2019, https://www.state.gov/us-security-cooperation-with-india.

93 Jerome Conley, 'Indo-Russian Military and Nuclear Cooperation: Implications for U.S. Security Interests', *INSS Occasional Paper*, USAF Institute for National Security Studies, February 2000; and Yogesh Joshi, 'Russia: An All-weather Defence Partner', BusinessLine, 2 July 2019, https://www.thehindubusinessline.com/opinion/russia-an-all-weather-defence-partner/article28263881.ece.

94 Nivedita Kapoor, 'Russia–Pakistan Relations and Its Impact on India', *Raisina Debates paper*, Observer Research Foundation, 3 July 2019, https://www.orfonline.org/expert-speak/russia-pakistan-relations-impact-india-52715.

95 Vidya Nadkarni, 'Russia: A Balancer in India–China Relations?', in Kanti Bajpai, Selina Ho and Manjari Chatterjee Miller (eds), *Routledge Handbook of China–India Relations*, pp. 380–95.

96 Gu Jing and Neil Renwick, 'Contested Partnership: China and India in a Changing BRICS', in Kanti Bajpai, Selina Ho and Manjari Chatterjee Miller (eds), *Routledge Handbook of China–India Relations*, pp. 349–62.

97 Zahid Ahmed, Sarfraz Ahmed and Stuti Bhatnagar, 'Conflict or Cooperation? India and Pakistan in Shanghai Cooperation Organisation', *Pacific Focus*, vol. 34, no. 1, April 2019, pp. 5–30.

98 C. Raja Mohan, 'India's Pivot to the United States', *East Asia Forum Quarterly*, vol. 12, no. 1, January–March 2020, pp. 6–8.

99 Rajesh Rajagopalan, 'Did India Lose China?', *Washington Quarterly*, vol. 42, no. 1, Spring 2019, pp. 71–87.

100 See, for example, Subrata K. Mitra and Srikanth Thaliyakkattil, 'Bhutan and Sino-Indian Rivalry: The Price of Proximity', *Asian Survey*, vol. 58, no. 2, March/April 2018, pp. 240–60.

101 See Sudha Ramachandran, 'China's Bhutan Gambit', *Diplomat*, 23 July 2020, https://thediplomat.com/2020/07/chinas-bhutan-gambit.

102 See Sukh Deo Muni and Tan Tai Yong (eds), *A Resurgent China: South Asian Perspectives* (Delhi: Routledge, 2012).

103 Zhu Yongbiao, 'China's Afghanistan Policy since 9/11: Stages and Prospects', *Asian Survey*, vol. 58, no. 2, March/April 2018, pp. 281–301.

Chapter Five

1   See Samuel P. Huntington, 'Arms Races: Prerequisites and Results', *Public Policy*, vol. 8, no. 1, 1958, pp. 41–86.

2   Laxman Kumar Behera, 'India's Defence Budget 2019–2020', *IDSA Issue Brief*, 8 June 2019, https://idsa.in/system/files/issuebrief/indias-defence-budget-lkbehera.pdf.

3   World Bank, *Global Economic Prospects* (Washington DC: World Bank, June 2020), p. 4.

4   For further reading, see William Choong, 'The Return of the Indo-Pacific Strategy: An Assessment', *Australian Journal of International Affairs*, vol. 73, no. 5, 2019, pp. 415–30.

5   US, Department of Defense, 'Indo-Pacific Strategy Report: Preparedness, Partnerships, and Promoting a Networked Region', June 2019, https://media.defense.gov/2019/Jul/01/2002152311/-1/-1/1/department-of-defense-indo-pacific-strategy-report-2019.pdf

6   Kei Koga, 'Japan's "Indo-Pacific" Question: Countering China or Shaping a New Regional Order', *International Affairs*, vol. 96, no. 1, 2020, p. 57.

7   Australian Government, '2017 Foreign Policy White Paper', 2017, p. 1, https://www.dfat.gov.au/sites/default/files/2017-foreign-policy-white-paper.pdf.

8   For further reading, see Joanne Wallis, 'Australia's One Step Forward, Two Steps Back in the Pacific', *East Asia Forum*, 21 June 2019, https://www.eastasiaforum.org/2019/06/21/australias-one-step-forward-two-steps-back-in-the-pacific.

9   US, Department of Defense, 'Indo-Pacific Strategy Report: Preparedness, Partnerships, and Promoting a Net-worked Region', p. 8.

10 Shri Narendra Modi, 'Keynote Address', 17th Asia Security Summit: The IISS Shangri-La Dialogue, 1 June 2018, https://www.iiss.org/events/shangri-la-dialogue/shangri-la-dialogue-2018.

11 Koga, 'Japan's "Indo-Pacific" Question: Countering China or Shaping a New Regional Order', p. 51.

12 Phillip Coorey, 'Australia Mulls Rival to China's "Belt and Road" with the US, Japan, India', *Australian Financial Review*, 18 February 2018, https://www.afr.com/politics/australia-mulls-rival-to-chinas-belt-and-road-with-us-japan-india-20180216-how7k5.

13 Andrew Tillet, 'Australia to Team Up with US, Japan in Regional Infrastructure Rival to China', *Australian Financial Review*, 31 July 2018, https://www.afr.com/politics/australia-to-team-up-with-us-japan-in-regional-infrastructure-rival-to-china-20180731-h13cqx.

14 Ian Hall, 'The Struggle to Maintain Momentum in the Australia–India Partnership', *Asan Forum*, 11 February 2019, http://www.theasanforum.org/the-struggle-to-maintain-momentum-in-the-australia-india-partnership.

15 Lavina Lee, 'Assessing the Quad: Prospects and Limitations of Quadrilateral Cooperation for Advancing Australia's Interests', Lowy Institute for International Policy, 19 May 2020, https://www.lowyinstitute.org/publications/assessing-quad-prospects-and-limitations-quadrilateral-cooperation-advancing-australia.

16 Dinakar Peri and Suhasini Haidar, 'India Open to Including Australia in Malabar Naval Exercise', *Hindu*,

3 June 2020, https://www.thehindu.com/news/national/india-open-to-including-australia-in-malabar-naval-exercise/article31740876.ece; and Rory Medcalf, 'Australia's Long Courtship of India Is Bearing Fruit', *Australian Financial Review*, 9 June 2020, https://www.afr.com/world/asia/australias-long-courtship-of-india-is-bearing-fruit-20200609-p550p5.

17 Ankit Panda, 'Australia Returns to the Malabar Exercise', *Diplomat*, 19 October 2020, https://thediplomat.com/2020/10/australia-returns-to-the-malabar-exercise.

18 See, for example, Ankit Panda, 'US, India, Japan, Philippine Navies Demonstrate Joint Presence in South China Sea', *Diplomat*, 11 May 2019, https://thediplomat.com/2019/05/us-india-japan-philippine-navies-demonstrate-joint-presence-in-south-china-sea.

19 Matthew Knott, 'Independence Actually: Marise Payne's Unmistakable Message to the US', *Sydney Morning Herald*, 29 July 2020, https://www.smh.com.au/world/north-america/independence-actually-marise-paynes-unmistakable-message-to-the-us-20200729-p55gfi.html.

20 C. Raja Mohan, 'The Case for Alliance', *Indian Express*, 14 September 2017, https://indianexpress.com/article/opinion/columns/the-case-for-alliance.

21 For example, while Beijing's island-building efforts in the South China Sea and the subsequent militarisation of these features has, in one view, augmented its ability to control these waters in all scenarios short of conflict, this programme can also be read as a sign of weakness: an attempt to compensate for its lack of an aircraft-carrier capability equivalent to that fielded by the US.

22 US, Department of Defense, 'Military and Security Developments Involving the People's Republic of China 2019', May 2019, p. 6, https://media.defense.gov/2019/May/02/2002127082/-1/-1/1/2019_CHINA_MILITARY_POWER_REPORT.pdf.

23 Aaron Mehta, 'America's Greatest Advantage against China Is Slowly Eroding', *Defense News*, 15 February 2019, https://www.defensenews.com/pentagon/2019/02/15/americas-greatest-advantage-against-china-is-slowly-eroding.

24 Jonathan Cheng, 'Beijing Scraps GDP Target, a Bad Sign for World Reliant on China Growth', *Wall Street Journal*, 22 May 2020, https://www.wsj.com/articles/china-scraps-gdp-target-for-2020-11590111014?emailToken=c6e2f392071dfe789584ff226930727ahw2JfRMq5JhA3H/GauavdMRsR-P5R7v11Gm6KuFiFWmZEGoM9vY-4PLgoI1aWnsmIwWU74MsEeFQSX+8673FIwkw%3D%3D&reflink=article_copyURL_share.

25 James Kynge and Jonathan Wheatley, 'China Pulls Back from the World: Rethinking Xi's "Project of the Century"', *Financial Times*, 11 December 2020, https://www.ft.com/content/d9bd8059-d05c-4e6f-968b-1672241ec1f6.

26 Tristan Kenderdine and Niva Yau, 'China's Policy Banks Are Lending Differently, Not Less', *Diplomat*, 12 December 2020, https://thediplomat.com/2020/12/chinas-policy-banks-are-lending-differently-not-less.

27 For further reading, see Bates Gill and Yanzhong Huang, 'Sources and Limits of Chinese "Soft Power"', *Survival: Global Politics and Strategy*, vol. 48, no. 2, Summer 2006, pp. 17–36.

28 Brian Wong, 'China's Mask Diplomacy', *Diplomat*, 25 March 2020,

https://thediplomat.com/2020/03/chinas-mask-diplomacy.

29 See Euan Graham, 'U.S. Naval Standoff with China Fails to Reassure Regional Allies', *Foreign Policy*, 4 May 2020, https://foreignpolicy.com/2020/05/04/malaysia-south-china-sea-us-navy-drillship-standoff.

30 Joseph S. Nye, Jr, 'No, the Coronavirus Will Not Change the Global Order', *Foreign Policy*, 16 April 2020, https://foreignpolicy.com/2020/04/16/coronavirus-pandemic-china-united-states-power-competition.

31 Donald K. Emmerson, 'ASEAN Stumbles in Phnom Penh', *East Asia Forum*, 23 July 2012, https://www.eastasiaforum.org/2012/07/23/asean-stumbles-in-phnom-penh-2.

32 David Tweed and David Roman, 'Chinese–ASEAN Meeting on South China Sea Ends in Confusion', *Japan Times*, 15 June 2016, https://www.japantimes.co.jp/news/2016/06/15/asia-pacific/chinese-asean-meeting-south-china-sea-ends-confusion.

33 See Seng Tan, 'The 3rd ADMM-Plus: Did the Media Get It Right?', *RSIS Commentary*, no. 257, 26 November 2015, https://www.rsis.edu.sg/wp-content/uploads/2015/11/CO15257.pdf.

34 For further reading, see Tim Bouverie, *Appeasing Hitler: Chamberlain, Churchill and the Road to War* (London: The Bodley Head, 2019).

35 For further reading, see IISS, *Asia-Pacific Regional Security Assessment 2019* (London: IISS, 2019), pp. 199–217.

36 For further reading, see Geoffrey Blainey, *The Causes of War* (New York: The Free Press, 1973), pp. 127–45.

37 Hal Brands, 'If America and China Go to War, It Won't Be an Accident', *Bloomberg*, 7 August 2020, https://www.bloomberg.com/opinion/articles/2020-08-07/war-between-china-and-america-won-t-happen-by-accident.

38 Deputy Secretary of Defense Dr Kathleen Hicks (@DepSecDef), tweet, 26 February 2021, https://twitter.com/DepSecDef/status/1365339647769993217.

39 See, for example, Stein Tonnesson, *Explaining the East Asian Peace: A Research Story* (Copenhagen: Nordic Institute of Asian Studies Press, 2017).

40 Donald Kagan, *On the Origins of War and the Preservation of Peace* (New York: Doubleday, 1995), pp. 567–8.

41 For further reading, see 'Hypersonic Weapons and Strategic Stability', *IISS Strategic Comments*, vol. 26, no. 4, March 2020, https://www.iiss.org/~/publication/23a21359-6cb1-4355-b6be-f6aba4a5c1e9/hypersonic-weapons-and-strategic-stability.pdf.

42 See Tim Huxley, 'Why Asia's "Arms Race" Is Not Quite What It Seems', World Economic Forum, 12 September 2018, https://www.weforum.org/agenda/2018/09/asias-arms-race-and-why-it-doesnt-matter.

43 For a discussion of this point, see Avery Goldstein, 'First Things First: The Pressing Danger of Crisis Instability in U.S.–China Relations', *International Security*, vol. 37, no. 4, Spring 2013, p. 67; and Robert Ayson and Desmond Ball, 'Can a Sino-Japanese War Be Controlled?', *Survival: Global Politics and Strategy*, vol. 56, no. 6, December 2014–January 2015, pp. 135–66.

44 Herman Kahn, *On Escalation: Metaphors and Scenarios* (New Brunswick and London: Transaction Publishers, 2010), p. 39.

45 Rebecca Hersman, 'Wormhole Escalation in the New Nuclear Age', *Texas National Security Review*, Summer 2020, https://tnsr.org/2020/07/wormhole-

escalation-in-the-new-nuclear-age.

46 See David A. Welch, 'Crisis Management Mechanisms: Pathologies and Pitfalls', *CIGI Papers*, no. 40, September 2014, pp. 7–8.

47 Errol Morris, *The Fog of War: Eleven Lessons from the Life of Robert S. McNamara* (Culver City, CA: Columbia TriStar Home Entertainment, 2003).

48 See Phil Williams, *Crisis Management: Confrontation and Diplomacy in the Nuclear Age* (New York: John Wiley & Sons, 1976), p. 191.

49 For further reading, see David F. Winkler, 'The Evolution and Significance of the 1972 Incidents at Sea Agreement', *Journal of Strategic Studies*, vol. 28, no. 2, April 2005, pp. 361–77.

50 For further reading, see Kevin Rudd, 'Beware the Guns of August – in Asia: How to Keep U.S.–Chinese Tensions from Sparking a War', *Foreign Affairs*, 3 August 2020, https://www.foreignaffairs.com/articles/united-states/2020-08-03/beware-guns-august-asia.

51 See Ian Storey, 'As US–China Tensions Rise, What Is the Outlook on the South China Sea Dispute in 2020–2021?', *South China Morning Post*, 8 September 2020, https://www.scmp.com/week-asia/opinion/article/3100563/us-china-tensions-rise-what-outlook-south-china-sea-dispute-2020.

52 For further reading, see Rush Doshi, 'Improving Risk Reduction and Crisis Management in US–China Relations', in Ryan Hass, Ryan McElveen and Robert D. Williams (eds), 'The Future of US Policy Towards China: Recommendations for the Biden Administration', Brookings *China Center Monograph*, November 2020, pp. 69–71.

53 For further reading, see Alastair Iain Johnston, 'The Evolution of Interstate Security Crisis Management Theory and Practice in China', *Naval War College Review*, vol. 69, no. 1, Winter 2016, pp. 29–71.

54 Malcolm Chalmers, 'The Debate on a Regional Arms Register in Southeast Asia', *Pacific Review*, vol. 10, no. 1, 1997, pp. 104–23.

INDEX

Adelphi books are published six times a year by Routledge Journals, an imprint of Taylor & Francis, 4 Park Square, Milton Park, Abingdon, Oxfordshire OX14 4RN, UK.

A subscription to the institution print edition, ISSN 1944-5571, includes free access for any number of concurrent users across a local area network to the online edition, ISSN 1944-558X. Taylor & Francis has a flexible approach to subscriptions enabling us to match individual libraries' requirements. This journal is available via a traditional institutional subscription (either print with free online access, or online-only at a discount) or as part of our libraries, subject collections or archives. For more information on our sales packages please visit www.tandfonline.com/page/librarians.

2021 Annual Adelphi Subscription Rates			
Institution	£881	US$1,629	€1,304
Individual	£302	US$517	€413
Online only	£749	US$1,314	€1,108

Dollar rates apply to subscribers outside Europe. Euro rates apply to all subscribers in Europe except the UK and the Republic of Ireland where the pound sterling price applies. All subscriptions are payable in advance and all rates include postage. Journals are sent by air to the USA, Canada, Mexico, India, Japan and Australasia. Subscriptions are entered on an annual basis, i.e. January to December. Payment may be made by sterling cheque, dollar cheque, international money order, National Giro, or credit card (Amex, Visa, Mastercard).

For a complete and up-to-date guide to Taylor & Francis journals and books publishing programmes, and details of advertising in our journals, visit our website: **http://www.tandfonline.com.**

Ordering information:
USA/Canada: Taylor & Francis Inc., Journals Department, 530 Walnut Street, Suite 850, Philadelphia, PA 19106, USA. **UK/Europe/Rest of World:** Routledge Journals, T&F Customer Services, T&F Informa UK Ltd., Sheepen Place, Colchester, Essex, CO3 3LP, UK.

Advertising enquiries to:
USA/Canada: The Advertising Manager, Taylor & Francis Inc., 530 Walnut Street, Suite 850, Philadelphia, PA 19106, USA. Tel: +1 (800) 354 1420. Fax: +1 (215) 207 0050. **UK/Europe/Rest of World**: The Advertising Manager, Routledge Journals, Taylor & Francis, 4 Park Square, Milton Park, Abingdon, Oxfordshire OX14 4RN, UK. Tel: +44 (0) 20 7017 6000. Fax: +44 (0) 20 7017 6336.